SCOTTISH HISTORY SOCIETY

FOURTH SERIES

VOLUME 12

Calendar of
Papal Letters to Scotland
of
Clement VII of Avignon
1378-1394

Dr. Annie I. Dunlop

CALENDAR OF

Papal Letters to Scotland of Clement VII of Avignon 1378-1394

edited by
Charles Burns

★

Annie I. Dunlop (1897-1973): a Memoir
by
Ian B. Cowan

★

★

EDINBURGH
printed for the Scottish History Society *by*
T. AND A. CONSTABLE LTD
1976

ISBN 9500260 8 5

Printed in Great Britain

PREFACE

The Great Schism, which originated in a disputed papal election, has always been regarded as one of the most crucial periods in the history of western Christendom, and to this day that election remains the greatest unresolved controversy of the later Middle Ages.

The stand taken by the Scottish nation throughout the Schism was particularly significant, yet, until recently, Scottish historians had explored only inadequately the original sources existing in the Vatican Archives.

During the academic year 1961-2, the University of Glasgow awarded me a research scholarship with the specific aim of examining the letter-books, or registers, of one of the rival popes, and of noting systematically all the entries concerning Scotland. A microfilm of this source material is deposited with the Department of Scottish History.

This project was instrumental in introducing me to the late Dr Annie I. Dunlop. It won her immediate and enthusiastic approval and she followed its progress with lively interest. Only a few months before her death, Dr Dunlop asked me, if I was still working hard for Scotland ! This Calendar of Papal Letters of Clement VII of Avignon relating to Scotland is the result of that work. I am deeply honoured by the decision of the Council of the Scottish History Society to associate the present calendar and its companion volume with the memory of such a dedicated and distinguished Scottish historian.

My sincere gratitude goes out to Monsignor Martino Giusti, Prefect of the Vatican Archives, for his permission to consult the original documentary sources, and to the Committee of the Ross Fund of the University of Glasgow for entrusting me with this research project. Help and encouragement have come from many colleagues and friends in Rome and in Scotland and to all of them I am deeply grateful. Deserving of special recognition are Dr Leslie J. Macfarlane, who first suggested the project ; Dr Grant G. Simpson and Dr Donald E. R. Watt for their valuable advice during the early preparatory stages ; Dr Hermann Diener of the German Historical Institute in Rome, with whom many of the problems connected with the records of the papal chancery were discussed. A special expression of thanks is reserved for Dr Ian B. Cowan, second only to Dr Annie I. Dunlop herself, for the interest he has shown in the preparation of this calendar and without whose patient and generous assistance it would never have reached completion.

Vatican Archives   CHARLES BURNS
May, 1976

*A generous contribution from the
Carnegie Trust for the Universities of Scotland
towards the cost of producing this volume
is gratefully acknowledged by the
Council of the Society*

CONTENTS

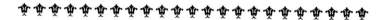

ANNIE I. DUNLOP
1897-1973

a *memoir* by Dr Ian B. Cowan

ANNIE ISABELLA CAMERON was born on 10th May 1897 at Glasgow, the eldest daughter of James Cameron and Mary Sinclair. Her father was a prominent civil engineer, whose many achievements included the building of the Glasgow underground railway system. Educated initially at a private school in Glasgow, she received part of her primary education at Strathaven Academy when her family moved from the city, but latterly attended the Glasgow High School for Girls before proceeding to the university of Glasgow from which she graduated MA with honours in history in 1919. After training as a teacher at Jordanhill College, she taught briefly in Sunderland and Edinburgh, but quickly realised that her real métier lay in the field of historical research to which she turned her attention in 1922.

The remaining fifty years of her life were to be devoted to this pursuit. Encouraged by the leading Scottish historians of the day, she quickly established herself as an expert record scholar. Under Professor R. K. Hannay, she embarked upon research for her PHD at the university of Edinburgh and it was to his advice that she attributed her life-long interest in fifteenth-century Scotland. Her subject matter for the doctorate which she obtained in 1924 was in Hannay's opinion 'a hard nut to crack, but well worth cracking'. Award of the PHD degree only confirmed her interest in its subject matter and for many years her thesis continued to be expanded and implemented after visits to archives throughout Europe. Finally in 1950 the work emerged as a singular contribution to our knowledge of the period as *The Life and Times of James Kennedy: bishop of St Andrews*. To her great pleasure she was asked by the prefect of the Vatican archives, Angelo Mercati, to present a copy of her work personally to Pope Pius XII – a gesture which in her eyes fittingly rounded off the affection and respect with which she had come to regard Kennedy – 'my bishop'.

The intervening years between acceptance of her thesis and final publication of its findings had been a period of prodigious activity. Initially she

A*

concentrated upon texts available in Edinburgh, and the editing of no fewer than three volumes of papers and correspondence which were to be published by the Scottish History Society between 1927 and 1932 testify to her diligence. In these endeavours she was encouraged by Principal Robert Rait of the university of Glasgow while other scholars quick to note her palaeographical skill were already encouraging her to venture further afield in search of Scottish material.

The opportunity to do so came with her appointment as a Carnegie Research Fellow in 1928. On the suggestion of Professor J. H. Baxter of St Andrews university, the Vatican archives was her first port of call. This proved to be a fortuitous decision, and while wider historical interests were never neglected, the study of ecclesiastical history in these archives quickly developed into the work of a life-time. Timid by disposition, the decision to live and work in Rome for an extended period could not have been an easy one, but once made was entered into with resolution. She not only studied in the archives but also enrolled in the Vatican School of Palaeography under its then distinguished professor, Father Bruno Katterbach, OFM. It was he who on one occasion declared that whereas some of his students spoke precipitately, the signorina never spoke at all. Life in an almost entirely male preserve presented obvious difficulties and the self confession 'Many a time at first I could have fain run away, but being a dour Scot and a Cameron Highlander to boot, I held my ground' reflects both the nature of the problem and the resolution of the writer. Perseverance brought its reward and she not only gained the coveted Diploma of the Vatican in Palaeography, but also acquired a life-long circle of friends both in Rome and throughout Europe.

In Rome itself she quickly established links with her fellow Scots in the city through membership of the Scots kirk, the minister of which, Dr McKinnon, had found her lodgings on first arrival and continued to act as a friend and mentor. She in turn acted as librarian of the church for two years and thereby established links with the congregation and its successive ministers, and every Sunday when in Rome she was to be found in the little church in the Via xx Settembre. She was a cherished member of its guild and was proud of her membership card which stated that she belonged to the presbyterian church in the parish of Rome and presbytery of Italy.

Her two and half years in Rome were not only happy but academically rewarding. A chance remark by a German scholar led her to examine the Registers of Supplications in relation to petitions made by Scots to the Pope. An equally fortuitous meeting with the Honourable E. R. Lindsay, who had also come to study this series led to fruitful editorial collaboration and the publication by the Scottish History Society of a volume of such petitions in 1934. Thereafter, a study of this series became the object of all future visits to the archives. Single-handed she eventually examined some seven hundred of these volumes which were themselves so massive that her diminutive frame could scarcely be seen behind them. The results of her endeavours are now lodged in the Department of Scottish History in the University of Glasgow and as she wished are freely available for consultation by scholars seeking to continue her researches.

Her own studies were by no means confined to Rome, however, and visits to libraries and archives in Munich, Florence, Paris and Vienna became something in the nature of an academic pilgrimage to other repositories throughout Europe – Dijon, Innsbrück, Bruges, Middelburg and Veere. Other visits were stimulated by the desire to see old friends. Attendance at the International Historical Congress in Poland in 1933 brought not only a devious journey as her Polish ship skirted the coast of Denmark rather than enter the Kiel Canal, but also brought a revival of friendships initiated in Rome. A return visit to an international conference of University Women at Cracow in 1936 strengthened these bonds and created a sense of affinity with Poland and the plight of her people which was always to remain with her.

A visit to Budapest with calls at Breslau, Cassel, Cologne and Brussels rounded off the itinerary for that year but the magnetism of Rome still remained and it alone soon became the object of her European pilgrimages. By 1936, however, private research on her previous scale was no longer possible. The termination of her Carnegie scholarship was followed by a further period of research at St Andrews University which culminated in the publication of *The Apostolic Camera and Scottish Benefices* for which she was awarded the degree of DLITT in 1934. With this achievement behind her, she now sought and obtained a more secure position in the Scottish Record Office in which she was to serve until her marriage in 1938. There in the midst of official duties which included the editing of a *Calendar of State Papers relating to Scotland and Mary, Queen of Scots* she continued to maintain her personal research interests, but the opportunity to pursue them in the Vatican archives was inevitably more restricted. Nevertheless, holidays were utilised to good purpose and in 1937 after an absence of three years she returned to work on the then unexplored registers of the Roman Rota in which legal experts in Scotland had shown an interest. Her pioneer efforts in this direction were not maintained and the examination which she began was not to be revived until shortly before her death. Since then, the richnesses which these records have revealed have more than justified the exploratory survey without which the task might never have been renewed.

Marriage in 1938 to George B. Dunlop, principal proprietor of the Kilmarnock Standard and a well known art collector, recreated the opportunity to concentrate on her own historical interests. The outbreak of war, however, prevented travel to foreign archives though this was not without its compensations as it provided the opportunity to digest and utilise much of the information which had been acquired in the past. The emergency also brought other demands. On the initiative of Professor V. H. Galbraith she undertook part-time teaching in history in the university of Edinburgh in 1942 and for the next six years commuted weekly during term from Fenwick in Ayrshire to Edinburgh to carry out her teaching duties, latterly in the department of Scottish History. Classes were small, and to her tutorials she brought not only her scholarship but a spirit of friendship exemplified more often than not by the provision of tea for her students. Lectures were also given to allied forces on leave in Scotland and the plight of her many friends in Europe, which gave her great concern, stimulated her to further literary efforts on their behalf. She had by now become a regular contributor to the Kilmarnock Standard and her 'Ayrshire Notes', later to be re-entitled 'Leaves from a Historian's Notebook' not only reflect her love of history but also her humanity.

In terms of historical publication these were necessarily fallow years although 1942, the year in which she was awarded the OBE for her services to scholarship, also saw the appearance of an Historical Association pamphlet on *Scots Abroad in the Fifteenth Century*. In addition, the writing of Bishop Kennedy went ahead and the end of hostilities found her anxious to return to the Vatican Archives to acquire the additional information which would allow her to put the finishing touches to this work. Despite many difficulties she succeeded in acquiring a visa to return to Rome in 1947. Likening herself to a medieval cleric who had made the journey some five centuries previously 'with perils and dangers by sea and road and the inconveniences caused by the waging of wars and internecine strifes' she set out on her travels. The journey proved to be no less difficult than that encountered by her medieval compatriots. Stranded late at night in Turin without any currency, refuge was eventually found in an Italian convent which she had aroused by error in searching for the YWCA. The remainder of her journey through war devastated Italy to Rome was no less difficult, and the train eventually arrived exactly one day late. A further struggle to obtain a permit to reside lasted another three days, and then, and only then was a return to the archives possible. The story that she was embraced by a Swiss Guard as she entered the precincts of the Vatican may be apocryphal, but the welcome was certainly warm and sincere. From the Prefect to the *bedelli* who once again brought the volumes of supplications to the seat under the prefect's desk which she quickly re-occupied by prescriptive right as the *nonna* (grandmother) of the *Archivio Vaticano*, she received the warmest of welcomes. Rome once again had become her second home, and thereafter few years were to pass without one or two visits to the eternal city.

The years immediately following 1947 were not, however, easy ones. Her book on Bishop Kennedy was completed in the shadow of increasing concern for the health of her husband following a serious operation. His death shortly after its publication, and only three weeks after the conferment upon her of the honorary degree of LLD by the university of St Andrews, came as a great blow to her morale. Her indomitable spirit revived, however, on the receipt of an invitation to deliver a series of lectures at Oxford where she spent a term at Lady Margaret Hall during the academic session 1950-1. Thereafter, her normal pattern of life was not only renewed, but, as air travel opened new horizons, became increasingly adventurous. During the course of the next twenty years she not only attended numerous historical gatherings at home and abroad, including the International Historical Conference in Sweden in 1960, but also undertook a lecture tour of the United States in 1955 and made many private visits to various parts of the world including Canada, India, Kenya, Rhodesia, Scandinavia, Finland, France, Germany, Portugal, Israel and Jordan. Each visit brought new acquaintances into her world-wide circle of friends. Stranded in Aden on Palm Sunday 1964, the Scots Kirk at Steamer Point provided not only a place of worship, but an introduction to the Scottish community whose hospitality was thereafter enjoyed. Such friendship eased many difficult journeys for her, and even the prospect of visiting Jordan and Israel at a time of diplomatic tension which required visitors to carry two passports in order to gain entry from one to the other found her unperturbed; experience had shown that a helping hand would never be far away.

Whatever part of the world she might visit, however, all roads eventually led to Rome and many of her trips began and ended in that city. A sojourn there inevitably meant residence in the friendly atmosphere of the British School. She had established contact there shortly after her first arrival and successive directors had always welcomed her presence. To staff and students alike Mrs Dunlop soon became a well known figure. Solicitous care was always shown for her welfare and even her dislike of pasta was accommodated by the special provision of a more frugal lunch of cheese, fruit and the inevitable pot of tea. Two of the staff above all epitomised the friendship and security which she experienced there. The *major domo* of the School – Sr Bruno Bonelli – who had guarded its integrity during the war, saw to her material needs by way of expediting finance, the franking of mail and even the repair of shoes, while Signorina Anna Fazzari, who had become secretary to the school in the immediate post-war period, ensured, despite rather erratic travel plans, that accommodation was always available.

Visits, however brief, always found Mrs Dunlop in the Vatican archives at which she was inevitably one of the first to arrive at eight o'clock sharp each morning. Even when the archives deferred its opening for a further fifteen minutes, this habit of a lifetime was not easily broken. Within the walls of the Archives both friendship and scholarship awaited her. The Prefect, after the death of her friend and mentor Mgr Angelo Mercati, whose dying blessing she had received and to whom in association with the memory of her husband she dedicated her second volume of *Scottish Supplications to Rome*, was Mgr Martino Giusti who had been one of her fellow students in the School of Palaeography. Other members of staff from the Cardinal Prefect to the doorkeeper were equally well known to her, but it gave her special pleasure when a fellow countryman, Mgr Charles Burns, became one of its archivists. Of the scholars known to her in the archives one in particular characterised the international nature of her acquaintances. This was Madame Skrowonska, a small black-clad figure like herself, whom she had met initially in Rome and who had greeted her with a large bouquet of flowers when she had stepped off the train at Warsaw on her Polish visit of 1933. Not until 1955, with Madame Skrowonska a refugee from her native land and resident in Rome, did their paths cross again. Thereafter, their reunions in the study room of the Vatican archives were always fraught with emotion as bearing down upon one another, and exchanging greetings in a mixture of Polish, French and Italian, their friendship was brought to life again.

Inevitably, however, as the years proceeded the circle of old friends grew smaller. Attendance at the Scots Kirk and the friendship of its minister, the Rev. A. J. Maclean, and his wife, remained one of the constant factors, but gradually visits to other acquaintances became fewer. The tea parties with the English speakers of the Association of the Laureate of the Italian Federation of University Women where 'everyone seemed to talk and no one to listen' do not seem to have been revived after the war. In their stead an invitation to dinner at the British School became the normal means of fulfilling social obligations. Occasionally friends would persuade her to accompany them to one of the city's many trattorias, but she had little appetite for such occasions, and conversation and a cup of tea in a small Roman bar was much more to her taste.

Throughout her life service to others was always to the fore. In a public capacity Mrs Dunlop served on numerous bodies. She was a member of the Royal Commission on the Ancient and Historical Monuments of Scotland from 1955 until shortly before her death, and served for several years as a member of the Advisory Council for Scottish Records. She also sat on the councils of the Scottish History Society and of the Scottish Church History Society of which she was honorary president from 1956 until her death. In a private capacity she was a local director of the Kilmarnock Standard and was active in membership of the British Federation of University Women and of clubs such as the University Women's, the Royal Overseas League and the St Rule (St Andrews). In university circles she served in one capacity or another each of the four ancient Scottish universities. In Aberdeen, she acted as external examiner in Scottish history, at Edinburgh as a member of the University Library Committee, for St Andrews she not only edited the *Acta Facultatis Artium* for the university, but also provided the biography of Kennedy as one of the quincentenary volumes associated with the celebrations commemorating the foundation of St Salvator's College. For a time the muniment room of the university became like a second home, to which a note of domesticity was added by the provision of the inevitable tea-pot through which friendship could be dispensed to all callers. The happiness experienced there was always remembered and this gratitude found final expression in the bequest of her books to the Scottish history class library. In her closing years it was, however, with her original *alma mater*, Glasgow, that she became most closely associated as with the status of a research fellow she helped to promote further investigation in the Vatican archives.

In all her activities personal generosity was always evident. After her husband's death, their house at Dunselma at Fenwick in Ayrshire became an old people's home in the care of the Church of Scotland and several paintings from her husband's extensive art collection were gifted to the university of Glasgow. Nor did her generosity stop there. The Scottish History Society, the British School at Rome and other charitable causes benefited financially from time to time and an idealistic group of young Scottish medievalists also found financial backing for their ventures.

In her latter years the greatest pleasure was found in the realisation that the work she had commenced would be carried on by others. She had always befriended and helped scholars visiting the archives for the first time, but when the Ross Fund Committee of the University of Glasgow initiated in 1962 a thorough investigation into the whereabouts of all pre-Reformation Scottish material in the Vatican archives, she at once became a prime supporter of this action. Her own research was thereafter directed towards that end and for the next eight years successive Ross Fund scholars were to owe to her their introduction to the Vatican archives and its riches. If in the three years before her death, she was unable to visit Rome and perform this service in person, her goodwill and her generosity always lay behind the venture. This lifetime in the Vatican archives and the propagation of the value of Scottish material which it contains was fittingly recognised on 13th April 1972 when Pope Paul VI conferred upon her for her services to scholarship in the Vatican archives the papal *Benemerenti* medal. Over forty years had passed since she had first entered these archives and nothing could have been more appropriate as her life drew to a close that recognition of her achievements should not only be recorded in her native Scotland but in the city which she had come to love. This award coupled with the distinctions bestowed upon her at home were hall-marks of a truly international scholar whose life came peacefully to a close on 23rd March 1973. It is through her scholarship that future generations of historians will make her acquaintance, but to those who remember her personally, the qualities which spring most quickly to mind, her gentleness, kindness and ever readiness to assist will remain as their abiding memories of this distinguished but unassuming scholar.

A bibliography of her writings

BOOKS

GENERAL HISTORY

The Life and Times of James Kennedy, bishop of St Andrews (Edinburgh, St Andrews University Publications, no. xlvi, 1950).

EDITIONS OF SOURCES

The Scottish Correspondence of Mary of Lorraine, 1543-1560 (SHS, 1927).

The Warrender Papers, 2 vols: vol i, 1301-1587; vol ii, 1587-1603 (SHS, 1931-2).

The Apostolic Camera and Scottish Benefices (Oxford, 1934).

'Bagimond's Roll for the Archdeaconry of Teviotdale' in *SHS Miscellany*, v (1933), 79-106.

Calendar of the State Papers relating to Scotland and Mary, Queen of Scots, xi (Edinburgh, 1936).

'Bagimond's Roll: Statement of the Tenths of the Kingdom of Scotland' in *SHS Miscellany*, vi (1939), 3-77.

Calendar of Scottish Supplications to Rome: 1423-1428 (SHS, 1956).

'Cassilis Papers from the Manuscripts of the Marquis of Ailsa' in *Ayrshire Archaeological and Natural History Society Collections*, 2nd series, iii (1950-54), 86-106.

'Correspondence of the First Earl of Dundonald' in *Ayrshire Archaeological and Natural History Soc. Collections*, 2nd series, iv (1958), 143-181.

Acta Facultatis Artium Universitatis Sancti Andree, 1413-1588 (Edinburgh, St Andrews University Publications, no. lvi, 1964, and in 2 vols, SHS, 1964).

IN COLLABORATION

King James's Secret (London, 1927) (with Sir Robert Rait).

Calendar of Scottish Supplications to Rome, 1418-1422 (with E. R. Lindsay) (SHS, 1934).

Calendar of Scottish Supplications to Rome, 1428-1432 (with I. B. Cowan) (SHS, 1970).

'Protocol Book of Mr James Colvill, 1545-1578' in *Ayrshire Archaeological and Natural History Soc. Collections*, 2nd series, x (1972), 1-76 (with John D. Imrie).

CONTRIBUTIONS TO BOOKS

'Vatican Archives, 1073-1560' in *An Introductory Survey of the Sources and Literature of Scots Law* (Stair Society, 1936), 274-281.

GENERAL EDITOR

The Royal Burgh of Ayr (Edinburgh, 1953).

PAMPHLETS

Memory's Chain: European Meditations, articles reprinted from the columns of the Kilmarnock Standard (Kilmarnock, 1940).

Hearts Desire for Poland, articles reprinted from the columns of the Kilmarnock Standard (Kilmarnock, 1941).

Scots Abroad in the Fifteenth Century, Historical Association Leaflet, no. 124 (London, 1942).

Lectures delivered to Canadian and USA Forces on leave: Mary, Queen of Scots etc. (Edinburgh, 1943).

The Jeopardy of the Jews in Europe (An address) (Edinburgh, 1943).

A cry from Europe – Articles (to reflect the course of international events since the Munich Crisis), reprinted from the columns of the Kilmarnock Standard (Kilmarnock, 1959).

Spring Flowers for a Chaplet: Being leaves from a historian's notebook, reprinted from the columns of the Kilmarnock Standard (Kilmarnock, 1959).

ARTICLES AND NOTES

'The Canongate Crafts: an agreement of 1610' in *Book of the Old Edinburgh Club*, xiv (1925), 25-44.

'Two Groups of Documents relating to John Baliol from the Vatican Archives' in *Papers of the British School at Rome*, xii (1932), 26-42.

'Scots at the Roman Court in the Fifteenth Century' in *Proceedings of the Royal Philosophical Society of Glasgow*, lxi (1932-3), 59-73.

'Scottish Students at Paris University, 1466-1492 [an abstract from vol 3 of the Liber Procuratorum Nationis Alemanniae of the University of Paris]' in *Juridical Review*, xlviii (1936), 228-55.

'Diploma of Nobility of Thomas Cunningham, 1727' in *Juridical Review*, l (1938), 51-74 (with Helena Polaczek).

'Registers of Supplications: *Registra Supplicationum*' in 'Miscellany Composed for H. W. Meikle' *Edinburgh Bibliographical Society Transactions*, ii (1938-45), 383-5.

'Life in a Medieval Cathedral' in *Journal of the Society of Friends of Dunblane Cathedral*, iv (1942-5), 70-86.

'Scottish Student Life in the Fifteenth Century' in *Scot. Hist. Rev.*, xxvi (1947), 47-63.

'The date of the birth of James III' in *Scot. Hist. Rev.*, xxix (1950), 212-13, and ibid., xxx (1951), 202-4.

'John Crannach, Bishop of Brechin 1436-1454' in *Book of the Society of the Friends of Brechin Cathedral*, vi (1953), 8-27.

'The Society's Centenary Celebrations' in *Dumfriesshire and Galloway Natural History and Antiquarian Society Transactions*, 3rd series, xl (1963), 13-16.

'Note on the Grey Friars at Kirkcudbright' in *Dumfriesshire and Galloway Natural History and Antiquarian Society Transactions*, 3rd series, xxxv (1956-7), 127-9.

'In the Footsteps of a medieval bishop' in *Alumnus Chronicle* (University of St Andrews), no. li (1960), 18-28.

'Remissions and Indulgences in Fifteenth Century Scotland' in *Recs. Scot. Church Hist. Soc.*, xv (1965), 153-167.

'Notes on the Church in the Dioceses of Sodor and Argyll' in *Recs. Scot. Church Hist. Soc.*, xvi (1968), 179-184.

REVIEWS

The University of St Andrews: a short history, by R. G. Cant, in *History*, xxxii (1947), 127-9.

Charters of the Abbey of Coupar Angus, ed. D. E. Easson, in *History*, xxxiv (1949), 170.

Mission de Beccarie de Pavie, Baron de Fourquevaux, by G. Dickinson, in *Scot. Hist. Rev.*, xxviii (1949), 82-83.

The Carnegie Family in Gothenburg, by Alexander A. Cormack, in *Scot. Hist. Rev.*, xxviii (1949), 86.

The Old Minute Book of the Faculty of Procurators in Glasgow, ed. J. S. Muirhead, in *Scot. Hist. Rev.*, xxix (1950), 101-2.

Collections of the Ayrshire Archaeological and Natural History Society, 1947-1949, 2nd series, vol i (1950), in *Scot. Hist. Rev.*, xxx (1951), 196-7.

Catalogue of Scottish Medieval Liturgical Books and Fragments, by David McRoberts, in *Scot. Hist. Rev.*, xxxiii (1954), 162-3.

The Letters of James V, ed. R. K. Hannay and Denys Hay, in *English Hist. Rev.*, lxx (1955), 636-9.

The Fetternear Banner, by David McRoberts, in *Scot. Hist. Rev.*, xxxvii (1958), 86-87.

Le Livre du Recteur de l'Académie de Genève, vol i, ed. S. Stelling-Michaud, in *Scot. Hist. Rev.*, xxxix (1960), 146-8.

The Vatican Archives, by Leslie MacFarlane, in *Scot. Hist. Rev.*, xxxix (1960), 157-8.

Education in Ayrshire through seven centuries, by William Boyd, in *Scot. Hist. Rev.*, xlii (1963), 54-56.

The Parishes of Medieval Scotland, by Ian B. Cowan, in *Scot. Hist. Rev.*, xlvii (1968), 87-88.

❀ ❀

INTRODUCTION

EARLY IN the nineteenth century some British scholars, under a mistaken impression that many original records had been taken to Rome at the time of the Reformation for safekeeping, began to show a lively interest in the collections of the Vatican Archives in the hope that those lost muniments would be rediscovered.[1] Of course that was not the case, but the search made at the time in response to their requests convinced the Prefect of the *Archivio Segreto Vaticano*, Monsignor Marino Marini, that nonetheless the papal archives did constitute an immensely rich source for British history, both civil and ecclesiastical, and that even a summary of the relevant entries in the papal records would be of inestimable value to British historians. He undertook to compile the summary personally and Pope Pius VII gave his assent to this quite singular project. The forty-eight volumes of Marini's transcripts are preserved in the British Museum to this day.[2]

Father Augustin Theiner succeeded Marini as Prefect in 1855 and his outstanding output of published historical sources soon aroused widespread interest in the Vatican collections. When his *Vetera monumenta Hibernorum et Scotorum historiam illustrantia* appeared in

[1] An interesting correspondence concerning this matter is to be found in the Vatican Archives, Secretariate of State, 1823, rubric 67.

[2] British Library, Add. MSS 15351-15398, with indexes in Add. MSS 15399-15401. The title of Marini's transcripts is 'Monumenta Britannica ex autographis Romanorum Pontificum registris ceterisque documentis deprompta'. Marini's original intention was to publish the fruits of his research with a suitable dedication to the British monarch, George IV, but there is no evidence that anything ever appeared in print. Correspondence about the project exists in the Vatican Archives, Secretariate of State, 1823, rubric 67, and *ibid.*, 1827, rubric 67. From one of Marini's letters it emerges that the originator of the idea was William Richard Hamilton, antiquary and diplomatist, who was British minister at the court of Naples from 1822 until 1825. His name is also associated with the recuperation of the Rosetta Stone from the French, and he organised the transport of the Elgin Marbles from Greece. See D[*ictionary of*] N[*ational*] B[*iography*], viii, 1118-19.

1864, the British Government was launching a project to publish 'all the materials illustrative of the history of Great Britain which are extant in foreign libraries and archives', and quite probably Theiner's monumental volume influenced the decision to appoint a researcher for the libraries and archives of Rome in the person of the Reverend Joseph Stevenson, the renowned Scottish antiquary and scholar.[1] His permission to consult the Vatican Library and Archives dates from September 1872.[2] Four years later, when he relinquished the post, Mr W. H. Bliss was appointed to his place and the same permission, hitherto enjoyed by Stevenson, was extended also to Bliss, at the instance of Cardinals Manning and Cullen.[3]

The name of William Henry Bliss will be associated forever with the *Calendar of entries in the Papal Registers relating to Great Britain and Ireland*, of which he was editor or joint-editor of the first five volumes of *Papal Letters*, and sole editor of the one volume of *Petitions to the Pope*.[4] While Marini and Theiner had drawn widely, but at random, from the vast range of records in the Vatican Archives, Bliss set himself to examine systematically the records of the papal chancery. Although his method of calendaring was inconsistent and has come in for severe criticism, the Bliss *Calendar* remains indispensable for research on the history of the pre-Reformation Church in the British Isles.

The papal chancery records are arranged in three distinct series of bound registers, the *Registra Vaticana*, the *Registra Avenionensia*, and the *Registra Lateranensia*.[5] This triple division and designation

---

[1] For Stevenson's earlier academic career, see *DNB*, xviii, 1127-9.

[2] The correspondence regarding the admission of Stevenson is in the Vatican Archives, Secretariate of State, 1872, rubric 47, ff. 63-79. This includes a printed 'Statement relative to Mr Stevenson's employment at Rome', issued by the Master of the Rolls on 9 July 1872, which explains the research policy of the British government with regard to European archives and libraries.

[3] The correspondence relative to the permission extended to Bliss is in the Vatican Archives, Secretariate of State, 1877, rubric 47, ff. 14-18, and *ibid.*, 1877, rubric 283, ff. 40-44. It was only in 1880 that Pope Leo XIII opened the papal archives for general consultation.

[4] The first five volumes of *Papal Letters* appeared between 1893 and 1904, and the volume of *Petitions to the Pope* appeared in 1896.

[5] The best study of this triple series of papal registers is by M. Giusti, *Studi sui registri di bolle papali*, Collectanea Archivi Vaticani (Vatican City, 1968), i. The most useful description of these registers in English is by L. Boyle, *A Survey of the Vatican Archives and of its Medieval Holdings*, Subsidia Medievalia (Toronto 1972), i, pp 103-48.

are quite fortuitous, and can even be considered unfortunate in that they bear no relation whatever to any original classification of the chancery, fail to distinguish from the extensive cameral and secretarial records which are included under these titles, and so in no way reflect the true nature or the provenance of the contents. For the entire thirteenth century the Vatican Registers form the single series of volumes, into which the letters dispatched by the popes have been elegantly copied on to parchment. For the fourteenth century, however, these are flanked by a parallel series of paper registers, the Avignon Registers. The third series, the Lateran Registers, also on paper, appears only at the end of the fourteenth century and so need not be taken into further consideration for the purposes of this present study.

The Avignon Registers[1] contain the original registration, equivalent to a file copy, of the outgoing letters of the chancery. At a later moment these registrations were recopied on to parchment in order to form a more permanent record. Obviously the parchment registers of fair-copies, being a step further removed from the original letters sent out, have always constituted a secondary series. They were placed alongside the other parchment registers of the previous century (for which there exists no equivalent paper series) and today form the continuation of the collection of *Registra Vaticana*.

The system of recopying the paper registers appears to have functioned efficiently until the middle of the century, but during the pontificate of Innocent VI (1352-62) it began to break down and gradually the fair-copy registers begin to represent less and less the total output of the chancery. At first only parts of the paper registers and then entire volumes are found to have no corresponding part in the parchment series of Vatican Registers. They are not even endorsed as ever having been copied, as was the accepted practice in the chancery until then. Consequently, the paper Avignon Registers, far from occupying a merely

---

[1] The best study of the Avignon Registers is by F. Bock, *Einführung in das Registerwesen des Avignonesischen Papsttums*, (Quellen und Forschungen aus italienischen Archiven und Bibliotheken, xxxi, Rome, 1941). In English an adequate and useful description can be found in Boyle, *Survey*, pp 114-31, including a complete list of the calendars published by the French School at Rome on pp 125-27.

ancillary position, emerge as the primary source in their own right.[1]

Unaware, perhaps, of the relationship of interdependence existing between the two chancery series, Bliss ignored the Avignon Registers when compiling the *Calendar* for the fourteenth century, and continued with his examination of the Vatican Registers of the period without reference to the parallel series. In this he was greatly mistaken, not only because the fair copies are not free from simple copyists' errors and misreadings, but rather because the original paper series contains considerably more letters, for reasons which are not always clear but cannot be explained simply by oversight.[2] Scholars soon adverted to the fact that in this regard the Bliss *Calendar* was seriously defective and incomplete, and Scottish historians became aware that, at least in the later Avignon Registers, there was still a major source of Scottish history as yet inadequately explored.[3]

The present volume of *Papal Letters to Scotland of Clement VII of Avignon, 1378-1394,* and the companion volume of *Papal Letters to Scotland of Benedict XIII of Avignon, 1394-1419,* now provide that long-desired calendar of entries in the papal registers relating to Scotland during the later Avignon period, and with their joint publication by the Scottish History Society a very significant want is supplied in the published sources of Scottish medieval ecclesiastical history.

The Papal Chancery at Avignon and its Records

Throughout the Middle Ages the popes relied principally on their chancery for the actual machinery of government. This was the department of the papal curia most directly involved in the practical aspect of governing the universal Church. Normally it was by letters that the popes maintained regular contact with local churches and conveyed their decisions to even the most remote places of Christendom. Over the centuries the chancery evolved into a highly competent and well organised secretariat, employing a large

---

[1] D. E. R. Watt, 'Sources for Scottish History of the Fourteenth Century in the Archives of the Vatican', *Scottish Historical Review,* xxxii (1953), p 113; Boyle, *Survey,* p 114.

[2] Boyle, *Survey,* p 117.   [3] Watt, 'Sources', p 115

personnel in the daily business of preparing and dispatching the ever-increasing volume of papal correspondence, which was conducted in accordance with set rules governing the style, script, dating and sealing of the documents. A system of registration guaranteed that a permanent record remained of this outgoing correspondence.[1]

The records of the Avignon chancery for the entire period 1305-1423, comprising both the paper registers of first registration and the parchment volumes of fair copies, consist today of some 555 volumes, distributed between the *Registra Avenionensia* and *Registra Vaticana* series.[2] Numerous fragments are dispersed among various holdings of the Vatican Archives and Library, or have found their way into collections possessed by other European archives and libraries;[3] quite clearly the Vatican records are not complete, but it is difficult to establish precisely to what extent they are deficient, or reconstruct within any near degree of accuracy the total original content.[4] Considering that almost all the forty-one paper registers of Clement v, inventoried in 1369,[5] are now lost, one is prepared to accept that major losses have been sustained, at least for some pontificates. These very losses, however, only reflect the turbulent times through which the papal archives have passed in the course of centuries and even an outline history of these collections shows why it is tantamount to miraculous that any record of those bygone days has survived at all.

[1] By the fourteenth century the pre-eminence of the chancery was steadily being eclipsed by the chamberlain, who functioned as the closest and most heeded advisor of the popes, consulted by them not only on matters of finance but more especially on political affairs. Under his direction various secretaries dealt with the political correspondence, or *litterae secretae*, which were prepared and registered *apud Cameram*. This gave rise to yet another series of registers containing papal letters, most of which have now found their way into the Registra Vaticana series. Prior to the pontificate of Pope John xxii (1316-34), only four volumes of the series, namely, Reg. Vat. 27, 31, 40 and 42, are attributed to the Camera. From the time of John xxii onwards, however, the situation changes radically, and many cameral registers are now included in this series.

[2] Giusti, *Studi*, pp 129, 138-41, 149-51.

[3] G. Battelli, '"Membra disiecta" di registri pontifici dei secoli xiii e xiv', *Mélanges Eugène Tisserant*, iv (Studi e Testi 234, Vatican City, 1964), pp 1-34.

[4] An attempt at reconstructing the chancery archive material for the period between 1339 and 1369 was made by F. Ehrle, *Historia Bibliothecae Romanorum Pontificum* (Rome, 1890), p 433.

[5] Ehrle, *Bibliotheca*, p 434, n. 6.

During the years when the popes resided at Avignon, the chancery records were deposited in the *turris*, or *magna turris*, situated at the south eastern corner of the central courtyard of the papal palace.[1] The 'Great Tower', which to this day retains its original austere and massive appearance, was among the first major works to be constructed, between 1335 and 1337, as part of the new palace of the popes. Built on solid rock, it rises to a height of 140 feet with walls of an average thickness of ten feet, flanked by buttresses and pierced by few windows, all of the narrow lancet type. Designed for security, this was the safest place in the palace and was under constant guard, because here the popes had their bedchamber, their treasury, library and muniments.

Unlike the regrettable fate of so many medieval episcopal and monastic records, the archive of the Avignon popes was never affected by fire, although the palace was not entirely immune from this danger. In fact on 14 November 1339, a fire destroyed the private kitchen which abutted on to the western façade of the newly constructed Great Tower ;[2] but perhaps the period of greatest threat was during the last months of 1398, when Benedict XIII was besieged in the palace and repeated attempts were made to tunnel under the ramparts and set fire to the central buildings from below ground.[3]

During the night of 12 March 1403, Benedict XIII managed to elude his assailants ; Avignon had seen its last pope. What happened to the papal records now becomes a matter of conjecture, but nothing appears to have been done about them immediately after the Schism ended with the election of Martin V in 1417, and presumably they remained undisturbed at Avignon throughout that time. As a consequence of the schismatic papacy, 'papal' records were now dispersed in various parts of Europe and opinions are divided as to whom should go the greatest credit for undertaking to reassemble them.[4] It has always been said that Martin V recovered the archive of Benedict XIII from Peniscola.[5] That does not mean,

---

[1] Ehrle, *Bibliotheca*, p 705.   [2] Ehrle, *Bibliotheca*, p 709.

[3] G. Mollat, 'Episodes du Siège du Palais des Papes au temps de Benoit XIII, 1398-1399', *Revue d'Histoire Ecclésiastique*, xxiii (1927), pp 489-501.

[4] A. Corbo, 'Martino V, Eugenio IV e la ricostituzione dell'archivio papale dopo Costanza', *Rassegna degli Archivi di Stato*, xxviii (Roma, 1968), pp 36-66.

[5] Corbo, 'Martino V', p 37.

however, that it was brought to Rome, but rather back to Avignon, where most of Benedict's registers remained until late on in the eighteenth century. Probably, it was not until 1441, under Eugenius IV, that a move was made to recover the papal archives from Avignon.[1] Although the archive of the Apostolic Camera was safely transported to Rome in 1443,[2] the bulk of the chancery material remained in the palace at Avignon and was destined to lie there for many years to come.

A century was to elapse before Pompeo Capello was sent by Pope Paul III to inspect what still remained in Avignon, which at that time was under constant threat from marauding French mercenaries. In 1542 Capello drew up the first detailed inventory to survive of all the registers of the Avignon chancery,[3] now relocated in the Tour de la Gâche on the western façade of the palace. Obviously, his list does not correspond with the modern arrangement of the registers; he lists them all together, but does distinguish materially between those written on parchment and those on paper. The list is not entirely free from anomalies and discrepancies, but there were approximately 595 registers extant, or, more precisely, 148 on parchment and 447 of paper. Capello's mission was not without some success and possibly resulted in the return to Rome of the earlier, thirteenth-century registers of the parchment series.

The intention of uniting all the papal records in one central archive persisted, but in reality the project continued to meet with setbacks.[4] Shortly after his election to the papacy in 1565, Pius V commissioned Mario Zazzarino to convey to Rome all the documents, books and registers that belonged to the Apostolic See and were still in the papal palace at Avignon.[5] The procès-verbal which was drawn up as the material was handed over to him by the papal legate, records that on 19 August 1566 157 volumina vitellina (the parchment

---

[1] M. Gachard, Les Archives du Vatican (Brussels, 1874), p 7.
[2] M. Bååth, 'L'inventaire de la Chambre Apostolique de 1440', Miscellanea Archivistica Angelo Mercati, (Studi e Testi 165, Vatican City, 1952), pp 135-57.
[3] F. Benoit, 'Les Archives du Palais des Papes d'Avignon du xve siecle à la fin de la domination pontificale', Mémoires de l'Académie de Vaucluse, xxiv (1924). Citations refer to an off-print of this article, published at Vaison, 1925.
[4] Gachard, Archives, p 8.
[5] Vatican Archives, Arm. XLII, 25, f. 488.

B

registers of Nicholas III, Clement V and the latter's successors at Avignon) were consigned for dispatch to Rome, where, upon arrival, they were deposited in the Vatican Library.[1] After this, only occasional volumes were returned, as, for instance, two registers of Gregory XI in 1583.[2] The great series of paper registers remained at Avignon. Regrettably, whoever prepared the inventory of the contents of the archive for the papal legate, Cardinal Ottavio Acquaviva, in 1594, passed over them in silence.[3]

A new era dawned with the establishment of the modern *Archivio Segreto Apostolico* by Paul V in 1611, and between then and 1616, in different phases, hundreds of registers of papal administration, including the parchment registers in the Vatican Library, were brought together in the Vatican Palace to form the first nucleus of what has become one of the richest and most important historical archives in the world.[4] The pope intended that everything be brought from Avignon and an inventory was compiled for that express purpose,[5] but in fact only the remainder of Benedict XIII's library came back to Rome in his lifetime.[6] Once again the bulk of the chancery records was left behind in Avignon and this situation went unchanged throughout the seventeenth century, although between the years 1631 and 1641 other consignments of records were effected, including the volumes of the *Obligationes* and *Collectoriae*, and possibly some registers of *Supplicationes* and some of *Bullae* of Clement V.[7] Later, in 1671, a considerable number of miscellaneous charters of the Apostolic Camera were added to the Vatican holdings, which by then had overflowed to the floor above the original archive, in the room adjacent to which this introduction is being written.

The turn of the century witnessed several important develop-

---

[1] Gachard, *Archives*, pp 10-11.   [2] *Ibid.*, p 11.

[3] Three examples exist of this inventory, which bears the title: Index librorum manuscriptorum, qui in Archivio Palatij Avenionensis reperti sunt tempore Legationis Ill^mi et Rev^mi D. D. Octavij Cardinalis de Acquaviva Anno Domini MDXCIIII. Two copies are in the Vatican Archives, Indice 147, ff. 60-118, and Fondo Borghese, IV, 164, ff. 66-137. The third copy, which was formerly Indice 146 of the Vatican Archives, is now Cod. Borghese 390, in the Vatican Library.

[4] F. Gasparolo, *Costituzione dell'Archivio Vaticano e suo primo indice sotto il pontificato di Paolo V. Manoscritto inedito di Michele Lonigo* (Studi e documenti di Storia e Diritto, viii, Rome, 1887), pp 3-64.

[5] Benoit, *Archives d'Avignon*, p 11.   [6] *Ibid.*, p 12.   [7] *Ibid.*, p 13.

ments: the archive at Avignon was completely reorganised and, during the first decade of the eighteenth century, the archivist, Joseph de Martin, compiled a general index of the paper chancery registers, which he calendared volume by volume, item by item. This index consists of twenty-eight volumes and covers the pontificates of the Avignon popes from Clement v to Clement vii, although, inexplicably, it lacks the entire pontificate of Gregory xi (1370-78), and extends only to the first pontifical year of Clement vii. It was completed in 1711 and sent to Rome.[1]

A new index was commissioned almost immediately. This is the index of Pierre de Montroy, which took eighteen years to complete, fills 85 large tomes, and provides succinct summaries of each papal letter, arranged alphabetically, diocese by diocese. By the end of the century this voluminous index joined Martin's index in the Vatican.[2]

Montroy was also responsible for having the registers bound in a more permanent form, as apparently before 1714 they consisted simply of loose fascicles, bundled together in parchment folders. Time had played havoc with them; entire registers had perished completely, or were irreparably affected by damp and mould. Some idea of their deplorable condition can be formed from Montroy's own annotations: 'Omnia ista volumina vetustate fere consumpta restauravi et decorari curavi', or 'Librum hunc, nudum, lacerum, pulvere, tinea et pluvia corrosum, in quaternionibus confuse disparatum, religari iussit', to cite only two examples from among many.[3] Before binding them, however, insufficient care was taken to allot to each pope what truly belonged to his pontificate, with the result that some registers are quite wrongly ascribed, or stray fascicles from one pontificate have been haphazardly bound into the registers of another.[4]

Between 1768 and 1774 the city of Avignon and the surrounding Comtat Venaissin were occupied by the troops of Louis xv, and when the papal territories were restored to the Holy See, it was discovered that once again the archive was reduced to a state of chaos and much of the material was dispersed. The Abbé Carlo Bonacca was appointed archivist and he set about the difficult task of

---

[1] Vatican Archives, Indici 642-69.   [2] Vatican Archives, Indici 557-641.
[3] J. -M. Vidal, Benoit xii (1334-42). Lettres communes et curiales, iii (Paris, 1911), p xxc.   [4] Vidal, Lettres communes, iii, p xxci.

reorganisation. Sometime later, a servant was discovered selling the precious records to local grocers and shopkeepers for wrapping paper, at the modest charge of a few *sous* per pound weight! When this was reported the reaction from Rome was swift and decisive: the miscreant was dismissed and the vice-legate was instructed to recover the records from their buyers.[1] Meantime the Abbé Bonacca began preparations for the transport of the entire archive to Rome. This had to be done with the maximum secrecy and he personally filled the chests with the registers. There were sixteen chests in all, containing 505 volumes, including 351 registers of bulls, thirteen registers of supplications, and the eighty-five volumes of Montroy's index. When the chests left Avignon on 25 February 1783, Bonacca accompanied them as far as Marseilles where they were loaded on to a ship destined for Civitavecchia. They reached Rome without mishap in mid-April and were deposited in the Vatican Archives.[2] When one reflects that only six years later the French Revolution broke out and swept all before it in an orgy of pillage and destruction, then the timely evacuation of the papal archive from Avignon appears all the more providential.

But who could have foreseen that within little over twenty-five years, those very same volumes would be packed again in chests and be back on the road to France? Rome fell to the army of Napoleon on 2 February 1808: exactly two years later (Pope Pius VII having been deported from Rome in the meantime) it was decided that all the archive material should be transported to France. The registers of bulls were among the first items to be taken, and the first convoy, comprising 117 chests of records, set off for Paris on 17 February. Altogether twenty-two convoys left Rome in the course of 1810, composed of a total number of 1,650 chests. In 1811 six more convoys brought the entire archive of the Apostolic Camera to Paris. By 1813 it is reckoned that the number of chests transported there amounted to 3,239, with an aggregate weight of 408,459 kilograms, or the equivalent of over 400 tons! Their stay in Paris was shortlived: with the final fall of Napoleon in 1815, it was possible for the Holy See to arrange for the restoration of all

---

[1] F. Ehrle, 'Die Uebertragung des letzen Restes des päpstlischen Archivs von Avignon nach Rom', *Historisches Jahrbuch*, xi (1890), pp 727-9.
[2] Benoit, *Archives d'Avignon*, p 21.

the archives and other moveable property removed from Rome and the Papal States. In fact the transport of the archives took almost two years to complete, but, by 24 July 1817, having sustained incalculable losses en route, the last of the records returned to the Vatican, and with that the long and far from uneventful history of the papal records of Avignon also comes to an end.[1] Since then they have been carefully preserved in the Vatican Secret Archives, without further upheaval, even throughout the period of the Italian 'Risorgimento', which despoiled the popes of the city of Rome and the Papal States, and not forgetting, in more recent times, the period of the Second World War, when the Vatican was under real threat of occupation by the Axis, or bombardment by the Allied Powers, but emerged unscathed.

Clement VII: Pope or Anti-pope?

Before proceeding further, something must be said about the pope whose official acts in relation to Scotland are listed and analysed in this calendar. Pope Clement VII of Avignon is not numbered among the legitimate occupants of the papacy. This is a stigma which the course of six centuries has not only failed to erase, but has even rendered rehabilitation well nigh impossible.[2] Yet the

[1] Gachard, *Archives*, pp 23-4; R. Ritzler, 'Die Verschleppung der päpstlichen Archiv nach Paris unter Napoleon I und deren Rückführung nach Rom in den Jahren 1815 bis 1817', *Römische historische Mitteilungen*, 6-7 (1962-64), pp 144-90.

[2] There has never been a definitive pronouncement regarding the legitimacy of the various popes, eight in all, who reigned during the Great Schism. In 1492, Rodrigo de Borja styled himself Alexander VI, in deference to Alexander V, the first pope of the 'Pisan obedience' (1409-10). In 1523, however, Giulio de' Medici immediately styled himself as Clement VII, a clear repudiation of any claims that Robert of Geneva might have had to the papacy. Logoz, *Clément VII*, p xxxvii, note 1, asserts that for almost two years after his election, Giulio de' Medici styled himself Clement VIII, but this appears to be quite untenable. There is an original bull in the Vatican Archives, A.A. Arm. I-XVIII, 2581, dated 26 November 1523 (the very day of the pope's coronation), to which is affixed the lead seal, bearing the inscription CLEMENS PP. VII. Since that time, there has been a long succession of popes, who have assumed the name 'Clement' upon their election to the papacy. The most recent was Pope Clement XIV (1769-74). The official list of Roman Pontiffs since 1947 classifies the popes of both the Avignonese and the Pisan obediences as 'anti-popes'. This became a deciding factor in 1958 when Angelo Roncalli assumed the name 'John' and styled himself Pope John XXIII, thereby excluding the second of the Pisan popes, Baldassarre Cossa, who bore the name John XXIII until his deposition by the Council of Constance in 1415.

meteor-like ascendency of Clement's early career had augured great things for him. Were it not for the fateful precipitation of events between the months of April and September 1378, both his later life and the subsequent history of all western Christendom might have been so very different.

Robert of Geneva, the future Pope Clement VII, was born in 1342 in the château of Annecy, the ancestral home of the counts of Geneva. He was the fifth son of Count Amadeus III and his wife Mahaut de Boulogne, and was christened Robert after his maternal grandfather, the count of Auvergne. His elder brothers were Aimon, Amadeus, Jean and Pierre, and his five younger sisters were Marie, Blanche, Jeanne, Yolande and Catherine.[1] His family was closely connected to the royal house of France and to many other princely and noble families.[2] As befitted a younger scion with little chance of succeeding to the family title, Robert was destined from childhood for the Church and he received the appropriate education in the household of his maternal uncle, the influential Cardinal Guy de Boulogne, in residence at the papal court in Avignon. To launch this nephew's career, the cardinal obtained a dispensation from Pope Clement VI that enabled Robert, then at the tender age of nine and so otherwise impeded by defect of canonical age, to accept almost any ecclesiastical position, or benefice, even those entailing cure of

[1] There is no major work on Clement VII in English. Until recently, the best accounts of his life were to be found in N. Valois, *La France et le Grand Schisme d'Occident*. 4 vols. (Paris, 1896-1902), and the article by G. Mollat, 'Clément VII (Robert de Genève)', in *Dictionaire d'histoire et de géographie ecclésiastiques*, xii (Paris, 1953), 1162-75. Recently, however, several interesting works have been published in Switzerland, which throw considerably more light on the personality of Clement VII. These are: P. Duparc, *Le Comté de Genève, IXe-XVe siècle* (Mémoires et Documents publiés par la Société d'Histoire et d'Archeologie de Genève, xxx, Geneva, 1955); L. Binz, *Vie religieuse et réforme ecclésiastique dans la diocèse de Genève pendant le Grand Schisme et la Crise Conciliare (1378-1450)*, (Mémoires et Documents publiés par la Société d'Histoire et d'Archéologie de Genève, xlvi, Geneva, 1973); and finally, R. Logoz, *Clément VII (Robert de Genève). Sa Chancellerie et le Clergé Romand au début du Grand Schisme (1378-1394)*, (Mémoires et Documents publiés par la Société de la Suisse romande, 3rd series, x, Lausanne, 1974). This last work contains an exhaustive bibliography on pp xxv-xxxv.

[2] The family could trace its descent back to Louis VII of France (1137-80). See Valois, *Grand Schisme*, i, p 109. After Robert of Geneva's election to the papacy, it was claimed that he was related to Robert II, king of Scots. Probably this lineal descent was traced back through Mary, countess of Boulogne, daughter of St Margaret and Malcolm III. See *Chron. Bower*, i, p 364. Belief in this auspicious family connection must have greatly influenced Robert II's decision to adhere to Clement VII.

souls.[1] Over the next ten years Robert accumulated a variety of sinecures, including a canonry and prebend of Astorga, and the annexed archdeaconry of Bergido, in Spain;[2] a canonry and prebend of Paris, where, in later life, he claimed to have resided at one time,[3] probably in order to attend the university and further his education; and the chancellorship of Amiens, where Guy de Boulogne, at an equally early age, had once held a canonry. Moreover, he was licensed to act as a papal notary[4] and was admitted to the ranks of the familiars of Pope Innocent vi. When the pope promoted him to the vacant diocese of Thérouanne[5], Robert of Geneva, aged nineteen, was simply a tonsured clerk, without having as yet received ordination to holy orders. No doubt the progressive grades of orders were conferred upon him in rapid succession (as in the case of St Thomas Becket and many other instances), and the mere fact that he no longer figures in records as 'bishop-elect', implies that he had de facto received episcopal consecration. Seven years later, on 11 October 1368, Robert was transferred to the important diocese of Cambrai,[6] situated within the confines of the Empire, which he retained until his elevation to the cardinalate. It is unlikely that he ever functioned as bishop in either of these dioceses, at least not in any permanent way, and probably the greater part of his time was spent at the papal court of Avignon.

Robert of Geneva did not have to wait long for the cardinalate

[1] The dispensation is dated 1 December 1351. Reg Vat 145, f. 123; Reg Vat 244-N, f. 133, n. 326. See E. Deprez, G. Mollat, *Clément VI. Lettres closes, patentes et curiales se rapportant à la France*, iii (Paris, 1959), p 228, n. 5133, where Robert's age is given incorrectly as being fourteen years.

[2] Reg Aven 151, ff. 63, 202. See A. Fierens, C. Tihon, *Lettres d'Urban V (1362-1370)*, i (1362-1366) (Analecta Vaticano-Belgica, ix, Rome, 1928), pp 151, n. 443 and p 237, n. 646.

[3] There is no Vatican source for this information, but Valois, *Grand Schisme*, i, p 81, note 3, quotes a bull of Clement VII, dated 24 April 1383, to the diocese of Paris, in which he asserts 'dum minori fungeremur officio, canonicatum et prebendam obtinuimus et residentiam fecimus personalem'; Paris, Archives Nationales, L 364, n. 24.

[4] Reg Suppl 33, f. 26v. The letter is dated 23 February 1360. Robert is described as being provost of the collegiate church of St Barthélemy at Béthune, Arras diocese.

[5] The bull of provision is dated 3 November 1361. Reg Aven 147, ff. 216v-17. See C. Eubel, *Hierarchia Catholica Medii Aevi*, i (Munster, 1913), p 351.

[6] Apparently, the registration of this provision is lost. Eubel, *Hierarchia*, i, p 160, gives the date as being 11 October 1368, but the reference to Reg Aven 167, f. 3v, is simply to the rubric listing the provisions, without supplying the dates.

to be conferred upon him. Pope Gregory XI, who esteemed Robert highly, created him a cardinal priest, with the Roman title of the basilica of the Twelve Apostles[1], in the first promotion of cardinals of his pontificate[2]. At the time Robert was only twenty-nine years of age. The cardinalate secured for him a place at the centre of one of the most splendid courts of all times. The 'cardinal of Geneva', the name by which he became more generally known, set up his official residence at Avignon in the Livrée de Giffon,[3] where he continued to live in the lavish style to which he had been accustomed from birth. His income as a cardinal was enormously augmented, especially by the share he received from the revenues that the papal curia exacted in the form of 'common services'[4]. His expenditure must also have been colossal. Like most other churchmen of his day, Robert of Geneva was ready to accept any lucrative benefice in order to help defray his endless expenses. He is known to have held the priories of Etoy, Payerne and Douvaine, but until all the chancery registers of Pope Gregory XI have been calendared, it remains impossible to estimate the full extent of his pluralism.[5] When his father, Count Amadeus, died in January 1367, he left in his testament the castle of Beauregard and Gaillard to his cadet son.[6]

The young cardinal was endowed by nature with a fine physique, coupled with a pleasant personality. Apparently he was of more than average height, but suffered from lameness and short-sightedness (or perhaps a squint), but these defects did not detract from his otherwise commanding appearance. His voice was deep and sonorous and he knew how to express himself with elegance in several languages, both in speech and in writing. His demeanour was affable and he possessed real qualities of diplomacy, being able

---

[1] At least since the third century this term has been used to designate the older churches of Rome. In this way, the cardinal priests, representing the 'presbyterium' of the City, were always assigned a titular church, a practice which continues to the present day.

[2] The consistory was held on 30 May 1371. See Eubel, *Hierarchia*, i, p 21.

[3] P. Pansier, *Les Palais cardinalices d'Avignon aux XIVme et XVme siècles*. Fasc. i (Avignon 1926-29), p 62.

[4] The 'common services' were so called because the revenue exacted from the abbots and bishops, whom the pope appointed, or confirmed, in bishoprics or abbeys of an annual income of more than 100 florins, was divided equally between the College of cardinals and the Apostolic Camera. See Boyle, *Survey*, p 157.

[5] Logoz, *Clément VII*, p 13.

[6] Duparc, *Comté de Genève*, p 304.

to delight those who approached him.[1] There is abundant evidence that he was a man of culture, with an appreciation of the fine arts and of music, and he took pleasure in the company of musicians and minstrels.[2] This does not mean that he was effeminate, or soft, because he is also said to have mixed easily with his men-at-arms.

This characteristic, perhaps, pointed him out as the most suitable person to entrust with the military mission to Italy at a particularly critical moment, when several cities of the Papal States were in open revolt against Pope Gregory xi and the territories themselves were threatened from Florence and Milan. Robert of Geneva set out from Avignon on 27 May 1376 with some 6,000 footmen and about 4,000 horsemen under his command, and by the beginning of July he reached Bologna, where an unsuccessful siege operation was begun, which later had to be abandoned. The cardinal marched instead on Faenza, Forli, Cesena and Rimini. On 1 February 1377 a riot of such ferocity broke out at Cesena against the Breton mercenaries, that the legate had to take refuge for his life in the citadel, leaving behind 400 of his men dead in the town. The garrison was reduced almost to the point of surrender, when it was relieved by Sir John Hawkwood, the notorious English *condottiere*. The Breton troops went berserk and revenged themselves on the towns-folk without the least regard for sex or age. Local chroniclers have reckoned the toll as being as high as 4,000 lives.[3] The papal legate, far from restraining his men, is accused of inciting them to commit further excesses and the atrocity earned for him the infamous title of 'butcher of Cesena'. There is no doubt that this reputation, deserved or undeserved, seriously damaged his cause in Italy in the immediate years that followed. In spite of this incident, the mission succeeded in its original purpose of pacification, and, on 13 March 1378, the cardinal of Geneva was able to rejoin the papal curia, which by that time had been re-established in Rome for little over a year.[4] Within only two weeks, however, the pope died and events

[1] Valois, *Grand Schisme*, p 81.
[2] E. Müntz, 'L'antipape Clément vii, essai sur l'histoire des arts à Avignon vers la fin du xive siècle', *Revue archéologique*, 3rd series, xi (1888), pp 8-18, 163-83.
[3] For a bibliography of this incident and a discussion of the degree of blame to be attached to Robert of Geneva, see Logoz, *Clément VII*, pp 19-20.
[4] Pope Gregory xi left Avignon on 13 September 1376. After a stormy and almost disastrous voyage by sea, he reached Rome on 17 January 1377.

began to take that catastrophic course, which altered drastically the life of Robert of Geneva and divided western Christendom for almost forty years, in what has come to be known as the Great Schism.

Stated in the most simple of terms, the key events took place in this order.[1] Pope Gregory XI died on 27 March 1378. Eleven days later the sixteen cardinals then present in Rome assembled in the Vatican Palace, and on the following morning, 8 April, they elected Bartolomeo Prignano, the archbishop of Bari, as pope. Since all the formalities of the election could not be completed that same day, his acceptance and enthronement only took place the next day. On the following Sunday he presided as pope in St Peter's basilica at the liturgy of Palm Sunday, at which the cardinals also participated, and a week later, on Easter Sunday, he was solemnly crowned as Pope Urban VI. The cardinals wrote to the emperor and to various other kings and princes notifying them of the election of the new pope. They also presented rolls of petitions to the pontiff, asking for numerous favours. During the month of May, one by one the cardinals obtained his permission to leave Rome, on the pretext of the excessive summer heat, and by 24 June all the non-Italian cardinals, together with many members of the papal curia, had reassembled at Anagni, a town in the Papal States, about forty miles south of Rome. From there they later publicly repudiated Urban, declaring his election to be null and void, and calling upon him to vacate the pacacy. When Urban VI refused to comply, the cardinals (including the three Italian members of the college) moved further south to Fondi, just outside the boundaries of the Papal State, where, on 20 September, they elected Cardinal Robert of Geneva as pope in a unanimous, one-ballot election. The next day he was proclaimed as Pope Clement VII and was crowned at Fondi on 31 October following.

[1] The election of Urban VI has been examined from every possible angle and a vast literature exists on this subject. The output of continental authors has been particularly abundant. For English readers, a neutral position with regards to the two rival popes is adopted by P. Hughes, *A History of the Church*, iii (1270-1517), (London, 1955), pp 229-46, and also by K. Fink, *Handbook of Church History*, iv, *From the High Middle Ages to the Eve of the Reformation* (Freiburg, 1969), pp 401-25; a more partisan position in favour of Urban VI is taken up by W. Ullmann, *The Origins of the Great Schism* (London, 1948). All three authors provide a full bibliography.

The elucidation and evaluation of these events, from the election of Urban VI to the open defection of the cardinals, constitute one of the greatest problems of medieval church history.

Pope Gregory XI, after little more than a year in Rome, had been persuaded by the cardinals to return, with the curia, to Avignon, and a decision had been taken to do so in the coming autumn. Then, on 27 March 1378, the premature death of the pope plunged the papacy into a critical situation.

At that time the college of cardinals was composed of twenty-three members, of whom six were still in residence at Avignon and one was absent on a diplomatic mission elsewhere in Italy. The remaining sixteen cardinals, all present in Rome at the moment of the pope's demise, consisted of eleven Frenchmen, four Italians and one Spaniard. Already the college was divided internally over the choice of a new pope: the numerically stronger Limousin faction wanted to secure the election of yet another pope of their 'nationality', which was the very thing that the Gallic faction was determined to thwart at all costs. So difficulties were already foreboded for the conclave.

This was the first papal election to be held in Rome for seventy-five years,[1] and among the populace there was an overriding sense of urgency that the cardinals must be persuaded to elect a Roman, or failing that, at least an Italian, as pope, who would keep the curia in Rome and not allow it to return to Avignon, thereby putting an end to French predominance in the government of the Church. In the days following upon the death of Pope Gregory XI, this proposition was put to the cardinals at an official level by the city officials. Consequently, before the cardinals ever entered the conclave, the question of finding a compromise candidate had already arisen and in their informal discussions the name of Bartolomeo Prignano, although not himself a cardinal, had probably been mentioned if not formally proposed.

That is how matters stood when the cardinals, having first had to pass through a noisy, menacing crowd to reach the Vatican, entered the conclave on the evening of 7 April 1378. Late into the night

---

[1] The previous election that was held in Rome was of Pope Benedict XI, on 12 October 1303. It is worth noting, that over the period 1198-1378, out of twenty-six papal elections, only six took place in Rome.

the rabble, by then much the worse of drink, kept up a constant fracas outside, shouting as before for the election of a Roman, or at least of an Italian. Early the next morning, as the liturgical preliminaries to the election were in progress, the din broke out afresh and the guardians of the conclave beseeched the cardinals to make haste – and to content the mob – otherwise there could be no guarantee for their safety. Seeing that a regular procedure was now impossible, the majority of the cardinals expressed a simple verbal assent to the election of an Italian in the person of Bartolomeo Prignano, archbishop of Bari and regent of the papal chancery. Not being a cardinal himself, Prignano had been excluded from taking part in the conclave and was not even present in the palace ; so he had to be summoned, along with several other prelates of the curia. Meantime the impatient crowd outside, sensing that the election had taken place and suspecting that the French cardinals had cheated them,[1] began to hammer furiously at the doors of the conclave. Inside, the cardinals hastily vested the only Roman cardinal, the ailing octogenarian Pietro Tebaldeschi, in the pontifical cope to act as a decoy and gain time. As the mob rushed into the chapel they left him enthroned and fled from the scene, intent only on saving their own lives. Not a thought was given to the pope-elect. On the next day, when word had spread that an Italian had been elected and a semblance of calm had returned to the Vatican, twelve of the cradinals reassembled to complete the formalities of announcing to Bartolomeo Prignano his election to the papacy and receiving his acceptance. At that moment, Prignano, who assumed the pontifical name of Urban VI, appeared to be as legitimate a pope as ever his predecessor, Gregory XI, had been. It has never been possible, therefore, to explain satisfactorily how the same cardinals came to abandon him and denounce their own electoral act as invalid.

Part of the explanation can be found, perhaps, in the hostile attitude adopted by the new pontiff towards the cardinals from the moment of his coronation. His outbursts of temper appear to have

---

[1] It has been argued that some confusion may indeed have been made between the title 'Barensis' of the archbishop of Bari, and Jean de Bar, a detested relative of the late Pope Gregory XI. Thinking that the latter had been elected the fury of the mob erupted against the French cardinals. See Logoz, *Clément VII*, p 45.

been so violent and uncontrolled that most historians agree that the former archbishop of Bari took leave of his senses upon election to the papacy. If, on the other hand, he had proved to be more indulgent towards the cardinal-electors, it is unlikely that they would ever have given a second thought to the irregular circumstances of his election, and, least of all, to the part played in it by the Roman crowd. When, however, the cardinals saw that they had no influence over Urban VI and that he would never be persuaded to leave Rome and return to Avignon, they then sought for legal grounds to overthrow the election and declare it null and void. In a solemn declaration they explained to the Church how they had been forced into performing what in effect had been no election at all, but a complete farce, on account of the real fear that the mob surrounding the conclave had instilled in them. They soon followed this up with a second declaration, that, as a consequence, the Apostolic See remained vacant and that Urban was an intruder and must return to private life. To put an end to the *sede vacante*, therefore, the cardinals, whose original composition was virtually unchanged,[1] proceeded to elect Robert of Geneva to the papacy, and with his election at Fondi the schism became a reality.

The action of the cardinals proved to be an appalling miscalculation. Perhaps they imagined that Urban VI, when faced with a pope whom the cardinals had elected unanimously, would soon abandon all pretence to being pope himself. It is unthinkable that they foresaw the disastrous consequences of their second conclave, but once they had chosen that road they could not turn back. The scandal of rival popes, solemnly excommunicating each other, lasted for almost the next half-century, to the incalculable detriment of the papacy itself and of ecclesiastical authority generally. Within only a matter of weeks the various nations of Christendom began to declare their support for one or other of the rival popes, motivated largely by the political advantages such support might bring. As early as 18 October 1378, even before Clement VII's coronation at Fondi, the

---

[1] The aged Cardinal Tebaldeschi died on 20 August, and the remaining fifteen original electors had been joined in the meantime by Cardinal Jean de la Grange, who had been absent on the diplomatic mission at the time of the April election. When he returned to Rome, already furious that his colleagues had elected an Italian, he had a violent and unfriendly reception from the new pope. Later, Urban VI declared that this cardinal was the chief architect of the Schism.

emperor had announced his support for Urban vi. On 5 November Richard ii of England also declared himself in favour of Urban. On 16 November Charles v of France, with the support of the university of Paris, announced his decision to adhere instead to the party of Clement vii, composed as it was of his own kinsman and the mainly French cardinal-electors. Robert ii, king of Scots, followed the example of the king of France, and was numbered among those kings *'qui potuerunt citius informare conscientias suas'*, and therefore *'noluerunt ulterius differe nec alios expectare, sed iam declaraverunt se velle obedire domino Clementi'*.[1] For the moment the kings of Castille, Aragon, Navarre and Portugal remained neutral, but eventually, after an exhaustive enquiry into the events of the two elections of 1378,[2] they too went over to the side of Clement vii, who, by that time, could also count on the support of Naples, Savoy and Sicily. The rest of Italy and the Scandinavian countries had already taken sides with Urban vi. The emperor denounced the cardinals as the *'destructores Christianae unitatis'*, and the Church remained torn apart until the Schism was healed by the election of Martin v in 1417 at the Council of Constance. Throughout the duration of the Schism, even when other nations wavered or changed sides altogether, Scotland remained steadfast in its allegiance to Clement vii, and later to his successor at Avignon, Benedict xiii, until eventually, the Scots were alone in their support of the 'Avignon pope'.

The election of Clement vii was hailed by the majority of the curial officials who deserted Urban vi and went over to the rival party. At first Clement's cause appeared to be the more promising, but after he failed to gain possession of Rome, it became clear that his position in Italy was untenable. Accompanied by the cardinals and other officials he returned to Avignon, where he spent the remainder of his life.[3] His pontificate was overshadowed by the

---

[1] Baxter, *Copiale,* p xxxvii, n. 1.

[2] Vatican Archives, Arm. liv, 14-39. The contents of this cupboard are fundamental for the history of the Great Schism. These volumes have been described by M. Seidlmayer, *Die spanischen Libri de Schismate des Vatikanischen Archivs,* (Gesammelte Aufsätze zur Kulturgeschichte Spaniens, viii, Munster, 1940), pp 199-262.

[3] Each step of Clement vii's return journey to Avignon is minutely described in Logoz, *Clément VII,* pp 131-2. After his re-entry there on 20 June 1379, the pope remained at Avignon throughout his entire pontificate, except for his occasional sojourns in the summer months at Sorgues, Châteauneuf-du-Pape, Villeneuve-lès-Avignon, Roquemaure, Carpentras, Beaucaire, Tarascon, and Aramon.

endless debates over the validity, or invalidity, of Urban's election, and, consequently, over the legitimacy of his own title to the papacy. Every effort was made to dissipate the uncertainty as to the legitimate pope; exhaustive enquiries were instituted and countless witnesses were interrogated. Through all the time that the Great Schism lasted, both 'obediences', the Roman and the Avignonese, could count among their supporters men of the greatest learning, both theologians and canonists, and also men of outstandingly holy lives. In spite of this it was never possible to clarify the issue so that no doubts remained in the majority of minds.

Clement VII enjoyed robust health throughout his life. Only once is it recorded that he required the services of a doctor. His death, therefore, at the age of only fifty-two was premature. After three days of slight indisposition, the pope suffered what has been described as a fit of apoplexy as he re-entered his rooms after hearing Mass, and, about ten o'clock on the morning of 16 September 1394, he died peacefully. Two days later a provisional interment took place in the cathedral of Avignon. Later, when the church of the Celestins was completed, his remains were exhumed and solemnly transferred to a fine monument that had been erected to his memory beside the tomb of Blessed Peter of Luxemburg, whom Clement VII himself had raised to the cardinalate at the age of seventeen, and who died at the papal court with a reputation of great sanctity. For four centuries Clement lay there undisturbed, but in the orgy of the French Revolution his tomb was broken into and his mortal remains were scattered on the street. The monument itself was completely destroyed and only the mutilated head of his recumbent effigy exists today.

The Registers of Clement VII[1]

The Avignon chancery registers for the period covered by the present calendar consist today of seventy-six paper and nine parch-

[1] The chancery registers of Pope Clement VII are described in minute detail by E. Göller, *Repertorium Germanicum*: i, *Clemens VII von Avignon (1378-1394)* (Berlin, 1916), pp 16*-29*. Likewise, a full analysis of these registers has been made by H. Diener, *Die Grossen Registerserien im Vatikanischen Archiv (1378-1523)*, in Quellen und Forschungen aus italienischen Archiven und Bibliotheken, li (Tübingen, 1972). pp 305-68.

ment volumes, corresponding to the Vatican Archives classification of *Registra Avenionensia* 205-40,[1] 242-5,[2] 247-74, and *Registra Vaticana* 291-307. Considering their chequered history and granted, therefore, that the series is not complete, the first question to be answered is, how incomplete are these records for Clement VII's pontificate? Is it possible, from a comparison of the several inventories made at different times in the past, to arrive at an estimate of the overall losses sustained, and even to indicate the pontifical years in which the gaps occur? Unfortunately, absolute trust cannot be placed in the figures provided by the various lists, almost all of which contain discrepancies of some sort, but the final analysis is probably not far from the truth.

The earliest extant inventory was compiled by Pompeo Capello in 1542, before any of the registers had left Avignon for Rome. It lists the registers of all the Avignon popes year by year, and those of Clement VII are given as follows:

Clementis VII. Bullarum Avenioni datarum libri 91, omnes in bombacina charta, sine rubricellis in capite.

De anno 1, libri 17	De anno 9, libri 4
De anno 2, libri 7	De anno 10, libri 5
De anno 3, libri 7	De anno 11, libri 7
De anno 4, libri 6	De anno 12, libri 7
De anno 5, libri 6	De anno 13, libri 5
De anno 6, libri 3	De anno 14, libri 6
De anno 7, libri 6	De anno 15, libri 5
De anno 8, libri 4	De anno 16, libri 2

Ex hiis libris tot bullae in membranis descriptae sunt quod 9 libri editi sunt cum suis rubricellis in capite. De anno 1, 2, 3, 4, 5, 6, 7, 8, 9, 10 – libri singulares 9.
Rotulus 1 bullarum similium.
Processus in causa schismatis post Gregorii XI obitum,

[1] Reg Aven 241 is entitled 'Clemens VII. An. VII. Pars III. Tom. XXXVII', but in fact the letters contained in it all belong to the pontificate of Pope Clement VI.
[2] Reg Aven 246 is entitled 'Clemens VII. An. VIII. Pars IV. Tom. XLII', but in fact its contents are entirely from the pontificate of Pope Clement VI, and this register has now been reclassified as Reg Aven 110.

inter Urbanum vi et Clementem vii, exorti in pluribus
libris, quinternis et schedulis scripturisque.[1]
There are some obvious discrepancies. A simple addition shows
that the total number of paper volumes should read ninety-seven,
and not ninety-one.[2] Likewise, if there was a parchment register
for each pontifical year, then surely the number of volumes should
be ten, and not nine? Today, in point of fact, there are only nine
parchment registers of Clement vii, there being none that corre-
sponds with his fourth pontifical year, but endorsements in one of
the paper registers of that fourth year attest that at least some
quires were copied out on parchment.[3] The paper registers are
described as being without indexes at the beginning, so presumably
the *rubricellae* were only inserted, when these volumes were properly
bound at the start of the eighteenth century.

The second inventory is the procès-verbal drawn up by Mario
Zazzarino, in 1566, when the parchment registers of the popes were
dispatched to Rome.[4] According to this list the registers of Clement
vii were ten in all, and for almost fifty years they were housed in
the Vatican Library. They were among the first things to be transferred to the new Vatican Archive, in 1611 as is recorded in the
inventory of Michele Lonigo: 'Regesta antiqua Pontificum olim
pro maiori parte lacerata, quae in Vaticana Bibliotheca asservabantur,
Sanctissimi Domini Nostri Pauli v pecunia restaurata, et de novo
cooperta, ac in novum Vaticanum Archivum eiusdem iussu
reposita. . . . Clementis 7¹ antipapae Libri 9'.[5] Zazzarino is in contra-

---

[1] There are five copies of Capello's list extant: Vatican Archives, Arm. xxxvii,
40, f. 371, and Indice 75, ff. 86v-87; Vatican Library, Codd. Barb. lat. 2312, f. 232-32v,
and Barb. lat. 3169, ff. 108v-9. The fifth ms is Vat. lat. 5302, but this codex is in such
a fragile condition that it was not possible to consult it and indicate the folios relevant
to the registers of Clement vii. The list is published in extenso by Benoit, *Archives
d'Avignon*, pp 26-31.

[2] There are slight difference between the various copies. In some the number of
registers for the third year is given as six, and for the twelfth year as five. Even so,
the total would not be ninety-one.

[3] In Reg Aven 229, which bears the title 'Clemens vii. An. iv. Pars ii. Tom. xxv',
from f. 180v to f. 459 there are endorsements to the effect that the quires have been
recopied on to parchment. On ff. 411 and 459, in the midst of a quire, a note has been
added 'Scriptus in pergamena usque hic'. [4] Gachard, *Archives*, pp 10-11.

[5] F. Gasparolo, *Costituzione dell'Archivio Vaticano e suo primo indice sotto il pontificato
di Paolo V. Manoscritto inedito di Michele Lonigo* (Studi e Documenti di Storia e Diritto,
viii, Rome, 1887), p 36. The original index of Lonigo is now in the Vatican Library,
ms Vat. lat. 10247.

C

diction to both Capello and Lonigo regarding the number of parchment registers. Are we to deduce that the register of Clement VII's fourth pontifical year disappeared between 1566 and 1611, or, in fact, was it already lost before the registers ever left Avignon? Unfortunately, there is no more precise information to be had regarding this parchment register, and so it must be considered as lost, though it is the only loss from the series of parchment registers of Clement VII. Lonigo lists a 'Regestum litterarum de Curia annorum 12 et 13 Clementis 7^1 antipapae'^{1} as also having come from the Vatican Library, when an exchange of paper volumes was made, but he makes no mention of other paper registers of Clement VII, although at some time at least another seven had been brought to Rome and added to the series of papal registers, where today they are classified as Reg Vat 300-307.

Meantime, in an undated, seventeenth-century account, the registers of Clement VII still in Avignon were inventoried as follows:

Clementis 7^1 Anni primi libri 16. Unus in quo Bulla qua Equitibus Rhodi permittitur ut ad victum necessaria ab infidelibus emant, attenta peniuria tritici: et alius in quo Bulla qua Ludovico Duci Andegaven., Regis in Britania et Aquitania locumtenenti, permittitur decimam exigere pro tuitioni regni.

Anni 2^1 6. Unus in quo Bulla super reconciliationem civitatis Florentiae cum Summo Pontifice.

Anni 3^1 quinque	Anni 4^1 sex
Anni 5^1 quinque	Anni 6^1 quatuor
Anni 7^1 tres	Anni octavi quinque
Anni noni quinque	Anni decimi quinque.

Unus in quo Bulla quomodo Cardinales creandi Pontificis causa in conclavi debeant manere.

Anni XI^1 quinque	Anni 12^1 quinque
Anni 13^1 4	Anni 14^1 unus
Anni 15^1 tres	Anni 16^1 unus.^{2}

The final list for comparison is that of the Abbé Carlo Bonacca, who provided the Cardinal Secretary of State with precise details

---

[1] Gasparolo, *Costituzione*, p 40. This register is Reg Vat 301.
[2] Vatican Library, MS Barb. lat. 6538, f. 23.

of the contents of each of the sixteen chests of archive material when these were sent to Rome in 1783.[1] The paper chancery registers, within each single pontificate, were numbered consecutively, and are listed by their ordinal numbers in this document. The seventh chest contained volumes 1-12 and 27-42 of Clement VII, a total of twenty-eight volumes. Bonacca adds a note to the effect that volumes 13-26 of this pope were missing, and apparently had been missing for a considerable number of years. He could not say if they had been already transferred to Rome, but there was no trace of them in Avignon. The next chest contained volumes 43-70, again twenty-eight volumes of Clement VII's pontificate in all, together with the first six volumes of his predecessor, Benedict XII (1334-42). Included with these were reputedly volumes 13-26 of Pope Clement XI, who reigned from 1700 until 1721, and of whose pontificate, according to Bonacca, the previous twelve volumes were missing. What a strange coincidence, that precisely those volumes that were missing from the pontificate of Clement VII, should turn up as registers of a pope, who lived over 300 years later ! The mystery of the missing registers is easily solved by checking on volumes 13-26 of Clement VII in the Avignon Registers, where the name of Clement XI (in whose pontificate these registers were bound for the first time) has carelessly been stamped on the spine of each volume instead of that of Clement VII. This episode, however, serves to illustrate that the data furnished by these various lists and inventories must be accepted with caution.

By putting all this information together and comparing it with the paper registers, as they are today, the following table results, from which a general conclusion can be drawn.

The table shows the gradual losses sustained in the number of registers of each pontifical year, which in almost all years is perfectly straightforward. Attention, however, should be paid to the figures for the sixth to the ninth years, which contrast with the progressive losses noted at all other times. Perhaps the explanation of this irregularity lies in the fact that some of these registers were mistakenly ascribed to the wrong years, for if we accept Capello's total of seventeen volumes for those four years, then, with sixteen extant today, the loss amounts to one register only. This would imply that

---

[1] Vatican Archives, Congregazione d'Avignone, 152, ff. 3-4.

the records for three of those years, probably the sixth, seventh and ninth, are in fact complete. So the overall picture that emerges is that for five pontifical years the registers are complete, whereas for the other years approximately one parchment and twenty-one paper registers have been lost. This means that over one-fifth of the chancery records for the pontificate of Clement VII has perished,

Pont. year	Capello's list (1542)	In Vatican before 1700	In Avignon in 17th cent.	Bonacca's list (1783)	Present Day	Number presumed lost
I	17		16	16	16	1
II	7		6	4	4	3
III	7		5	3	3	4
IV	6		6	4	4	2
V	6		5	3	3	3
VI	3		4	4	4	
VII	6	1	3	4[2]	4	1
VIII	4		5	4[3]	3	
IX	4		5	5	5	
X	5		5	4	4	1
XI	7		5	4	4	3
XII	7	1	5	5	6	1
XIII	5		4	4	4	1
XIV	6	3	1	2	5	1
XV	5	2	3	3	5	0
XVI	2	1	1	1	2	0
	97	8[1]	79	70	76	21

[1] These registers are now Reg Vat 300-7.
[2] Reg Aven 241, which is really a register of Clement VI.
[3] Reg Aven 110, but at one time classified as Reg Aven 246, and later identified as belonging to the pontificate of Clement VI.

which is an appreciable loss. It is worth noting, however, that, at least so far as Scottish entries are concerned, no letter has been found in the parchment registers for which there is no corresponding letter in the paper series.

The Registers of Benedict XIII

It seems appropriate to include, at this point, a similar analysis of the chancery registers of Benedict XIII (the immediate successor of Clement VII at Avignon), from which the contents of the companion volume to the present calendar have been derived.

Only eighty-four registers, corresponding to the modern classification of *Registra Avenionensia* 278-349 and *Registra Vaticana* 321-332, have survived from the long and turbulent pontificate of Benedict XIII (1394-1414). These all belong to the paper series of first registration and there is no indication that a parallel series of parchment registers ever existed for this period, probably because the practice of making fair copies on parchment had already ceased during the pontificate of Clement VII. From a comparison of the same extant inventories, some idea can be formed of what proportion these registers represent of the complete series of records. It remains difficult, however, to indicate with accuracy, from the figures available, the pontifical years in which the greatest losses have been sustained.

The first list for comparison is taken from the inventory drawn up by Pompeo Capello, in 1542. It provides the following description of Benedict XIII's registers:

De anno	1, libri 21.	De anno	14, libri 4.
De anno	2, libri 6.	De anno	15, libri 3.
De anno	3, libri 5.	De anno	16, libri 3.
De anno	4, liber 1.	De anno	17, libri 3.
De annis	5, 6 et 7 desunt libri.	De anno	18, libri 2.
De anno	8, liber 1.	De anno	19, libri 2.
De anno	9, libri 4.	De anno	20, libri 2.
De anno	10, libri 19.	De anno	21, libri 3.
De anno	11, libri 5.	De anno	22, liber 1.
De anno	12, libri 5.	De anno	23, liber 1.
De anno	13, libri 4.	De anno	24, liber 1.

De anno 29 et 1º inclusive de omnibus liber 1.

Libri 25 computorum.

Libri registri supplicationum 13.

Rotuli 2 magni bullarum plumbatarum originalium.[1]

There are no obvious discrepancies in this list and the total of 97 volumes is accurate, in contrast to Capello's faulty addition of Clement VII's registers in the preceding section.

The first transport of chancery records from Avignon to Rome, in 1566, consisted exclusively of the *volumina vitellina*, which Mario Zazzarino described only summarily in his procès-verbal. As it is unlikely that a series of parchment volumes ever existed for the pontificate of Benedict XIII, it is not surprising that his name does not figure on the list with those of his predecessors. This is corroborated by the fact that no mention is made of registers of Benedict XIII by Michele Lonigo, in 1611, when the original nucleus of archive material was transferred from the Vatican Library to the newly-founded Vatican Archives.

A new inventory of the chancery registers that still remained in the papal palace at Avignon was prepared sometime in the course of the seventeenth century. It lists the volumes of Benedict XIII's pontificate as follows:

Benedicti XIII adsunt Anni primi, libri 22.

Anni 2[1], septem. Unus in quo Bulla qua taxantur expensae episcoporum in visitationibus.

Anni 3[11], sex. Unus in quo Bulla super concordia Ursinorum et Coloniensium.

Anni 4[1], tres.	Anni 5[1], duo.
Anni 6[1], unus.	Anni 7[1], unus.
Anni 8[1], unus.	Anni noni, duo.
Anni 10[1], quindecim.	Anni XI, quinque.
Anni 12[1], 4[r].	Anni 13[1], quatuor.
Anni 14[1], duo.	Anni 15[1], tres.
Anni 16[1], tres.	Anni 17[1], tres.
Anni 18[1], duo.	Anni 19[1], duo.

---

[1] Vatican Archives, Arm. XXXVII, 40, f. 371, and Indice 75, ff. 87v-88; Vatican Library, Codd. Barb. lat. 2312, f. 232-3, and Barb. lat. 3169, f. 109. Cod. Vat. lat. 5302, which contains a fifth MS of Capello's list, is illegible. The list is published in Benoit, *Archives d'Avignon*, pp. 30-1.

Anni 20[1], duo. Unus in quo Bulla qua conceditur Regi
Castello quarta pars fructuum ecclesiasticorum pro ex-
pellendis a Regno Sarracenis.

Anni 21[1], tres.   Anni 23, unus.[1]

Before the end of the century at least twelve volumes were
brought to Rome, and added to the collection of chancery and
cameral registers which were already housed in the Vatican Archives.
The transfer must have taken place sometime before the remaining
seventy-two registers were bound early in the eighteenth century,
because there is no evidence that volumes were subsequently
removed from the series.

The final inventory for comparison is that of the Abbé Carlo
Bonacca, in which he describes in detail the contents of each of the
sixteen chests on the eve of their departure for Rome in 1783. The
ninth chest contained the first eighteen registers of Benedict XIII,
together with two registers of his predecessor Benedict XII (1334-
42), and volumes 13-26 of Clement VII, wrongly ascribed by the
binder to Clement XI (1700-21), and repeated by Bonacca. The
remaining registers of Benedict XIII followed in the next two
chests: volumes 19-50 in the tenth chest, and volumes 51-72 in the
eleventh.[2]

When the information provided by these various lists is put
together and compared with the registers as they are today, the
following table results, from which a general conclusion can be
drawn.

A drastic reversal of fortune and the mounting defections from
his obedience are clearly reflected in these records of Benedict XIII.
Their early history is quite separate from that of the other registers
of the Avignon chancery and it poses questions, which for the
present must remain unanswered. Benedict XIII was besieged in
the papal palace at Avignon for over four years, from 1398 onwards,
and this isolation accounts for the almost complete interruption of
normal communications throughout that entire period, from the
fifth to the eighth pontifical year. Two registers, Reg Aven 305 and
306, contain the only letters dated during those years. In March

[1] Vatican Library, MS Barb. lat. 6538, f. 22v.

[2] Vatican Archives, Congregazione d'Avignone, 152, ff. 4-4v.

Pont. year	Capello's list (1542)	In Avignon in 17th cent.	In Vatican before 18th cent.	Bonacca's list (1783)	Present day	Number presumed lost
I	21	22		20	20	
II	6	7	1	3	4	
III	5	6		3	3	
IV	1	3	1	1	2	
V	—	2				4
VI	—	1		1	1	
VII	—	1				
VIII	1	1		1	1	
IX	4	2	2	1	3	
X	19	15	5	9	14	5
XI	5	5		5	5	
XII	5	4		4	4	
XIII	4	4		3	3	
XIV	4	2		3	3	
XV	3	3	1	2	3	
XVI	3	3		2	2	
XVII	3	3		2	2	
XVIII	2	2		2	2	4
XIX	2	2		2	2	
XX	2	2		3	3	
XXI	3	3		3	3	
XXII	1	—	1	1	2	
XXIII	1	1		1	1	
XXIV	1	—	1	—	1	
XXIX	1	—	—	—	—	
	97	94	12	72	84	13

1403, however, the pope managed to escape under cover of dark-ness. It seems highly unlikely that he took his registers with him. By then they must have consisted of approximately thirty-five bulky volumes: did they remain behind in Avignon throughout the rest of his pontificate, or were they retrieved later? Having regained his freedom, Benedict XIII did his utmost to reassert his authority and there was a notable increase in the volume of correspondence handled by the papal chancery. At one time, apparently, there were four registers for the ninth pontifical year and as many as nineteen for the tenth year. The pope abandoned Avignon as the seat of government and spent the remaining years of his life wandering around the south of France, until finally he established his court at Peniscola, an isolated promontory to the north of Valencia in the kingdom of Aragon. By this time, most countries of the Avignon obedience, Scotland being the notable exception, had withdrawn their support from Benedict XIII and the diminishing number of registers bears witness to this steady decline. When the pope died in 1423 there were at least sixty-three registers for this latter period of his pontificate. Unfortunately, it is impossible to say at what precise date, or under what circumstances, these volumes were reunited with the parent series in Avignon, but their transport may have been organised by Cardinal Pierre de Foix, legate of Martin V, when he brought the library of Benedict XIII back to France in 1429.

Since, during this earlier period, some losses may have gone unrecorded, a doubt remains regarding the reliability of the figures provided by Capello in 1542, whether they correspond to the full number of registers that originally pertained to each year. More-over, when his list is compared with the inventory of the seventeenth century, several anomalies become immediately apparent, especially in the contradictory figures given over the first ten years of the pontificate. There is always the possibility that in the interval some registers may have been ascribed to different years. Of greater significance, however, is the fact that fundamentally both totals agree. Although the table is not perfectly straightforward, it appears that the registers are complete for at least eight pontifical years, with approximately only thirteen volumes dispersed from the remaining years. This represents a loss of less than one-seventh of the chancery registers of Benedict XIII, which is an even smaller proportion than what was calculated for the pontificate of Clement VII.

As regards the quantity of documentation, the records of Clement VII and Benedict XIII compare very favourably with those of their predecessors, as the following table clearly demonstrates :[1]

	John XXII	Benedict XII	Clement VI	Innocent VI	Urban V	Gregory XI	Clement VII	Benedict XIII
Provisions or collations :								
Bishoprics	10	3	10	1	4	3	11	13
Cathedral dignities	5		15	6	4	3	26	51
Canonries with prebends	13		9	4	1	1	17	49
Canonries with expectation of a prebend	36	2	40	13			52	26
Parish churches	4		19	2	3	5	40	91
Perpetual vicarages	1		3	1	1	1	35	49
Monastic offices	1		2	1			11	55
Reservations :								
Canonries	3	7					9	16
Benefices	17		50	2	1		73	91
Plenary indulgences	1		50	18			27	10
Dispensations :								
Illegitimacy	14	2	11		1	5	23	3
Marriage	21	6	14	9	10	7	18	66
Indults	13		21	1	2	5	24	225
Confirmations	9		2	5	2	5		97
New foundations	3		2				5	2
Litigations	8	2	2	3	4	10	19	65
Universities			2				8	11
Papal chaplains			1		1		8	30

In spite of the losses inflicted on the Avignon archives, the pontificates of Clement VII and Benedict XIII appear to be the best documented of all the popes of the fourteenth century, a factor that

[1] The survey is based entirely on the *Calendar of Papal Letters*, vols. ii–iv (1305–78) for the pontificates prior to Clement VII.

makes the publication of these calendars by the Scottish History Society all the more significant.

Method of Editing

These chancery registers are not chronicles, or diaries of events. They were compiled to fulfil a juridical function and not to serve as historical records. In calendaring the Scottish entries, however, only the details of historical importance have been extracted from them and the repetitive legal formulas omitted. Obviously, meticulous care has been taken to include all proper names, academic degrees, grades of holy orders and ecclesiastical office, together with details of parentage and relationships of consanguinity and affinity, whenever they occur. The original spelling of both proper and place names has been retained, except for the benefices of mandatories and frequent references to certain abbeys, where the modern form has been preferred. The assessed value of benefices is included as being at least indicative, even though it may seldom have corresponded closely with the true state of affairs.

The calendar is arranged chronologically, and not according to the series of registers and their folios as was done in the Bliss *Calendar*. The date is given in both its modern form and according to the style used by the papal chancery for dating the original bulls, and then entered in the registers. Only when more than one entry occurs under the same date have they been placed according to their order in the registers, with precedence given to the Avignon Registers over the Vatican Registers. During the pontificate of Clement VII what appears to be a stricter control over the dispatch of papal letters was introduced into the practice of the chancery. The first date, given after *Datum* etc., was accompanied by two subsequent dates, entered in the registers, sometimes by a different hand, under the headings of *Expedita* and *Tradita parti*,[1] together with the name, or simply the initial, of the official responsible for making these entries. Normally the intervals between the three dates are a matter of only days, or weeks at the most, but periods of some years are not uncommon.

[1] In the calendar these dates are respectively represented as 'expedited' and 'consigned'.

There may be a connection between these dates and the payment of fees due to the Apostolic Camera. A comparison of the letters and the cameral records may provide a clue to the solution of this problem, but until a fuller study is made of the Avignon chancery during the period of the Schism it is premature to attempt a satisfactory explanation of the real significance of these dates. The practice continued throughout the pontificate of Benedict XIII but ceased with his death.

In order to make the calendar as complete as possible, an attempt has been made to trace any stray records that can be identified with the chancery of Clement VII and have found their way into the collections of other archives and libraries,[1] so that, as regards his letters to Scotland the present work can be considered definitive. Only two categories of records have been excluded: those of the Apostolic Camera, which are quite different in nature and content and require to be published separately; and the supplications to the pope. Because of the close affinity of supplications to letters, at first it was intended to unite the two in one volume, arranged chronologically, so as to facilitate consultation and reduce cross-references, but this proposal had to be rejected. It is hoped, however, that a separate volume will appear, devoted entirely to the supplications prior to Pope Martin V (1417-31), which, in fact, will be a completely revised and augmented edition of the Bliss *Calendar of Petitions to the Pope*, at least in so far as Scotland is concerned.

The Contents of the Calendar

The pontificate of Pope Clement VII (1378-94), after those of his predecessors Innocent III (1198-1216) and John XXII (1316-34),

---

[1] In order to render the calendar as complete as possible, an attempt has been made to examine all the records which can be attributed to the chancery of Clement VII. Consequently, the following collections have been investigated: Vatican Archives, Reg Aven 205-40, 242-5, 247-77, 279, ff. 230-43v, 289, f. 69; Reg Vat 291-309; the Bullarium Generale, Instrumenta Miscellanea, and Archivum Arcis collections. Vatican Library, Barb. lat. 2101. The search was extended to include the collections of the British Museum and Public Record Office, London, and the Scottish Record Office, Edinburgh. The editions of Scottish medieval chartularies have been examined. It was possible, by means of the 'Schedario Baumgarten' in the possession of the Vatican School of Paleography and Diplomatic, to extend the range and include the collections of many other European archives and libraries.

and of his successor at Avignon, Benedict XIII (1394-1423), was the fourth longest pontificate of the entire Middle Ages. As has been shown, with regards to the Church in Scotland it is the most amply documented pontificate of the fourteenth century, and so it seems appropriate to include a brief analysis of the contents of this calendar of his letters.

The calendar follows a chronological order although this is not the arrangement of the letters in the registers. The original practice of the papal chancery was to group the letters, regardless of their contents, simply according to the pontifical year in which they were dispatched. From 1243 onwards, the letters were distinguished into *litterae secretae*[1] and *litterae communes*. At the beginning of the fourteenth century, a rudimentary system of classification by subject matter was introduced for the registration of the 'common letters'. This system was gradually amplified and perfected. By the time of Clement VII the classification table in use in the papal chancery comprised twenty-three headings. This permitted the registration of the various types of letter to be made simultaneously on separate quires, each quire being dedicated exclusively to a specific subject. The sets of quires, when completed, were put in order and bound according to pontifical years. The following titles, or headings, figure in the registers of Clement VII:

> De curia
> De litteris dominorum cardinalium
> De provisionibus prelatorum
> De dignitatibus vacantibus
> De dignitatibus vacaturis (de canonicatu sub expectatione
>   praebendae ac dignitatis)
> De dignitate, personatu vel officio vacaturo
> De praebendis vacantibus

---

[1] There are no extant registers of litterae secretae of Clement VII, although occasional marginal references in the registers of litterae communes prove that such registers did exist: e.g. 'cassata quia alibi in eisdem secretis registrata', or simply 'registrata in secretis'. This accounts for the complete absence of political correspondence in the calendar. In a forthcoming *Miscellanea Paleographica, Diplomatica et Archivistica. Studi in onore di Giulio Battelli. Storia e Letteratura* 140-1, a contribution promised by Pierre Gasnault is entitled 'Trois lettres secrètes sur papier de Clément VII (Robert de Genève) et une supplique originale signée par ce pape'.

De praebendis vacaturis (de canonicatu sub expectatione
   praebendae)
De beneficiis vacantis
De beneficiis vacaturis
De beneficiis cum cura vel sine cura vacaturis
De regularibus
De religionis ingressu (de monachis et monialibus recipien-
   dis)
De beneficiis religiosorum vacaturis
De diversis formis
De conservatoriis
De indultis, privilegiis et dispensationibus
De fructibus percipiendis
De tabellionatus officio
De absolutione plenaria
De altari portatili
De licentia testandi
De communibus

These headings provide a basic outline for a general survey of the
numerous letters, especially of the provisions and reservations,
calendared in this volume.

During the sixteen years of his pontificate, Clement VII provided
bishops to almost all the episcopal sees of Scotland. The only two
exceptions were the diocese of Moray and the diocese of Ross,
where the bishops were already in office before Clement's election
and survived the duration of the pontificate.[1] After elevating Bishop
Walter Wardlaw to the cardinalate in 1383, the pope allowed him
to retain his see *in commendam*, and this concession was renewed on
two more occasions before the cardinal's death. There is only one
instance when presumably the pope provided to the bishopric but
for which no record has been found. This is the provision of Matthew
de Glendinning as bishop of Glasgow in succession to Wardlaw. The
fact that a record survives in the registers of the rival pope, Boniface
IX, appointing John Framysden to the same see,[2] makes this gap,
in an otherwise fully documented series of episcopal provisions, all

---

[1] Alexander Bur, bishop of Moray, 1362-97; Alexander de Kylwos, bishop of Ross,
1371-98.
[2] Reg Lat 13, ff. 163-4; *CPL*, iv, 383.

the more regrettable. The scandal of 'competing provisions' was one of the characteristic and deplorable aspects of the Schism. The provision of Thomas de Rossy as bishop of Galloway in 1379 is a good example of the confusion and litigation that followed as a natural result of the divided papacy. Unfortunately, this was not an isolated case, and parallel to the provisions which Clement VII made to Scottish bishoprics, were the provisions that his rivals of the 'Roman obedience' at least attempted to make to these sees,[1] although this aspect is not documented in the records of the 'Avignon obedience' and so does not figure in the calendar.

Pope Clement VII also provided to many other major benefices, dignities and offices of the Scottish Church, and thirty-two letters of this kind have been discovered in the chancery registers. There are letters appointing eleven deans, two precentors, one chancellor, two treasurers, and sixteen archdeacons. Once again, the papal records appear to be remarkably complete, for there are only three instances during the pontificate where there is reason for suspecting that provision was made by the pope although the relevant records have not been found in the registers. The first two cases involve Walter Trail, later to become bishop of St Andrews, who petitioned the pope for a canonry of Dunkeld and the office of archdeacon.[2] This was granted him *motu proprio* on 26 February 1379, but no letter of provision corresponding to this date appears among the registrations. This provision is known to have been unfruitful. Trail petitioned the pope a second time, on 18 November 1380, for a canonry of Dunkeld and the deanship.[3] His request was granted, according to the entry in the register of supplications, but no corresponding entry has been found in the register of letters. Moreover, there is no evidence elsewhere that Trail ever obtained possession of these benefices, so it is possible that the letters of provision in both instances were never issued in fact. The third case is that of John Sinclair, who is said to have been provided by the pope as precentor of Ross,[4] but no record of this appears to have been kept in the papal archives.

[1] For notes on the bishops provided to Scottish sees by Urban VI and his successors at Rome, see J. Dowden, *The Bishops of Scotland*, 45-46, 94-95, 269-70, 288, 316, 375-6.
[2] Reg Suppl 47, f. 141v; *CPP*, i, 540.   [3] Reg Suppl 61, f. 4v; *CPP*, i, 555.
[4] *Fasti Ecclesiae Scoticanae Medii Aevi*, ed. D. E. R. Watt (Scottish Record Society. 1969), p 275.

A considerable part of the calendar, over 250 entries, consists of provisions or collations to canonries and prebends, to parish churches and vicarages, to countless other benefices in the single, or common gift of bishops, chapters, abbots and convents, and in simple papal reservations of the same. On analysis, the following picture emerges of papal intervention in each of the dioceses of Scotland, during the sixteen years of Clement VII's pontificate.

In the diocese of Aberdeen, the pope provided bishops to the bishopric on two occasions (pp 50, 150). Likewise, provisions were made of two deans (pp 52, 128), and to three parish churches, four perpetual vicarages, four canonries and prebends, and nine canonries with expectation of prebends.

In the diocese of Argyll, the pope provided once only to the bishopric (p 122), the deanery (p 143), and the treasurership (p 158), and thrice to the archdeaconry (pp 135, 142, 149). He also provided to seven parish churches and to two canonries and prebends.

In the diocese of Brechin, papal provision was made to the bishopric (p 89), the deanery (p 187), the precentorship (p 184), and on three occasions to the archdeaconry (pp 94, 161, 182). The pope also made provisions to two perpetual vicarages, two canonries with prebends, and two canonries with expectation of prebends. Reservation was made of one benefice in the gift of the bishop and chapter of Brechin.

In the diocese of Caithness, there is evidence of the provision of the bishop (p 68), and of provisions to two canonries with expectation of prebends.

In the diocese of Dunblane, apart from the provision of the bishop (p 49), and the dean (p 59), there is evidence that the pope provided to one perpetual vicarage, to one canonry and prebend, and to two canonries with expectation of prebends.

In the diocese of Dunkeld, Clement VII provided only once to the bishopric (p 160), and thrice to the deanery (pp 72, 148, 161), but apart from these provisions, it appears that he reserved only one benefice in the gift of the bishop.

In the diocese of Galloway, Bishop Thomas de Rossy was provided by the pope to this bishopric, in the disputed succession to Adam de Lanark (pp 26, 70). The pope also made provisions to the archdeaconry (p 163), and to four parish churches, one perpetual vicarage, and on one occasion a benefice in the gift of the bishop was reserved.

In the diocese of Glasgow, there is evidence of the conferring of the bishopric *in commendam* upon Cardinal Walter de Wardlaw (pp 100, 119, 123). The pope also provided to the precentorship (p 135), the treasurership (p 115), and the archdeaconry (p 164), and further provisions were made to seven parish churches and to eight perpetual vicarages, to nineteen canonries with prebends and to seventeen canonries with expectation of prebends. Moreover, five benefices in the gift of the bishop were reserved by the pope.

In the diocese of The Isles, the pope provided once to the bishopric (p 130), and to the archdeaconry (p 157), and on four occasions to both parish churches and perpetual vicarages. Two benefices in the gift of the bishop were reserved by the pope.

In the diocese of Moray, there is evidence that the pope provided deans on two occasions (pp 100, 160) and once only to the archdeaconry (p 20). There were no papal provisions to parish churches or to perpetual vicarages, but provisions were made to seven canonries with prebends, and to twelve canonries with expectation of prebends.

In the diocese of Orkney, the bishop was provided by the pope (p 101), but there is no further evidence of papal provisions to parishes, vicarages, canonries, or prebends, and no benefices appear to have been reserved by the pope. This is not altogether surprising, as the diocese of Orkney may well have belonged to the 'other obedience', and the promotion of Robert de Sinclair as bishop was more in name, than in fact.[1]

In the diocese of Ross, the pope confirmed provision of the chancellor (p 183), and provided two archdeacons (pp 72, 172), but no provisions were made to parishes, or vicarages. On three occasions, however, he made provisions to canonries with prebends, and twice to canonries with expectation of prebends.

In the diocese of St Andrews, the bishop (p 111), and two archdeacons (pp 24, 41), received their provision from the pope. There is evidence for further papal provisions to fifteen parish churches and to an equal number of perpetual vicarages. No provisions, however, were made to canonries, on account of the fact

[1] Watt, *Fasti*, p 251.

that the regular clergy served the cathedral, as also in the cathedral of Whithorn, but a total of twenty-nine reservations were made of benefices. Ten of these were in the gift of the bishop of St Andrews alone, and nineteen were in the common gift of the bishop and priory.

Considering the duration of Clement VII's pontificate and the added fact that the records for the period are so complete, then the evidence of papal intervention does not appear excessive. In certain years, apparently, it was almost non-existent. Moreover, one must bear in mind that in the majority of the provisions to parishes and vicarages it was the recipients who had petitioned the pope initially for provision, or for confirmation of a collation already made by the local ecclesiastical authority. Papal provisions appear to have been used as a precaution against possible contestation of tenure, rather than as an effective means by which the pope ensured that worthy men were appointed or abuses corrected. Several examples can be found in the calendar, where papal provision was not automatically successful. Likewise, the recipients of papal reservations on benefices were not always contented immediately, and sometimes were even forced into petitioning the pope a second time to grant them precedence over all other claimants. The calendar contains a goodly number of cases of litigation, which was one of the besetting evils of the medieval Church.

In the realm of monastic life, the calendar provides evidence of papal provisions to many of the greater and lesser houses of the regular clergy. Clement VII provided abbots to the abbeys of Holyrood (pp 25, 127), Lindores (pp 49, 81), Dunfermline (pp 85, 142), Arbroath (p 107), Inchaffray (p 130), Balmerino (p 175), Newbattle (p 176), and Saddell (p 195). Priors were provided to the priories of Coldingham (pp 25, 159), Oronsay (p 85), St Andrews (pp 122, 200), and Portmoak *alias* Loch Leven (pp 129, 179, 184). The pope appointed a provost to the newly erected collegiate church of Lincluden (pp 153, 158). The state of the monastic houses, judged by the contents of these papal letters, does not appear to have been healthy. In many instances, when the pope intervened and provided an abbot or prior, it was explicitly to put an end to scandalous abuses, although even in such cases his authority was not always respected. The calendar also contains confirmations by the pope of the appropriation of parishes and vicarages by various abbeys and priories. This diverting of revenues in itself is indicative of some process of decline, due to mounting economic pressure.[1]

The calendar sheds light on many other aspects of the life of the medieval Church and of the Scottish people. The piety of the faithful can be seen in the numerous grants of a plenary indulgence to be gained at the hour of death – the equivalent, today, of receiving the Papal Blessing; in the indults to have Mass celebrated upon a portable altar, so, presumably, at home, in their keeps and manors; or, of having a confessor of their personal choice. On the other hand, some degree of impiety is implied in the number of dispensations requested from impediments to the reception of holy orders, such as illegitimacy, or to the contracting of valid marriage. The latter, which frequently enter into the degrees of consanguinity and affinity, will provide interesting details for the genealogist. And, no doubt, the special indulgences which Clement VII granted for the restoration of the fabric of three Scottish cathedrals, for the upkeep of several poor-houses and popular shrines, not to forget the repair of a bridge in Cowal, will furnish information hitherto unknown to local historians.

[1] *Calendar of Scottish Supplications to Rome*, 1428-1432, ed. A. I. Dunlop and I. B. Cowan (Scottish History Society, 1970), p xii.

TABLE OF ABBREVIATIONS

B.A.	Bachelor of Arts.
B.DEC.	Bachelor of Decreets.
B.LEG.	Bachelor of Laws.
B.THEOL. . . .	Bachelor of Theology.
B.U.J.	Bachelor of Both Laws.
D.DEC.	Doctor of Decreets.
D.U.J.	Doctor of Both Laws.
LIC.ART. . . .	Licentiate in Arts.
LIC.DEC. . . .	Licentiate in Decreets.
LIC.JUR.CIV. . . .	Licentiate in Civil Law.
LIC.LEG.	Licentiate of Laws.
LIC.U.J.	Licentiate in Both Laws.
M.A.	Master of Arts.
M.THEOL. . . .	Master of Theology.
O.CARM. . . .	Carmelite Order.
O.CIST.	Cistercian Order.
O.CLUN.	Cluniac Order.
O.F.M.	Order of Friars Minor (Franciscans).
O.P.	Order of Preachers (Dominicans).
O.PREMON. . . .	Premonstratensian Order.
O.S.A.	Order of St Augustine.
O.S.A.E.	Hermits of St Augustine.
O.S.B.	Order of St Benedict.
O.VALLIS CAUL. . .	Order of Vallis Caulium.

Abdn Reg . . .	*Registrum Episcopatus Aberdonensis* (Spalding and Maitland Clubs, 1845).
Cambuskenneth Registrum .	*Registrum Monasterii S. Marie de Cambuskenneth* (Grampian Club, 1872).
Chron. Bower . . .	*Johannis de Fordun Scotichronicon cum Supplementis et Continuatione Walteri Bower,* ed. W. Goodall (Edinburgh, 1759).

CPL . . . . *Calendar of Entries in the Papal Registers relating to Great Britain and Ireland: Papal Letters*, ed. W. H. Bliss and others (London, 1893-   ).

CPP . . . . *Calendar of Entries in the Papal Registers relating to Great Britain and Ireland: Petitions to the Pope*, ed. W. H. Bliss (London, 1896).

Coupar Angus Chrs. . . *Charters of the Abbey of Coupar Angus*, ed. D. E. Easson (SHS, 1947).

Cowan, *Parishes* . . *The Parishes of Medieval Scotland*, ed. Ian B. Cowan (Scottish Record Society, 1967).

Highland Papers . . *Highland Papers*, ed. J. F. N. Macphail (SHS, 1914-34).

Inchaffray Chrs.. . . *Charters, Bulls and other Documents relating to the Abbey of Inchaffray*, ed. J. Dowden and J. Maitland Thomson (SHS, 1908).

Paisley Registrum . . *Registrum Monasterii de Passelet* (Maitland Club, 1832).

Reg Aven . . . Registra Avenionensia in Vatican Archives.

Reg Supp . . . Registra Supplicationum in Vatican Archives.

Reg Vat . . . . Registra Vaticana in Vatican Archives.

SHS . . . . Scottish History Society.

SRO Vat Trans. . . Transcripts from the Vatican Archives in Scottish Record Office.

1 CLEMENT VII

1 November, 1378   Reg Aven 218, 63v-64v

To the abbot of Dunfermline, the chancellor of Paris and the arch-deacon of Aberdeen. Mandate to collate John de Lychon, B.LEG., in his second year of reading laws, who is born of nobility of the diocese of Brechin, two leagues from the city of Brechin, to the canonry and prebend of Brechin vacant by the death of the late William de Dalgarnoch, to which John was provided originally by Gregory XI on 13 April, 1377, but the subsequent death of the pope prevented the letters being issued and the present collation is to have effect as from that original date, notwithstanding that he is rector of the parish church of Lechnot, Brechin diocese, and also received from Gregory XI an expectative grace of a benefice with cure in the gift of the bishop of St Andrews.
Fondi, Kal. Nov., anno 1.

3 November, 1378   Reg Aven 206, 37v-38v

To Andrew de Trebron, LIC.LEG., canon of St Donatien, Bruges. Provision to a canonry of the church of St Donatien, Bruges, Tournai diocese, with expectation of a prebend, notwithstanding that he holds the parish church of Kynwll, St Andrews diocese; granted at the petition of Robert, king of Scots.
Fondi, 3 Non. Nov., anno 1.
Concurrent mandate to the provost of St Mary's, Bruges, the dean of Liège and the official of Tournai.

3 November, 1378   Reg Aven 217, 172-3

To Adam de Tynnygham, canon of Moray, familiar of the pope.

Provision, made *motu proprio*, to a canonry of Moray with expectation of a prebend and dignity, or office, with or without cure.[1]
Fondi, 3 Non. Nov., anno 1.
Concurrent mandate to the archdeacon of Brechin, the treasurer of Glasgow and William de Calabre, canon of Aberdeen.

6 November, 1378   Reg Aven 206, 156-6v

To the chanter of Moray. Mandate to provide John de Crauford, clerk of St Andrews diocese, to a canonry of Aberdeen with expectation of a prebend.[2]
Fondi, 8 Id. Nov., anno 1.

6 November, 1378   Reg Aven 206, 193-3v

To the chanter of Moray. Mandate to provide William de Camera, clerk of Aberdeen diocese, to a canonry of Aberdeen with expectation of a prebend.[3]
Fondi, 8 Id. Nov., anno 1.

6 November, 1378   Reg Aven 206, 193v-4

To the chancellor of Paris. Mandate to provide William de Crauford, clerk of St Andrews diocese, to a canonry of Glasgow with expectation of a prebend.[4]
Fondi, 8 Id. Nov., anno 1.

6 November, 1378   Reg Aven 206, 194v-5

To the chancellor of Paris. Mandate to provide William de Camera *senior*, B.A., clerk of Aberdeen diocese, at present studying at Paris, to a canonry of Dunkeld with expectation of a prebend.[5]
Fondi, 8 Id. Nov., anno 1.

[1] See *CPP*, i, 547.   [2] See *CPP*, i, 550.
[3] See *CPP*, i, 550.   [4] See Reg Supp 51, 235v.
[5] See *CPP*, i, 550.

6 November, 1378 Reg Aven 213, 65v-66v

To the official of Glasgow. Mandate to reserve to Thomas de Loqunorsward, priest of Dunkeld diocese, a benefice with cure in the gift of the bishop of St Andrews, to the value of 40 marks sterling, but provided that he resigns the perpetual vicarage of the parish church of Logi, Dumblane diocese, to which he was provided by Gregory xi.[1]
Fondi, 8 Id. Nov., anno 1.

6 November, 1378 Reg Aven 213, 66v-67

To the official of Glasgow. Mandate to reserve to John de Meldon, priest of St Andrews diocese, a benefice with cure usually assigned to the secular clergy in the gift of the abbot and convent of Abirbrochok, o.s.b., together or separately, to the value of 40 marks sterling.[2]
Fondi, 8 Id. Nov., anno 1.

6 November, 1378 Reg Aven 213, 67-67v

To the official of Aberdeen. Mandate to reserve to John Marascalli, rector of the parish church of Dagwendonyr, Aberdeen diocese, (who claims to have acted as proctor for many years during the minority of the future Clement vii for the Scottish benefices that the latter held by papal dispensation), a benefice with cure in the gift of the bishop of St Andrews, that is not a canonry and prebend of the cathedral, to the value of 60 marks sterling. John must resign his parish church upon obtaining possession, but not the canonry of Glasgow and prebend of Glasgow Minor.[3]
Fondi, 8 Id. Nov., anno 1.

14 November, 1378 Reg Aven 205, 503v-4v

To William de Trebron, m.a., b.theol. formatus, canon of Glasgow. Provision, made *motu proprio*, to a canonry of Glasgow

[1] See *CPP*, i, 550.   [2] See *CPP*, i, 550.
[3] See *CPP*, i, 550.

with expectation of a prebend and dignity, parsonage, or office, with or without cure, even if elective, but provided it is not the greatest dignity of the cathedral after that of the bishop.[1]

Fondi, 18 Kal. Dec., anno 1.

Concurrent mandate to the dean of St Agricola, Avignon, and the officials of Paris and St Andrews.

14 November, 1378   Reg Aven 210, 98-98v

To William de Trebron, M.A., B.THEOL. formatus, priest of Moray diocese. Reservation of a benefice, even if a canonry and prebend, and dignity, or office, in the gift of the archbishop, dean and chapter of Rouen, together or separately, to the value of £120 Tournois with cure, or £80 Tournois without cure, provided it is not the greatest dignity of the cathedral after that of the bishop. The provision made today of a canonry of Glasgow with expectation of a prebend and dignity, parsonage, or office, is hereby rendered null.

Fondi, 18 Kal. Dec., anno 1.

Concurrent mandate to the dean of Paris, the archpriest of St Didier, Avignon, and the official of Paris.

15 November, 1378   Reg Aven 211, 266-6v

To the chancellor of Glasgow. Mandate to reserve to John Petyern, priest, perpetual vicar of the parish church of Chambusnathan, Glasgow diocese, a benefice with cure, usually assigned to the secular clergy in the gift of the abbot and convent of Paisley, O.S.B., together or separately, to the value of 30 marks sterling, on condition that he resigns his vicarage upon obtaining possession.

Fondi, 17 Kal. Dec., anno 1.

15 November, 1378   Reg Aven 217, 237-8

To Thomas de Barry, LIC.ART., priest, canon of Aberdeen. Provision to a canonry of Aberdeen with expectation of a prebend

Cf. *CPP*, i, 539 where it is wrongly dated 10 Kal. Dec. (see Reg Supp 54, 205).

and dignity, parsonage, or office, with or without cure, even if elective, that is not the greatest dignity of the cathedral after that of the bishop, notwithstanding that he has a canonry of Glasgow, a canonry and prebend of Dunbarr, St Andrews diocese, and a canonry, prebend and the subdeanship of Ross, which is not a dignity or parsonage and is without cure.[1]
Fondi, 17 Kal. Dec., anno 1.
Concurrent mandate to the bishop of Glasgow, the archdeacon of Ross and the treasurer of Glasgow.

15 November, 1378   Reg Aven 218, 268v-9

To Hugh de Dalmehoy, subdeacon, canon of Glasgow. Provision to a canonry of Glasgow with expectation of a prebend ; at the petition of the cardinal deacon of S. Eustacio, to whom he is a notary.
Fondi, 17 Kal. Dec., anno 1.
Concurrent mandate to the abbots of Dunfermline and Holyrood and the archdeacon of Angers.

16 November, 1378   Reg Aven 206, 314-14v

To Walter, bishop of Glasgow. Faculty to confer on six worthy persons of his own choice six canonries of his church of Glasgow and to reserve an equal number of prebends, even should any of these persons hold one or two benefices already.
Fondi, 16 Kal. Dec., anno 1.

16 November, 1378   Reg Aven 205, 445-6

To Walter, bishop of Glasgow. More ample faculty to confer on four worthy persons of his own choice four dignities, or offices, of his church of Glasgow, if vacant at present or whenever vacant, even though one of them is normally elective, but provided none of them is the greatest dignity of the cathedral after that of the bishop.
Fondi, 16 Kal. Dec., anno 1.

---

[1] See *CPP*, i, 545.

16 November, 1378   Reg Aven 206, 454v-5v

To the bishop of St Andrews. Mandate to confer on persons presented to him by Robert, king of Scots, canonries in the following dioceses, distributed also in the following manner, and with reservation of an equal number of prebends : two canonries of Glasgow, and likewise two of Dunkeld, Aberdeen, Moray, Ross, Caithness, Brechin and Dunblane.
Fondi, 16 Kal. Dec., anno 1.

16 November, 1378   Reg Aven 209, 92v-93v

To the bishop of Glasgow. Mandate to reserve to eight worthy persons, presented to him by Robert, king of Scots, eight benefices, to the value of 40 marks sterling with cure, or 25 marks sterling without cure, in the following dioceses and distributed in the following manner : two benefices in St Andrews, and likewise two in Sodor, Lismore and Whithorn.
Fondi, 16 Kal. Dec., anno 1.

17 November, 1378   Reg Aven 206, 307v-8

To the bishop of Dunblane. Mandate to provide John Lethe, priest, canon of Glasgow, to a canonry of Dunkeld with expectation of a prebend, notwithstanding that he holds a canonry of Glasgow and the prebend of Rufen and is said to have obtained the parish church of Hawyk, Glasgow diocese.[1]
Fondi, 15 Kal. Dec., anno 1.

17 November, 1378   Reg Aven 206, 308-9

To the official of Glasgow. Mandate to provide Alexander de Wardlaw, clerk of Glasgow diocese, to a canonry of Moray with expectation of a prebend.[2]
Fondi, 15 Kal. Dec., anno 1.

[1] Cf. *CPP*, i, 547.   [2] Cf. *CPP*, i, 548.

17 November, 1378   Reg Aven 206, 311v-12v

To the chancellor of Paris. Mandate to provide Thomas Trayl, clerk of Aberdeen diocese, to a canonry of Moray with expectation of a prebend.[1]
Fondi, 15 Kal. Dec., anno 1.

17 November, 1378   Reg Aven 208, 193-3v

To the official of Glasgow. Mandate to reserve to Walter de Wardlaw, canon of Glasgow, a benefice usually assigned to the secular clergy in the gift of the bishop of St Andrews, to the value of 40 marks sterling with cure, or 30 marks sterling without cure, but provided it is not a canonry and prebend of the cathedral, and notwithstanding that he holds a canonry of Glasgow and the prebend of Casturtarris.[2]
Fondi, 15 Kal. Dec., anno 1.

17 November, 1378   Reg Aven 208, 192v-3

To the official of Glasgow. Mandate to reserve to Henry de Archonreley, clerk of Glasgow diocese, a benefice in the gift of the bishop of St Andrews, to the value of 30 marks sterling with cure, or 18 marks sterling without cure, but provided it is not a canonry and prebend of the cathedral.[3]
Fondi, 15 Kal. Dec., anno 1.

17 November, 1378   Reg Aven 205, 505v-6v

To the official of St Andrews. Mandate to provide Symon de Crech, M.A., also said to be proficient in canon law, rector of the parish church of Cullas, St Andrews diocese, to a canonry of Dunkeld with expectation of a prebend, provided he resigns his parish upon obtaining possession of a parsonage, or office, with cure, but notwithstanding that he holds the perpetual chaplaincy of the chapel of Forgrundenyny, Dunkeld diocese.[4]
Fondi, 15 Kal. Dec., anno 1.

[1] Cf. CPP, i, 548.   [2] Cf. CPP, i, 548.
[3] Cf. CPP, i, 548.   [4] See CPP, i, 546.

17 November, 1378   Reg Aven 209, 89v-90v

To Thomas Wys, M.A., clerk of Moray diocese, who for two years
has attended lectures in both canon and civil law. Reservation of a
benefice usually assigned to the secular clergy in the gift of the abbot
and convent of Londoris, O.S.B., together or separately, to the value
of 37 marks sterling with cure, or 26 marks sterling without cure.[1]
Fondi, 15 Kal. Dec., anno 1.
Concurrent mandate to the dean of St Agricola, Avignon, and the
chanter and official of Moray.

17 November, 1378   Reg Aven 211, 473-4

To William de Falkelandi M.A., priest, perpetual vicar of the parish
church of Kehehindbi, St Andrews diocese. Reservation of a
benefice in the gift of the bishop, prior, chapter, canons and parsons
of St Andrews, together or separately, even pertaining to the
cathedral, but not a canonry and prebend, to the value of 40 marks
sterling with cure, or 30 marks sterling without cure, provided he
resigns the perpetual vicarage upon obtaining possession of a
benefice with cure.
Fondi, 15 Kal. Dec., anno 1.
Concurrent mandate to the abbot of Dunfermline, the dean of
St Agricola, Avignon, and the official of St Andrews.

17 November, 1378   Reg Aven 213, 43v-44

To the chancellor of Paris. Mandate to reserve to Thomas de
Eddenham, B.U.J., M.A., and scholar of canon law, canon of Caithness,
a benefice usually assigned to the secular clergy in the gift of the
bishop, prior and chapter of St Andrews, O.S.A., together or
separately, to the value of 37 marks sterling with cure, or 26 marks
sterling without cure, notwithstanding his canonry and prebend of
Caithness, the value of which does not exceed 30 gold francs.[2]
Fondi, 15 Kal. Dec., anno 1.

[1] See *CPP*, i, 546.   [2] See *CPP*, i, 545.

17 November, 1378   Reg Aven 213, 156v-7

To the official of Paris. Mandate to reserve to William de Nary, M.A., scholar of canon law, clerk of St Andrews diocese, a benefice in the gift of the bishop of St Andrews, to the value of 37 marks sterling with cure, or 26 marks sterling without cure.[1] Fondi, 15 Kal. Dec., anno 1.

17 November, 1378   Reg Aven 213, 391-2

To John de Caron, M.A., LIC.U.J., canon of Aberdeen. Reservation of a benefice with or without cure usually assigned to the secular clergy, even if a dignity, parsonage, administration, or office, in the gift of the bishop and chapter of St Andrews, O.S.A., together or separately, notwithstanding that he holds canonries and prebends of Aberdeen and Moray, but provided he resigns the parish church of Rathen, St Andrews diocese, upon obtaining possession of a benefice with cure, a dignity, or a parsonage. Fondi, 15 Kal. Dec., anno 1. Concurrent mandate to the bishop of Dunblane, the abbot of Dunfermline and the archdeacon of Brechin.

17 November, 1378   Reg Aven 217, 198-8v

To William de Fothyneyn, M.A., scholar of canon law, canon of Glasgow. Provision to a canonry of Glasgow with expectation of a prebend, parsonage, or office, in the gift of the bishop and chapter of Glasgow, together or separately, to the value of 37 marks sterling with cure, or 26 marks sterling without cure.[2] Fondi, 15 Kal. Dec., anno 1. Concurrent mandate to the abbot of Paisley the archdeacon de Vallibus, Cahors diocese, and the chancellor of Glasgow.

17 November, 1378   Reg Aven 217, 199v-200v

To William Gerland, M.A., scholar of canon law, priest, canon of Moray, perpetual vicar of the parish church of Newtyle, St Andrews

[1] See CPP, i, 546.   [2] See CPP, i, 545.

diocese, and chaplain of Duffus castle, Moray diocese. Provision to a canonry of Moray with expectation of a prebend, parsonage, or office, with or without cure, provided he resigns his vicarage upon obtaining possession of a benefice with cure, but notwithstanding his chaplaincy.[1]

Fondi, 15 Kal. Dec., anno 1.

Concurrent mandate to the abbot of Kinloss, the dean of St Agricola, Avignon, and the official of Aberdeen.

17 November, 1378   Reg Aven 219, 214-14v

To the official of Paris. Mandate to provide William de Camera, M.A., rector of the parish church of Halys, St Andrews diocese, who is nobly born and a student of canon law, to a canonry of Moray with expectation of a prebend, provided another has not an acquired right to it until 5 Id. Oct., anno 4 [11 Oct., 1382], and notwithstanding his parish church or that he has a similar provision to a canonry of Dunkeld with expectation of a prebend.

Fondi, 15 Kal. Dec., anno 1; expedited, 6 Id. Mar., anno 10 [10 March, 1388]; consigned, 3 Id. Mar., anno 10 [13 March, 1388].

18 November, 1378   Reg Aven 211, 290v-1

To the abbot of Lindores. Mandate to reserve to Stephen de Camera, priest of St Andrews diocese, a benefice with or without cure, usually assigned to the secular clergy, in the gift of the prior and chapter of St Andrews, O.S.A., together or separately, to the value of 25 marks sterling.

Fondi, 14 Kal. Dec., anno 1.

18 November, 1378   Reg Aven 211, 291-1v

To the official of Dunkeld. Mandate to reserve to John Kay, priest, perpetual vicar of the parish church of Bancheryterny, Aberdeen diocese, a benefice with cure in the gift of the bishop of St Andrews, provided it is not a canonry and prebend, to the value of 40 marks

[1] See *CPP*, i, 545.

sterling and on condition that he resigns his vicarage upon obtaining possession.
Fondi, 14 Kal. Dec., anno 1.

18 November, 1378   Reg Aven 211, 291v-2

To the official of Glasgow. Mandate to reserve to Andrew Homelyn, priest of Glasgow diocese, a benefice with cure in the gift of the bishop of Glasgow, that is not a canonry and prebend of the cathedral, to the value of 30 marks sterling.
Fondi, 14 Kal. Dec., anno 1.

18 November, 1378   Reg Aven 211, 323-3v

To the official of Dunkeld. Mandate to reserve to Symon Homly, priest of Glasgow diocese, a benefice with cure usually assigned to the secular clergy in the gift of the abbot and convent of Calkow, o.s.b., together or separately, to the value of 25 marks sterling.
Fondi, 14 Kal. Dec., anno 1.

18 November, 1378   Reg Aven 212, 592-2v

To the bishop of Dunkeld. Mandate to reserve to Guy de Turre, clerk of Léon diocese, a benefice with or without cure, even a rural deanery, in the gift of the bishop, dean and chapter of Vannes, provided it is not a canonry and prebend of the cathedral, to the value of £40 Tournois with cure, or £30 Tournois without cure.
Fondi, 14 Kal. Dec., anno 1.

18 November, 1378   Reg Aven 217, 164-5

To Walter Bricii, priest, canon of Glasgow, subcollector of the Apostolic Camera in the city and diocese of St Andrews. Provision to a canonry of Glasgow with expectation of a prebend and dignity, parsonage, or office, even one with cure and elective, notwithstanding that he suffers defect of birth being the son of a priest and an unmarried woman, or that he holds the perpetual vicarage

E

of the parish church of Cader, Glasgow diocese, which he must resign upon obtaining possession of a benefice with cure.
Fondi, 14 Kal. Dec., anno 1.
Concurrent mandate to the abbot of Dunfermline, the dean of St Agricola, Avignon, and the official of Glasgow.

18 November, 1378   Reg Aven 218, 276v-7v

To the official of Glasgow. Mandate to provide Thomas de Peblis, rector of the parish church of Bechorowl, Glasgow diocese, to a canonry of Glasgow with expectation of a prebend.
Fondi, 14 Kal. Dec., anno 1.

18 November, 1378   Reg Aven 218, 305v-6

To the official of Glasgow. Mandate to reserve to Adam de Peblis, canon of Glasgow, a prebend of Glasgow, notwithstanding that he already holds a canonry and prebend of Glasgow and the parish church of Essy, St Andrews diocese, but on condition that he resign the first prebend upon obtaining possession of this other prebend.
Fondi, 14 Kal. Dec., anno 1.

18 November, 1378   Reg Aven 218, 497-7v

To the bishop of Glasgow. Mandate to provide Robert Fourbour, clerk of Glasgow, to a canonry of Aberdeen with expectation of a prebend.
Fondi, 14 Kal. Dec., anno 1.

19 November, 1378   Reg Aven 205, 221v-2v

To Robert Flemyng, priest, rector of the parish church of Inverarity, St Andrews diocese. Provision to the parish church of Inverarite, St Andrews diocese, vacant by the death of the late Andrew Ox at the papal court; which Walter de Coventre, a former rector, retained unlawfully for more than a year together with the deanship of Aberdeen, which is a dignity with cure.
Fondi, 13 Kal. Dec., anno 1.

Concurrent mandate to the archdeacon of Brechin, the treasurer of Glasgow and the official of St Andrews.

19 November, 1378   Reg Aven 205, 510-11

To David de Trebrim, canon of Moray, well versed in both laws having studied assiduously for six years at Orleans and Oxford. Provision to a canonry of Moray with expectation of a prebend, and dignity or office without cure, provided the dignity is not the greatest of the cathedral after that of the bishop ; at the petition of king Robert.

Fondi, 13 Kal. Dec., anno 1.

Concurrent mandate to the dean of St Agricola, Avignon, the archdeacon of Dunkeld and John de Forg, canon of Moray.

19 November, 1378   Reg Aven 213, 28-29

To the official of St Andrews. Mandate to reserve to John Neuet, priest of St Andrews diocese, a benefice with cure usually assigned to the secular clergy in the gift of the abbot and convent of Abirbroyog, o.s.b., to the value of 37 marks sterling ; at the petition of king Robert.

Fondi, 13 Kal. Dec., anno 1.

19 November, 1378   Reg Aven 213, 38-39

To the official of St Andrews. Mandate to reserve to Robert Sherex, priest of Aberdeen diocese, a benefice with cure usually assigned to the secular clergy in the gift of the prior and chapter of St Andrews, o.s.a., together or separately, to the value of 37 marks sterling ; at the petition of king Robert.

Fondi, 13 Kal. Dec., anno 1.

19 November, 1378   Reg Aven 213, 135v-6

To the official of St Andrews. Mandate to reserve to John Wrich, priest of St Andrews diocese, a benefice with cure usually assigned to the secular clergy in the gift of the abbot and convent of

Dumformelyne, o.s.b., together or separately, to the value of 37 marks sterling; at the petition of king Robert.
Fondi, 13 Kal. Dec., anno 1.

19 November, 1378   Reg Aven 213, 136v-7

To the bishop of Dunkeld. Mandate to reserve to Patrick Lyon, clerk of St Andrews, a benefice in the gift of the bishop of St Andrews, to the value of 37 marks sterling with cure, or 26 marks sterling without cure; at the petition of king Robert.
Fondi, 13 Kal. Dec., anno 1.

19 November, 1378   Reg Aven 218, 493-3v

To the official of St Andrews. Mandate to provide James Lyon, M.A., perpetual vicar of the parish church of Edinburgh, St Andrews diocese, to a canonry of Aberdeen with expectation of a prebend; at the petition of king Robert.
Fondi, 13 Kal. Dec., anno 1.

19 November, 1378   Reg Aven 218, 502v-3

To the official of Brechin. Mandate to provide Walter Bell, priest, scholar of canon law, perpetual vicar of the parish church of Erselton, St Andrews diocese, to a canonry of Dunkeld with expectation of a prebend; at the petition of king Robert.
Fondi, 13 Kal. Dec., anno 1.

20 November, 1378   Reg Aven 207, 319v-20

To the official of St Andrews. Mandate to reserve to Thomas de Carnoten, priest of St Andrews diocese, a benefice usually assigned to the secular clergy in the gift of the abbot and convent of Donrfemelyn o.s.b., together or separately, to the value of 25 marks sterling with cure, or 18 marks sterling without cure.[1]
Fondi, 12 Kal. Dec., anno 1.

---

[1] See *CPP*, i, 541.

20 November, 1378   Reg Aven 217, 245-5v

To Robert Wysse, priest, canon of Moray, perpetual vicar of the parish church of Fordoun, St Andrews diocese. Provision to a canonry of Moray with expectation of a prebend, and dignity, parsonage, or office, with or without cure, provided the dignity is not the greatest of the cathedral after that of the bishop, on condition that he resigns his vicarage upon obtaining possession of a dignity, parsonage, or office with cure, and notwithstanding his canonry of Aberdeen, which was collated by ordinary authority.[1]
Fondi, 12 Kal. Dec., anno 1.
Concurrent mandate to the dean of Ross, the chancellor of Aberdeen and the treasurer of Glasgow.

20 November, 1378   Reg Aven 218, 508-9

To the chanter of Moray. Mandate to provide John de Forg, priest, canon of Moray, to a canonry of Ross with expectation of a prebend, notwithstanding that he holds a canonry and prebend of Moray, together with the perpetual vicarage of the parish church of Forg, same diocese, and the leper house of Rothnen, Aberdeen diocese, in the foundation of which house it was ordained that it be assigned in perpetuity as an ecclesiastical benefice.[2]
Fondi, 12 Kal. Dec., anno 1.

21 November, 1378   Reg Aven 219, 268-9

To William Makmorin, B.U.J., canon of Glasgow. Provision to a canonry of Glasgow with expectation of a prebend, and dignity, or office, with or without cure, even if elective, but provided it is not the greatest dignity of the cathedral after that of the bishop.[3]
Fondi, 11 Kal. Dec., anno 1; expedited, 17 Kal. Oct., anno 16 [15 Sept., 1394].
Concurrent mandate to the abbot of Melrose, and the provosts of Autun and of St André, Grenoble.

---

[1] See *CPP*, i, 545.   [2] See *CPP*, i, 548.
[3] See Reg Supp 56, 122v-3.

22 November, 1378   Reg Aven 205, 398v-9v

To William Gerland, M.A., priest, canon of Caithness, at present studying canon law at Paris. Provision to a canonry of Caithness with expectation of a prebend, and a parsonage, or office, with or without cure, on condition that he resigns the perpetual vicarage of the parish church of Neutill, St Andrews diocese, which involves cure, and notwithstanding that he holds the chaplaincy of the chapel of Duffus castle, Moray diocese.[1]
Fondi, 10 Kal. Dec., anno 1.
Concurrent mandate to the deans of Caithness and of St Agricola, Avignon, and the precentor of Moray.

22 November, 1378   Reg Aven 212, 158-9

To Henry de Cornton, priest, canon of Dunkeld. Reservation of a benefice usually assigned to the secular clergy in the gift of the bishop, prior, chapter and canons of St Andrews, O.S.A., together or separately, to the value of 40 marks sterling with cure, or 25 marks sterling without cure, on condition that he resign the perpetual vicarage of the parish church of Kyllebethach, Aberdeen diocese, and notwithstanding that he holds a canonry and prebend of Dunkeld.[2]
Fondi, 10 Kal. Dec., anno 1.
Concurrent mandate to the abbot of Dunfermline, the dean of St Agricola, Avignon, and the archdeacon of Brechin.

22 November, 1378   Reg Aven 213, 579-9v

To the official of Glasgow. Mandate to reserve to John Forman, clerk of St Andrews diocese, scholar of laws, a benefice usually assigned to the secular clergy in the gift of the bishop, prior and chapter of St Andrews, O.S.A., together or separately, to the value of 25 marks sterling with cure, or 18 marks sterling without cure.[3]
Fondi, 10 Kal. Dec., anno 1.

---

[1] See *CPP*, i, 543.   [2] See Reg Supp 53, 63v.
[3] Cf. Reg Supp 56, 129.

22 November, 1378   Reg Aven 215, 120-20v

To John, bishop of Dunkeld. Indult to confer on four worthy persons of his own choice four canonries of his church of Dunkeld, with reservation of an equal number of prebends.
Fondi, 10 Kal. Dec., anno 1.

22 November, 1378   Reg Aven 215, 121-1v

To John, bishop of Dunkeld. Indult to reserve to any of the four persons included in the previous indult, or to any other worthy persons, two dignities of his church of Dunkeld, with or without cure, but provided that neither is the greatest dignity of the cathedral after that of the bishop.
Fondi, 10 Kal. Dec., anno 1.

22 November, 1378   Reg Aven 215, 150-50v

To William, bishop of St Andrews. Indult to reserve to six worthy persons of his own choice six benefices, with or without cure, even if dignities, parsonages, or offices, of his cathedral, city and diocese of St Andrews.
Fondi, 10 Kal. Dec., anno 1.

22 November, 1378   Reg Aven 217, 170-1

To William de Salthand, M.A., priest, canon of Aberdeen. Provision to a canonry of Aberdeen with expectation of a prebend, and dignity, parsonage, or office, with or without cure, even if the dignity is elective, but provided it is not the greatest dignity of the cathedral after that of the bishop, and on condition that he resign the perpetual vicarage of the parish church of Kehthmidby, St Andrews diocese, and renounce his expectative grace to a benefice, with or without cure, in the gift of the bishop, prior and chapter of St Andrews, concerning which the letters have not yet been issued, upon obtaining possession of a dignity, parsonage, or office, with cure.
Fondi, 10 Kal. Dec., anno 1.

Concurrent mandate to the dean of St Agricola, Avignon, the archdeacon of Brechin and the official of Aberdeen.

22 November, 1378   Reg Aven 219, 150-50v

To the official of St Andrews. Mandate to provide Patrick de Forgrund, priest, rector of the parish church of Flysk, St Andrews diocese, to a canonry of Glasgow with expectation of a prebend.[1]
Fondi, 10 Kal. Dec., anno 1.

24 November, 1378   Reg Aven 207, 13

To Andrew Yowng, clerk of Aberdeen diocese. Reservation of a benefice usually assigned to the secular clergy in the gift of the abbot and convent of Abirbrochok, o.s.b., together or separately, to the value of 25 marks sterling with cure, or 18 marks sterling without cure.[2]
Fondi, 8 Kal. Dec., anno 1.
Concurrent mandate to the chancellor of Aberdeen, and to Walter Trayl and Alexander de Karon, canons of Aberdeen.

27 November, 1378   Reg Aven 212, 352v-3

To the official of Glasgow. Mandate to reserve to Robert de Inverlothan, priest, perpetual vicar of the parish church of Inverlothan, Glasgow diocese, a benefice usually assigned to the secular clergy in the gift of the abbot and convent of Calkow, o.s.b., together or separately, to the value of 25 marks sterling with cure, or 18 marks sterling without cure, on condition that he resigns his vicarage upon obtaining possession of a benefice with cure.[3]
Fondi, 5 Kal. Dec., anno 1.

27 November, 1378   Reg Aven 212, 353v

To the official of Glasgow. Mandate to reserve to John Vaus, priest of Glasgow diocese, a benefice usually assigned to the secular clergy

---

[1] See *CPP*, i, 540.   [2] Cf. *CPP*, i, 540.
[3] See *CPP*, i, 548.

in the gift of the abbot and convent of Passleto, o. CLUN, together or separately, to the value of 25 marks sterling with cure, or 18 marks sterling without cure.[1]
Fondi, 5 Kal. Dec., anno 1.

27 November, 1378   Reg Aven 217, 502v-3

To the official of Glasgow. Mandate to collate John Scherar, priest of St Andrews diocese, to the parish church of Kynnel, same diocese, vacant by the transfer of William Ramsey, the last rector, to the parish church of Tanadas, also same diocese.
Fondi, 5 Kal. Dec., anno 1; expedited, 14 Kal. Feb., anno 13 [19 Jan., 1391]; consigned, 13 Kal. Feb., anno 13 [20 Jan., 1391].

28 November, 1378   Reg Aven 209, 88-89

To William de Monifoch, priest of St Andrews diocese. Reservation of a benefice usually assigned to the secular clergy in the gift of the abbot and convent of Abbyerbroth, o.s.b., together or separately, to the value of 25 marks sterling with cure, or 18 marks sterling without cure.
Fondi, 4 Kal. Dec., anno 1.
Concurrent mandate to the treasurer of Glasgow, to John Skalpy, canon of Dunkeld, and to John de Drwm, canon of Brechin.

18 December, 1378   Reg Aven 220, 65-81v;
                                                     Reg Vat 291, 41v-58v

To Guy, cardinal priest of S. Croce in Gerusalemme, papal nuncio. Appointment as papal nuncio to the kingdoms of England, Ireland and Scotland, the province of Flanders, the cities and dioceses of Liège, Utrecht, Cambrai and Tournai.
Fondi, 15 Kal. Jan., anno 1.[2]
CPL, iv, 229-36.

---

[1] See *CPP*, i, 548.
[2] There follows a long list of extensive faculties granted to the nuncio under this same date to facilitate his mission. Additional faculties, forty-six in all, were also granted under this date (Reg Aven 219, fos. 278v-80v, 298v-9, 302-4v, 307v, 313v-15, 316v-17v, 320v, 321v-2, 325-5v, 333-4, 340, 379-9v).

4 January, 1379   Reg Aven 220, 500

To William de Kethe, marshal of Scotland, and Margaret his wife, Aberdeen diocese. Indult for a plenary remission of their sins to be granted at the hour of death by a confessor of their own choice. Fondi, 2 Non. Jan., anno 1.

8 January, 1379   Reg Aven 205, 39-40

To Hugh de Dalmehoy, archdeacon of Moray, in subdeacon's orders. Provision to the archdeaconry of Moray with its annexed canonry and prebend, vacant by the death at the papal curia of Godfrey Synclare, (*alias de Novavilla*), at the petition of Pierre, cardinal of S. Eustacio, of whom Hugh is the notary, familiar and commensal. Hugh must resign the parish church of Dysert, St Andrews diocese, to which he was provided by Gregory XI and held for a long time, until deprived by another, regarding which he hopes to introduce an appeal before the papal tribunal. The parish church of Kyngorne, same diocese, was granted him by Gregory XI in substitution for Dysart, when it became vacant by the death of the late Andrex Ox, though letters confirming this were never issued, and upon obtaining possession of the archdeaconry, this substitution must be considered as null and void.
Fondi, 6 Id. Jan., anno 1.
Concurrent mandate to the dean of Aberdeen, the archdeacon of Angers, and the chancellor of Dunkeld.

8 January, 1379   Reg Aven 218, 10v-11v

To Walter Trayl, LIC.U.J., M.A., official of Glasgow, canon of Aberdeen. Provision to a canonry and prebend of Aberdeen, notwithstanding that he already holds a canonry and prebend of Ross and a canonry of Glasgow and the office of treasurer, which he obtained from Gregory XI, but provided he resigns the perpetual vicarage of the parish church of Monyfoch, St Andrews diocese.
Fondi, 6 Id. Jan., anno 1.
Concurrent mandate to the dean of Glasgow, the precentor of Aberdeen, and Peter Boerii, canon of Moray.

14 January, 1379   Reg Aven 215, 50

To the bishop of Moray. Faculty to dispense Reginald Cheyn, donzel, and Murielle, damsel, daughter of Sir William de Keth, of Moray and Aberdeen dioceses, from the impediment to marriage arising from the third and fourth degrees of consanguinity.
Fondi, 19 Kal. Feb., anno 1.
SRO Vat. Trans., iv, no. 46.

18 January, 1379   Reg Aven 205, 38v

To the abbot of Dundrennan, the prior of St Mary's Isle (usually governed by a prior) and the prior of Whithorn. Mandate to provide Richard de Drunfres, priest of Glasgow diocese, to the parish church of Bochil, Galloway diocese, vacant because Maurice Macmoran, who held it for more than a year, neglected to be ordained priest within the prescribed limit of time.
Fondi, 15 Kal. Feb., anno 1.

18 January, 1379   Reg Aven 205, 39

To John de Carryk and Nicholas de Irewyn, canons of Glasgow, and the official of Glasgow. Mandate to collate Thomas Ewer, priest, rector to the parish church of Huton, Glasgow diocese, to the parish church of Glenkarn, same diocese, vacant because John de Trabron, who had lawful possession for more than a year, neglected to be ordained priest within the prescribed limit of time; provided Thomas resigns the parish church of Hutton.
Fondi, 15 Kal. Feb., anno 1.

18 January, 1379   Reg Aven 205, 200v

To the official of Aberdeen. Mandate to collate Laurence Trayl, priest of St Andrews diocese, to the perpetual vicarage of the parish church of Monyfech, same diocese, vacant by the free resignation of Walter Trayl, treasurer of Glasgow.
Fondi, 15 Kal. Feb., anno 1.

18 January, 1379   Reg Aven 206, 536v-7v

To Master Laurence Kanth, priest, canon of Brechin, papal chaplain. Provision to a canonry of Brechin with expectation of a prebend, notwithstanding that he holds the perpetual vicarage of Lantforgrund parish, St Andrews diocese.
Fondi, 15 Kal. Feb., anno 1.
Concurrent mandate to the abbot of Arbroath, the treasurer of Glasgow and John Bothurk, canon of Aberdeen.

18 January, 1379   Reg Aven 209, 180v-1

To Andrew de Kyle, priest of Glasgow diocese. Reservation of a benefice usually assigned to the secular clergy in the gift of the abbot and convent of Aberbrothok, O.S.B., together or separately, to the value of 25 marks sterling with cure, or 18 marks sterling without cure.
Fondi, 15 Kal. Feb., anno 1.
Concurrent mandate to the dean of Aberdeen, the dean of St Agricola, Avignon, and the official of St Andrews.

22 January, 1379   Reg Aven 215, 49v

To the bishop of Glasgow. Faculty to dispense John de Keeth, donzel, and Mary de Cheyn, damsel, of Aberdeen and Moray dioceses, from the impediment to marriage arising from the third degree of affinity, with absolution from the excommunication incurred through attempting marriage without a dispensation, and with legitimation of their offspring.
Fondi, 11 Kal. Feb., anno 1.
SRO Vat. Trans., iv, no. 47.

12 February, 1379   Reg Aven 205, 256-6v

To the abbot of Paisley, the archpriest of St Didier, Avignon, and William Ade, canon of Brechin. Mandate to collate John de Tonyrgayth, B.DEC., priest, canon of Glasgow, to the parish church of Westyrkyr, Glasgow diocese, vacant by the death of Adam

Blytheman, last rector, on condition that he resigns the parish church of Drunok, same diocese.[1]
Fondi, 2 Id. Feb., anno 1.

21 February, 1379   Reg Aven 215, 70v

To the bishop of St Andrews. Mandate to consecrate the bishop-elect of Dunkeld, with faculty to absolve him from any excommunication, censure, or interdict, incurred through his adherence to Urban VI.
Fondi, 9 Kal. Mar., anno 1.
SRO Vat. Trans., i, no. 34.

22 February, 1379   Reg Aven 215, 71

To John, bishop-elect of Dunkeld. Permission to receive episcopal consecration from any bishop in communion with the Apostolic See.
Fondi, 8 Kal. Mar., anno 1.

2 March, 1379   Reg Aven 205, 244v-5

To William de Ortolano, D.U.J., papal chaplain, judge of the papal palace, canon of Châlons. Mandate to collate David de Trebrim, proficient in canon law, canon of Moray, to the parish church of Disert, St Andrews diocese, vacant by the free resignation of Hugh de Dalmehoy, upon receiving provision as archdeacon of Moray, and notwithstanding that after the death of William de Licho, last rector, a dispute arose between John de Lichon, subdeacon of St Andrews diocese, and the said Hugh de Dalmehoy over the priorities of their respective provisions to this parish church. The earlier provision [19 Nov., 1378] to a canonry of Moray with expectation of a prebend, and dignity, parsonage, or office, is hereby nullified.
Fondi, 6 Non. Mar., anno 1.

6 March, 1379   Reg Aven 213, 641v-2

To Laurence Kanth, priest, perpetual vicar of the parish church of

---

[1] See *CPP*, i, 547.

Longforgrund, St Andrews diocese. Reservation of a benefice usually assigned to the secular clergy in the gift of the bishop, prior and chapter of St Andrews, O.S.A., together or separately, to the value of 50 marks sterling with cure, or 30 marks sterling without cure, notwithstanding that he already has a provision to a canonry of Brechin with expectation of a prebend, but on condition that he resigns his vicarage; at the petition of Charles, king of France.
Fondi, 2 Non. Mar., anno I.
Concurrent mandate to the bishops of Glasgow and Dunblane, and Peter Bosquerii, canon of Thérouanne.

10 March, 1379   Reg Aven 219, 487v-8

To Andrew de Trebrim, LIC.LEG., archdeacon of St Andrews. Provision to the archdeaconry of St Andrews, vacant by the promotion of John to the bishopric of Dunkeld, with dispensation to hold it together with the parish church of Kyniwell, St Andrews diocese, for the period of one year, after which time he must resign the parish in exchange for some other compatible benefice.
Fondi, 6 Id. Mar., anno I.
Concurrent mandate to the archdeacon of Rheims, Simon de Ketenes, canon of Aberdeen, and the official of St Andrews.

15 March, 1379   Reg Aven 215, 258-8v

To the archdeacons of Autun and Dunkeld, and the official of St Andrews. Mandate to enforce the statutes of Benedict XII and procure that William de Angus, monk of the abbey of Londorris, O.S.B., St Andrews diocese, be sent to a university.
Fondi, Id. Mar., anno I.
SRO Vat. Trans., i, no. 35.

20 March, 1379   Reg Aven 205, 69-69v;
                                              Reg Vat 291, 112-12v

To the bishops of St Andrews and Glasgow. Mandate to cite Robert de Clakkston, prior of Goldingham, O.S.B., St Andrews

diocese, and the others concerned, and to enquire into the many crimes of which the prior is accused and his felonies against king Robert, whose ancestors founded and built the priory, endowing it with a barony. If the charges are found to be true, they are to deprive and remove the prior and collate Michael de Inverkethin, monk of Demfermehon Abbey, to the office of prior at the petition of king Robert.
Fondi, 13 Kal. Apr., anno 1.
CPL, iv, 236.

20 March, 1379   Reg Aven 216, 76v-77

To the bishops of St Andrews and Glasgow. Mandate to summon Robert de Clakkston, prior of Goldingham, O.S.B., St Andrews diocese, and his accomplices, to appear before them and answer the charges against them of sacrilege, robbery, murder and the like of which they are accused. If they are found guilty, then the bishops are empowered to deprive and remove the prior from office and place them all under ecclesiastical censure.
Fondi, 13 Kal. Apr., anno 1.

13 June, 1379   Reg Aven 219, 454-4v

To David Bell, abbot of Holyrood, O.S.A., St Andrews diocese. Provision to the office of abbot of the abbey of Holyrood, vacant by the death of Abbot John. David Bell is a professed monk of the abbey of the Isle of Masses, O.S.A., Dunblane diocese, and is in priest's orders.
Avignon, Id. Jun., anno 1.
Concurrent mandate to the bishop of St Andrews, the convent of Holyrood, the vassals, and to Robert, king of Scots.

6 July, 1379   Reg Aven 219, 340v

To Guy, cardinal priest of S. Croce in Gerusalemme, papal nuncio. Grant of plenipotentiary powers to the nuncio in order to further facilitate his mission to England, Scotland, Wales and Ireland.
Avignon, 2 Non. Jul., anno 1.

15 July, 1379   Reg Aven 217, 524-4v

To the bishops of Glasgow and St Andrews. Mandate to enquire into the refusal by Ingeram, archdeacon of Dunkeld, to accept his provision to the bishopric of Galloway, vacant by the death of Adam, last bishop. Having ascertained the facts of Ingram's refusal, they are to provide Thomas de Rossy, priest, professor O.F.M., M.THEOL., papal penitentiary, to the vacant bishopric.
Avignon, Id. Jul., anno 1.

19 July, 1379   Reg Aven 215, 121v

To John, bishop of Dunkeld. Indult to celebrate Mass on a portable altar, or have it celebrated in his presence by a worthy priest.
Avignon, 14 Kal. Aug., anno 1.

19 July, 1379   Reg Aven 215, 121v

John, bishop of Dunkeld. Indult to reconcile churches after their desecration.
Avignon, 14 Kal. Aug., anno 1.

19 July, 1379   Reg Aven 215, 122

To John, bishop of Dunkeld. Indult to celebrate Mass, or have it celebrated in his presence, before dawn.
Avignon, 14 Kal. Aug., anno 1.

19 July, 1379   Reg Aven 215, 122

To John, bishop of Dunkeld. Indult to choose his own confessor.
Avignon, 14 Kal. Aug., anno 1.

19 July, 1379   Reg Aven 215, 122

To John, bishop of Dunkeld. Indult to celebrate Mass, or have it celebrated in his presence, even in places that are under interdict.
Avignon, 14 Kal. Aug., anno 1.

19 July, 1379   Reg Aven 224, 397v

To John, bishop of Dunkeld. Faculty to dispense ten men and as many women of his diocese from the matrimonial impediment arising from the fourth degree of consanguinity or affinity. Avignon, 14 Kal. Aug., anno 1.

19 July, 1379   Reg Aven 215, 122v

To all Christ's faithful. Indulgence of one year and forty days is granted to all who visit the cathedral church of Dunkeld on certain feasts, and one hundred days indulgence during certain octaves, and contribute towards the repair of the fabric, which is in a ruinous condition on account of the wars and pestilence in those parts. Avignon, 14 Kal. Aug., anno 1.
sro Vat. Trans., i, no. 36.

25 July, 1379   Reg Aven 220, 172v

To Symon de Preston, knight, St Andrews diocese. Indult for a plenary remission of his sins to be granted at the hour of death by a confessor of his own choice. Avignon, 8 Kal. Aug., anno 1.

27 July, 1379   Reg Aven 216, 28v;
                                Reg Vat 291, 65v

To abbot David and the convent of Holyrood, o.s.a., St Andrews diocese. Indult, granted at the petition of king Robert, whose principal chaplains the abbots are pro tempore, that the abbot and his successors may vest with the mitre, ring, and other pontifical insignia, and likewise may impart the final blessing solemnly in the monastery, in priories subject to it, and in parishes and other churches belonging to the abbot and convent together or separately, even though not subject pleno iure, provided that no bishop or papal legate also be present. Avignon, 6 Kal. Aug., anno 1.
CPL, iv, 236.

F

3 August, 1379   Reg Aven 215, 141

To Hugh de Dalmehoy, archdeacon of Moray. Confirmation, made at the petition of the cardinal deacon of S. Eustacio, of Hugh's provision to the archdeaconry of Moray, which was open to the accusation of subreption through not having mentioned in his second petition the fact of a previous provision to a canonry of Glasgow with expectation of a prebend.
Avignon, 3 Non. Aug., anno 1.

28 August, 1379   Reg. Aven 220, 501v

To Michael, rector of the parish church of Crichton, St Andrews diocese. Indult for a plenary remission of his sins to be granted at the hour of death by a confessor of his own choice.
Avignon, 5 Kal. Sept., anno 1.

29 August, 1379   Reg Aven 219, 341v

To Guy, cardinal priest of S. Croce in Gerusalemme, papal nuncio. Faculty to grant a plenary indulgence to everyone within his jurisdiction, who is at the point of death as a result of the great epidemic, or pestilence that is raging in those places.
Avignon, 4 Kal. Sept., anno 1.

13 September, 1379   Reg Aven 205, 133v-4

To the abbots of Kilwinning and Paisley, and William Ade, canon of Glasgow. Mandate to collate Laurence Laverole, priest of Dunkeld diocese, at present studying canon law, to the perpetual vicarage of the parish church of Dalri, Glasgow diocese, vacant because Duncan Pety, who had lawful possession for more than a year, neglected to be ordained priest within the prescribed limit of time, and notwithstanding moreover that the late Robert de Denys also obtained lawful possession for more than a year, but likewise neglected to be ordained priest within the prescribed limit of time.[1]
Avignon, Id. Sept., anno 1.

[1] Cf. CPP, i, 540-1.

13 September, 1379   Reg Aven 220, 503

To Robert Senescalli, second son of Robert, king of Scots, earl of Fife and Menteith. Indult for a plenary remission of his sins to be granted at the hour of death by a confessor of his own choice. Avignon, Id. Sept., anno 1.

15 September, 1379   Reg Aven 216, 125v-6;
                                       Reg Vat 291, 157-8

Ad perpetuam rei memoriam. Union of the perpetual vicarage of the parish church of Clacmanam, St Andrews diocese, annual value 10 marks sterling, vacant by the provision of Maurice de Stratherne to the dignity of archdeacon of Dunblane, to the abbey of Cambuskyneth, O.S.A., which enjoys the right of patronage and to which the rectory of Clacmanan is already appropriated. This measure is to relieve the penury of the abbey, which has been despoiled of its chalices, books and other altar ornaments during the wars, and the belltower of which, after being struck by lightening, has collapsed on the choir leaving it in ruins. Avignon, 17 Kal. Oct., anno 1.
CPL, iv, 236.

20 September, 1379   Reg Aven 220, 503v

To Ellen de Carryk, prioress of the priory of North Berwick, O.CIST., St Andrews diocese. Indult for a plenary remission of her sins to be granted at the hour of death by a confessor of her own choice. Avignon, 12 Kal. Oct., anno 1.

20 September, 1379   Reg Aven 220, 503v

To Joan de Donyeliston, prioress of the priory of Manuel, O.CIST., St Andrews diocese. Indult for a plenary remission of her sins to be granted at the hour of death by a confessor of her own choice. Avignon, 12 Kal. Oct., anno 1.

20 September, 1379   Reg Aven 220, 503v

To Matilda de Leys, nun of the priory of North Berwick, O.CIST., St Andrews diocese. Indult for a plenary remission of her sins to be granted at the hour of death by a confessor of her own choice. Avignon, 12 Kal. Oct., anno 1.

22 September, 1379   Reg Aven 215, 173

To the official of Glasgow. Mandate to confirm the provision made by ordinary authority by Walter, bishop of Glasgow, to his nephew Henry de Wardlau, of a canonry of Glasgow and the prebend of Auldroxisburch, vacant by the death of Thomas Theoderici, and of which Henry has had peaceful possession for over three months. Since Theoderici was a papal familiar and a sub-collector of the Apostolic Camera, upon his death provision was therefore reserved to the pope, and Henry fears that his tenure could be challenged in the future. Avignon, 10 Kal. Oct., anno 1.

22 September, 1379   Reg Aven 217, 471v-2

To the abbot of Dunfermline. Mandate to collate Andrew de Balmentacol, clerk of Dunkeld diocese, to the perpetual vicarage with cure of the parish church of Langton, St Andrews diocese, vacant because Richard de Cokburne, who had lawful possession for more than a year, neglected to be ordained priest within the prescribed limit of time. Andrew is hereby dispensed from the impediment arising from defect of age, being only eighteen years old.[1] Avignon, 10 Kal. Oct., anno 1.

24 September, 1379   Reg Aven 220, 173

To Simon Laverok and Brigid his wife, Dunkeld diocese. Indult for a plenary remission of their sins to be granted at the hour of death by a confessor of their own choice. Avignon, 8 Kal. Oct., anno 1.

[1] See *CPP*, i, 543.

24 September, 1379   Reg Aven 220, 173

To Peter Ferfith, priest of Glasgow diocese. Indult for a plenary remission of his sins to be granted at the hour of death by a confessor of his own choice.
Avignon, 8 Kal. Oct., anno 1.

1 October, 1379   Reg Aven 205, 145-6

To the abbots of Lindores and Scone, and the official of St Andrews. Mandate to collate Laurence Laverok, priest of Dunkeld diocese, to the perpetual vicarage of the parish church of Abirnethy, Dunblane diocese, the annual value of which is £10 sterling, which has been detained unlawfully by a certain Michael, still in his minority, born of the late Geoffrey Manysson, priest of the same diocese; upon obtaining possession Laurence must resign the perpetual vicarage of the parish church of Dalry, Glasgow diocese, which was assigned to him recently [13 September, 1379].[1]
Avignon, Kal. Oct., anno 1.

1 October, 1379   Reg Aven 207, 444v-5

To the official of St Andrews. Mandate to reserve to John de Balnanys, priest of Dunblane diocese, perpetual beneficiary of the parish church of Abrinecthy, same diocese, a benefice usually assigned to the secular clergy in the gift of the abbot and convent of Londorys, o.s.b., together or separately, to the value of 25 marks sterling with cure, or 18 marks sterling without cure, notwithstanding the perpetual benefice, which is without cure and is called a prebend in those parts.[2]
Avignon, Kal. Oct., anno 1.

2 October, 1379   Reg Aven 215, 226v-7

To the bishop of Glasgow. Mandate to confirm, at the petition of Abbot William and the convent of Cambuskynneth, o.s.a., St

[1] See CPP, i, 541-2.   [2] See CPP, i, 542.

Andrews diocese, the donation made by his predecessor Bishop John, to Cambuskenneth Abbey of the right of patronage over the parish church of Kylmoronok, Glasgow diocese, hitherto exercised by the late king Robert, vacant by the free resignation of the late John de Lyndesai, last rector, into the bishop's hands. A suitable portion of the income must be set aside for the maintenance of a perpetual vicar, who is to be presented by the abbot and convent.[1]
Avignon, 6 Non. Oct., anno 1.
SRO Vat. Trans., i, no. 37.

3 October, 1379   Reg Aven 215, 179v-80

To the bishop of Moray. Mandate to decide, without further appeal, in the case of John de Carralle, canon of Ross, against Bishop Alexander of Ross, Bishop William of St Andrews, John de Caron and John Pulcer, priests, and Robert Kannord and Thomas Madore, laics, of St Andrews and Brechin dioceses, regarding the revenues, fruits, and tithes which he derives from a canonry of Ross and the prebend of Colyrodin and from the parish church of Mockard, St Andrews diocese.
Avignon, 5 Non. Oct., anno 1.
SRO Vat. Trans., i, no. 38.

17 October, 1379   Reg Aven 215, 218v-19

To Gerard, prior of France of the Hospital of St John of Jerusalem and lieutenant of Juan, master of the said Hospital and of the convent of the Hospital at Rhodes. Whereas Robert Mercer, lord of Inirpery, Dunblane diocese, informed the pope's predecessor, Gregory XI, how the late Robert, master of the Hospital of St John of Jerusalem, at that time only prior of France and master-elect, with the counsel and consent of the other hospitallers and for the good of the said Hospital, granted all the houses, obventions, rents, proceeds, rights and all other goods, which the Hospital possessed in the realm of Scotland, on lease for ten years from then [24 June, 1374] onwards

---

[1] See CPP, i, 542-3.

for an annual rent of 400 gold florins of Florence, to be paid to the master on a certain date [Ascension Day] each year at Paris, and this contract was confirmed subsequently by Gregory XI [21 Jan., 1375]. Recently, however, Robert Mercer has made present the fact, that although he was ready to pay the rent in full, Robert, prior of England of the Hospital, David de Marre, archdeacon of Lothian, and Robert de Erskyn, knight of St Andrews diocese, have impeded him and impede him still from having peaceful possession of those properties, and through having had to have recourse to litigation over this, he has incurred considerable expenses and burdens to his great loss and detriment. Wherefore he has petitioned the pope to apply a suitable remedy and Charles, king of France supports this plea. Therefore the pope ordains that the terms of the original contract be observed inviolate and the said prior, archdeacon and knight must be prevented from hindering Robert from paying the rents due for the past, or for the future, because it is not opportune that any other remedy be adopted.
Avignon, 16 Kal. Nov., anno 1.

17 October, 1379   Reg Aven 220, 173v

To Elizabeth de Recte, wife of Sir William de Lyndesay, St Andrews diocese. Indult for a plenary remission of her sins to be granted at the hour of death by a confessor of her own choice.
Avignon, 16 Kal. Nov., anno 1.

17 October, 1379   Reg Aven 220, 173v

To John de Cornton, layman of St Andrews diocese. Indult for a plenary remission of his sins to be granted at the hour of death by a confessor of his own choice.
Avignon, 16 Kal. Nov., anno 1.

17 October, 1379   Reg Aven 220, 173v

To Henry de Cornton, canon of Dunkeld. Indult for a plenary

remission of his sins to be granted at the hour of death by a confessor of his own choice.
Avignon, 16 Kal. Nov., anno 1.

17 October, 1379   Reg Aven 220, 173v

To Alan de Erskyne, knight, lord of Inchmartin, St Andrews diocese. Indult for a plenary remission of his sins to be granted at the hour of death by a confessor of his own choice.
Avignon, 16 Kal. Nov., anno 1.

26 October, 1379   Reg Aven 215, 241-2

To the bishops of St Andrews and Glasgow. Mandate to enquire into the state of the leper hospital and other pious foundations, which are situated on the borders of Scotland and England within the domains of William, earl of Douglas, and which formerly were suitably endowed, but on account of the continual warfare in those parts have now become so ruinous that they are uninhabitable, and to grant the lands to the said earl so that a church with tower and bells may be constructed in a safer place, endowed for a dean and twelve priests who will form the chapter of the church, with collegiate rank, and over which the earl and his heirs will enjoy right of patronage.[1]
Avignon, 7 Kal. Nov., anno 1.
SRO Vat. Trans., i, no. 39.

26 October, 1379   Reg Aven 215, 242-3

To the bishop of St Andrews. Mandate to confirm the foundation and endowment made by Archibald de Douglas, knight, earl of Galloway, of a hospital and chapel for the poor, situated within the precincts of the monastery of Holywood, in memory of king Robert and king David, of Edward de Bruys, brother of the said king Robert, of his own forebear James, lord of Douglas, his ancestors and all the faithful departed, the revenues to be derived

---

[1] Cf. *CPP*, i, 537-8 where it is wrongly dated 1378 (see Reg Supp 54 156-7).

from the lands of Crosnychell and Treqhert between the rivers Des and Nyth and devoted to the sustenance of the sick and maintenance of a suitable chaplain, who will act as master of the hospital, with the obligation of celebrating Mass daily and administering the other sacraments. This foundation was planned originally by the late Edward de Bruys, but remained unrealised on account of the wars and his own death, and it has the consent of king Robert and Bishop Walter of Glasgow.[1]
Avignon, 7 Kal. Nov., anno 1.
SRO Vat. Trans., i, no. 40.

26 October, 1379   Reg Aven 215, 241

To Gilbert de Grenlaw, LIC.ART., canon of Moray. Absolution from any incapacity or infamy incurred through obtaining provision to the parish church of Liston, St Andrews diocese, vacant by the death at the papal curia of John Rayton, last rector, in virtue of papal letters in which Gilbert is described as being M.A., whereas he is only LIC.ART., and he does not wish his tenure to be disputed on grounds of subreption. He may retain all the revenues he has derived up to the present, but he must resign the parish forthwith.[2]
Avignon, 7 Kal. Nov., anno 1.

26 October, 1379   Reg Aven 218, 53-53v

To Walter Trayl and Alexander de Caron, canons of Aberdeen, and John Liche, canon of Dunkeld. Mandate to collate Adam de Tynyngham, dean of Aberdeen and papal familiar, to the canonry and prebend of Glasgow, vacant by the promotion of John, papal collector in Scotland, to the bishopric of Dunkeld; to which canonry Adam was already provided by ordinary authority, when provision was reserved to the pope.[3]
Avignon, 7 Kal. Nov., anno 1.

---

[1] Cf. *CPP*, i, 538 where it is wrongly dated 1378.
[2] Cf. *CPP*, i, 538 where it is wrongly dated 1378.
[3] Cf. *CPP*, i, 538 where it is wrongly dated 1378.

26 October, 1379   Reg Aven 215, 183v

To Thomas de Thaok, monk of the abbey of Balmerino, o.cist., St Andrews diocese. Dispensation from illegitimacy of birth, having been born of a priest and an unmarried woman, so that he may exercise all the functions of a monk and even accept the office of abbot, if elected.
Avignon, 7 Kal. Nov., anno 1.

26 October, 1379   Reg Aven 216, 187-7v

To the bishop of Glasgow. Mandate to enquire into the litigation between Andrew de Tribrine, priest of St Andrews diocese, and the abbot and convent of Combuskynech, o.s.a., same diocese, regarding the parish church of Kynnoull, St Andrews diocese, to which Andrew was provided by the pope when it became vacant by the death of the late Bric de Kreyc, last rector. The bishop of St Andrews, however, had previously united the parish to Cambuskenneth abbey to augment the revenues, and the bishop of Glasgow is to confirm this union, if he judges it expedient.[1]
Avignon, 7 Kal. Nov., anno 1.
Printed: *Camb. Reg.*, no. 165.

26 October, 1379   Reg Aven 217, 486-7

To the chancellor of Paris. Mandate to reassign to Gilbert de Grenlaw, lic.art., canon of Moray, the parish church of Liston, St Andrews diocese, vacant by the death of the last rector, John de Raycon, at the papal curia, to which Gilbert was provided originally by Gregory xi, but in the papal letters was erroneously described as being m.a., whereas he is only lic.art., notwithstanding that he has retained the living in the meantime and drawn the revenues.[2]
Avignon, 7 Kal. Nov., anno 1.

---

[1] See also Reg Aven 222, 409-10; Reg Vat 291, 218v-19 [*CPL*, iv, 237]; Reg Vat 292, 47-7v [*CPL*, iv, 238]; cf. *CPP*, i, 539 and *Camb. Reg*, no. 165 where it is wrongly dated 1378.
[2] Cf. *CPP*, i, 538 where it is wrongly dated 1378.

26 October, 1379   Reg Aven 218, 411v-12

To John de Carall, canon of Moray. Provision to a canonry of
Moray with expectation of a prebend, notwithstanding that he holds
the parish church of Mathard, St Andrews diocese, and a canonry
and prebend of Ross.

Avignon, 7 Kal. Nov., anno 1.

Concurrent mandate to the bishops of Avignon, Dunkeld and
Aberdeen.

13 November, 1379   Reg Aven 223, 357v-8v

To John de Caron, LIC.U.J., canon of Glasgow. Provision to a canonry of Glasgow and the prebend of Stabor, vacant by the death of William de Grenlaw, papal collector, at which the living first passed to Giles, cardinal bishop of Frascati, and when vacated a second time by his death, to the late James Senescalli, clerk of Glasgow diocese, who in turn died before the letters of provision had been issued. John de Caron already holds canonries and prebends of Moray and Aberdeen, together with the parish church of Rathdo, St Andrews diocese, and recently letters have been issued reserving to him a benefice with or without cure in the gift of the bishop and chapter of St Andrews.[1]
Avignon, Id. Nov., anno 2.
Concurrent mandate to the bishop of St Andrews, the dean of Aberdeen, and the dean of St Agricola, Avignon.

17 November, 1379   Reg Aven 222, 393-3v;
                                Reg Vat 292, 33v

To William Gerland, M.A., priest, canon of Moray. Confirmation of his provision to a canonry of Caithness with expectation of a prebend, parsonage, or office, with or without cure [22 Nov., 1378], notwithstanding that no mention was made of another provision to a canonry of Moray with a similar reservation [17 Nov., 1378], or that he holds the perpetual chaplaincy of Duffus castle, Moray diocese, but on condition that he resign the perpetual vicarage of the parish church of Nautill, St Andrews diocese, and that as soon

[1] See Reg Supp 57, 1v-2; 60, 21v.

as he obtains a parsonage, or office, in virtue of one of these provisions, other provision to a parsonage, or office, becomes void. Avignon, 15 Kal. Dec., anno 2.
CPL, iv, 237-8.

19 November, 1379   Reg Aven 223, 94; 224, 323, 328

To Margaret, countess of Douglas and Mar. Indults for a plenary remission of her sins to be granted at the hour of death by a confessor of her own choice, who may dispense her and her household from observing abstinence from flesh meat on certain days. Avignon, 13 Kal. Dec., anno 2.

2 January, 1380   Reg Aven 221, 246v-7v

To the official of St Andrews. Mandate to collate Alexander de Gathoy, priest of St Andrews diocese, to the parish church of Kinel, same diocese, vacant by the transfer of William de Ramsay, last rector, to the parish church of Tanadas, also St Andrews diocese. Andrew was provided to the living by ordinary authority by Bishop William of St Andrews, but he has petitioned for confirmation because doubts have subsequently arisen about the validity of his tenure on account of the provision being reserved to the pope. Avignon, 4 Id. Jan., anno 2.

8 January, 1380   Reg Aven 222, 362v ;
Reg Vat 292, 9v

To John de Caron, LIC.U.J., M.A., priest, canon of Moray. Permission to take the doctorate in civil and canon laws at Avignon, or at any other university of his preference, notwithstanding the constitutions and statutes to the contrary of the universities of Orleans and Paris, which John swore to observe when he graduated with a licentiate of civil law at Orleans and of canon law at Paris. Avignon, 6 Id. Jan., anno 2.
CPL, iv, 237.

28 January, 1380   Reg Aven 222, 618-19;
                                        Reg Vat 292, 242-2v

Ad perpetuam rei memoriam. Confirmation, granted at the petition
of Alexander, bishop of Aberdeen, Adam de Tyningham, dean,
and the chapter of Aberdeen, of the gift made by William de Keth,
lord of the barony of Alden, of an annual pension of six marks
sterling, to be paid in two equal portions at Pentecost and on the
feast of St Martin *in yeme* [11 Nov.] from his lands of Achidonald
in the said barony of Alden, for the endowment of a perpetual
chaplaincy in the choir of the cathedral of Aberdeen in memory of
William de Calabre, canon of Aberdeen, who was a notable bene-
factor of the said William de Keth.
Avignon, 5 Kal. Feb., anno 2.
CPL, iv, 240; printed : *Abdn. Reg.*, i, 124-6.

28 January, 1380   Reg Aven 222, 620v;
                                        Reg Vat 292, 244-4v

To the abbot and convent of St Mary de Cambuskenneth, o.s.a.
Reconfirmation of the union of the parish church of Clacmanan,
St Andrews diocese, to Cambuskenneth Abbey to relieve the
poverty of the monastery [as in Reg Aven 216, 125v-6 above],
notwithstanding that in the original confirmation the value of the
parish was stated to be 10 marks sterling, whereas in fact it is 15
marks sterling.
Avignon, 5 Kal. Feb., anno 2.
CPL, iv, 240.

5 February, 1380   Reg Aven 224, 393-3v

To Andrew Badly, monk of the abbey of Melrose, o.cist.,
Glasgow diocese. Permission to study canon law for seven years.
Avignon, Non. Feb., anno 2.
sro Vat. Trans., i, no. 41.

10 February, 1380   Reg Aven 212, 525-6

To Duncan Petit, b.u.j., archdeacon of Galloway. Reservation of a

benefice with or without cure, even if a canonry and prebend, dignity, parsonage, or office, and elective, in the gift of the bishop of St Andrews, the annual value of which does not exceed 100 marks sterling.
Avignon, 4 Id. Feb., anno 2.[1]
Concurrent mandate to the abbot of Kilwinning, the archdeacon of Brechin, and the official of Glasgow.

10 February, 1380   Reg Aven 221, 15v-18v ;
Reg Vat 292, 247v-50

To Guy, cardinal priest of S. Croce in Gerusalemme, papal nuncio. Faculties granted to the nuncio to facilitate his mission to England and Scotland and elsewhere.
Avignon, 4 Id. Feb., anno 2.
CPL, iv, 240-2.

10 February, 1380   Reg Aven 223, 194-4v

To Thomas Senescalli, archdeacon of St Andrews. Provision to the office of archdeacon of St Andrews, vacant by the promotion of John to the bishopric of Dunkeld ; at the petition of king Robert, who is his natural father.[2]
Avignon, 4 Id. Feb., anno 2.
Concurrent mandate to the bishop of Glasgow, the abbot of Dunfermline and the official of St Andrews.

10 February, 1380   Reg Aven 223, 364

To Thomas Senescalli, canon of Glasgow. Provision to a canonry of Glasgow and the prebend of Stobow, vacant by the death of his brother James Senescalli ; at the petition of king Robert, who is his natural father.[3]
Avignon, 4 Id. Feb., anno 2.

[1] See CPP, i, 553. In the register this letter is cancelled out and *Alibi est is suo loco* is noted in the left-hand margin and *anno primo* in the right-hand margin, but another registration of this letter has not been found in the first pontifical year. A similar concession to Petit occurs on 29 February, 1380 in Reg Aven 224, 383-4v.
[2] See CPP, i, 551.   [3] See CPP, i, 551.

Concurrent mandate to the bishop of Glasgow, the abbot of Dunfermline and the official of St Andrews.

11 February, 1380   Reg Aven 224, 351-2

To Robert Wyse, priest, canon of Aberdeen. Confirmation of his provision to a canonry of Aberdeen made by ordinary authority by bishop Alexander, with an annual pension of 10 marks sterling derived from certain lands pertaining to the church; the original episcopal instrument of provision [3 Oct., 1377], is repeated *in extenso*.
Avignon, 3 Id. Feb., anno 2.
SRO Vat. Trans., i, no. 42.

14 February, 1380   Reg Aven 222, 505v-6;
                                Reg Vat 292, 137v-8

To the bishops of Glasgow and St Andrews. Mandate to enquire what tax should be levied on the prelates and clergy of Scotland to help king Robert pay off the heavy ransom incurred by the late king David. King Robert has appealed to the pope for a tithe from the Church because the realm is impoverished by continual warfare and a great sum of money remains to be paid.
Avignon, 16 Kal. Mar., anno 2.
CPL, iv, 238-9.

15 February, 1380   Reg Aven 223, 92v

To Alexander de Stracton, squire, and Catherine his wife, St Andrews diocese. Indult for a plenary remission of their sins to be granted at the hour of death by a confessor of their own choice.
Avignon, 15 Kal. Mar., anno 2.

15 February, 1380   Reg Aven 223, 96v

To John Barber, archdeacon of Aberdeen. Indult for a plenary remission of his sins to be granted at the hour of death by a confessor of his own choice.
Avignon, 15 Kal. Mar., anno 2.

18 February, 1380   Reg Aven 221, 647v

To Sir Thomas Walhope, under-sheriff of Perth, St Andrews diocese. Indult for a plenary remission of his sins to be granted at the hour of death by a confessor of his own choice.[1]
Avignon, 12 Kal. Mar., anno 2.

23 February, 1380   Reg Aven 222, 194v-5v

To the official of Moray. Mandate to reserve to William Wysse, priest of Moray diocese, a benefice usually assigned to the secular clergy in the gift of the abbot and convent of Longodorso, o.s.b., St Andrews diocese, together or separately, to the value of 25 marks sterling with cure, or 18 marks sterling without cure.[2]
Avignon, 7 Kal. Mar., anno 2.

29 February, 1380   Reg Aven 224, 384-4v

To Duncan Petyt, B.U.J., archdeacon of Galloway. Permission to hold another benefice with cure, even if a dignity, parsonage, or office, together with the office of archdeacon of Galloway, which is a dignity with cure, for a period of three years; at the petition of king Robert, to whom he acted formerly as secretary.
Avignon, 2 Kal. Mar., anno 2.

2 March, 1380   Reg Aven 224, 323v

To all Christ's faithful. Indulgence of one hundred days is granted, at the petition of bishop Alexander and the chapter of Aberdeen, to all those who assist with the repair of that part of the cathedral called the nave, which on account of its antiquity has collapsed.
Avignon, 6 Non. Mar., anno 2.
Printed: *Abdn. Reg.* i, 131-2.

2 March, 1380   Reg Aven 224, 323v-4

To David de Bennyn, monk of the abbey of Melrose, O.CIST.,

---

[1] This indulgence is listed in the rubrics of the next register, Reg Aven 222, 18.
[2] See *CPP*, i, 554.

G

Glasgow diocese. More ample dispensation, having already been dispensed from illegitimacy of birth, being born out of wedlock, in order to receive holy orders, so that he may exercise all the functions of a monk and even accept the office of abbot, if elected.

Avignon, 6 Non. Mar., anno 2.

2 March, 1380   Reg Aven 224, 324v

To all Christ's faithful. Indulgence of seven years and seven quarantines is granted to all who visit the cathedral church of Aberdeen on certain feasts, their vigils and their octaves, and one year and forty days indulgence on certain lesser days, and contribute towards the reconstruction of the nave, which has collapsed on account of its antiquity.

Avignon, 6 Non. Mar., anno 2.
Printed : *Abdn. Reg.* i, 132-3.

4 May, 1380   Reg Aven 224, 391

To the bishop of St Andrews. Faculty to dispense Robert, earl of Fyff, and Murielle, daughter of Sir William de Keth, marshal of Scotland, from the matrimonial impediment of public honesty, because Robert has had carnal relations with a woman related to Murielle in the fourth degree of consanguinity.

Avignon, 4 Non. Maii, anno 2.
SRO Vat. Trans., iv, no. 48.

4 May, 1380   Reg Aven 224, 391

To the bishop of Dunblane. Faculty to dispense from the matrimonial impediment involving Robert, earl of Fyff, and Murielle, daughter of Sir William de Keth [identical with the dispensation described above].

Avignon, 4 Non. Maii, anno 2.
SRO Vat. Trans., iv, no. 49.

5 May, 1380   Reg Aven 222, 505v ;
                                     Reg Vat 292, 137v

To all Christ's faithful. Indulgence of one year and forty days is
granted to all who visit the chapel of the poor hospital of St John
the Evangelist de Hochtyrrogale, St Andrews diocese, on certain
feasts and their octaves, and fifty days indulgence during the six
days after Pentecost, and contribute towards its maintenance.
Avignon, 3 Non. Maii, anno 2.
CPL, iv, 238.

5 May, 1380   Reg Aven 222, 505 ;
                                     Reg Vat 292, 137-7v

To John de Congallis, priest, rector of the parish church of
Kinlochgoil, Argyll diocese. Dispensation to hold another benefice,
even involving cure, together with his parish church for a period
of three years ; at the end of which time he is to exchange it, or his
parish, for another benefice compatible with the one retained, or
else resign his parish. John is said to have studied canon law at Paris
for over three years.
Avignon, 3 Non. Maii, anno 2.
CPL, iv, 238.

5 May, 1380   Reg Aven 223, 379v-80

To Dugall Petri, canon of Argyll. Provision to a canonry of Argyll
and the erection of the parish church of Kilmorir in Lorn, Argyll
diocese, to the canonical status of a prebend, which he may retain,
while the cure is exercised by a perpetual vicar, and notwithstanding
that he also holds a canonry and prebend of Dunkeld.
Avignon, 3 Non. Maii, anno 2.
Concurrent mandate to the archdeacons of Dunkeld and Dunblane,
and the official of St Andrews.

5 May, 1380   Reg Aven 224, 396

To the chapter of Argyll. Erection of the parish church of Kilmorr

in Lorn, Argyll diocese, into a canonical prebend of the same diocese, at the petition of Dugall Petri, rector of the said parish.
Avignon, 3 Non. Maii, anno 2.
SRO Vat. Trans., i, no. 43 ; printed *Highland Papers*, iv, 137-8.

5 May, 1380   Reg Aven 224, 390v-1

To the chancellor of Dunblane. Faculty to dispense ten men and as many women of the domains of Robert, earl of Fyff, second son of Robert, king of Scots, from the matrimonial impediment arising from the third and fourth degrees of consanguinity or affinity, that by arranging marriages between the contesting families an end may be put to the feuds, murders and factions existing in those parts.
Avignon, 3 Non. Maii, anno 2.
SRO Vat. Trans., iv, no. 50.

5 May, 1380   Reg Aven 224, 544v

To Malachy Ysaach, monk of the monastery of Ardchattan, O.VALLIS CAUL., Argyll diocese. Dispensation from illegitimacy of birth, having been born out of wedlock, so that he may excercise all the functions of a monk and even accept the office of abbot, if elected.
Avignon, 3 Non. Maii, anno 2.

5 May, 1380   Reg Aven 224, 544v

To the bishop of Dunblane. Mandate to confirm the union of the parish church of St Columba de Thiriachinsula, Sodor diocese, to the monastery of Ardkatan, O.VALLIS CAUL., usually governed by a prior, which union was made by ordinary authority of the bishop of Sodor and confirmed by the archbishop of Nidaros, acting as metropolitan, and of which the monastery has now enjoyed peaceful possession for more than one hundred years.
Avignon, 3 Non. Maii, anno 2.
SRO Vat. Trans., i, no. 44; printed : *Highland Papers*, iv, 138-40.

7 May, 1380   Reg Aven 223, 470-70v

To the bishop of Brechin. Mandate to reserve to John Scot, clerk of Dunkeld, a canonry of Moray with expectation of a prebend. Avignon, Non. Maii, anno 2; expedited, 10 Kal. Aug., anno 9 [23 July, 1387]; consigned, 4 Non. Aug., anno 9 [2 Aug., 1387].

8 May, 1380   Reg Aven 222, 563v;
                                    Reg Vat 292, 192-2v

To William de Camera, clerk of Aberdeen diocese. Confirmation of the reservation made to him by Guy, cardinal priest of S. Croce in Gerusalemme, papal nuncio of a benefice usually assigned to the secular clergy in the gift of the bishop and chapter of St Andrews, O.S.A., together or separately, to the value of 25 marks sterling with cure, or 18 marks sterling without cure, notwithstanding that at the time of granting this expectative grace the nuncio had not yet entered the kingdom of Scotland, or that William is also provided to a canonry of Dunkeld with expectation of a prebend [6 November, 1378].
Avignon, 8 Id. Maii, anno 2.
CPL, iv, 239.

2 June, 1380   Reg Aven 222, 192v-3

To the bishop of Dunblane. Mandate to reserve to Robert Kann, priest, perpetual chaplain of the parish church of St Nicholas de Erol, St Andrews diocese, value not exceeding 8 marks sterling, a benefice usually assigned to the secular clergy in the gift of the abbot and convent of Abribrochat, O.S.B., same diocese, together or separately, to the value of 25 marks sterling with cure, or 18 marks sterling without cure.[1]
Avignon, 4 Non. Jun., anno 2.

16 June, 1380   Reg Aven 221, 438-8v

To John de Daldowy, priest, canon of Aberdeen. Provision to a

[1] Cf. CPP, i, 554.

canonry of Aberdeen with expectation of a prebend. John is said to have studied canon law for a year.
Avignon, 16 Kal. Jul., anno 2.
Concurrent mandate to the bishop of Dunblane, and the abbots of Dunfermline and Cambuskenneth.

14 July, 1380   Reg Aven 222, 163-3v

To the official of St Andrews. Mandate to reserve to John de Flisk, priest, perpetual chaplain of the chapel of Dunbulg and perpetual vicar of the parish church of Dunbulg, St Andrews diocese, a benefice usually assigned to the secular clergy in the gift of the abbot and convent of Londors, o.s.b., same diocese, together or separately, to the value of 25 marks sterling with cure, or 18 marks sterling without cure, provided he resigns his vicarage upon obtaining possession of a benefice with cure.
Avignon, 2 Id. Jul., anno 2.

15 August, 1380   Reg Aven 224, 430v

To Peter Enrici, priest of Dunblane diocese. More ample dispensation, having already been dispensed from illegitimacy of birth, being born of a priest and an unmarried woman, in order to receive holy orders and hold a benefice with or without cure, so that he may now hold two benefices, even if one of them be a canonry and prebend.
Avignon, 18 Kal. Sept., anno 2.

1 September, 1380   Reg Aven 222, 100-0v

To the bishop of Dunblane. Mandate to collate John Emrici, priest of Dunblane, to a benefice usually assigned to the secular clergy in the gift of the abbot and convent of Londoris, o.s.b., St Andrews diocese, together or separately, to the value of 25 marks sterling with cure, or 18 marks sterling without cure.[1]
Avignon, Kal. Sept., anno 2.

[1] See Reg Supp 59, 89.

11 September, 1380   Reg Aven 221, 25-26;
                                      Reg Vat 292, 255v-6

To Guy, cardinal priest of S. Croce in Gerusalemme, papal nuncio.
Faculty, which he may exercise even when outside the territories
of his nunciature, to summon those ecclesiastics, secular or regular,
of the kingdoms of England and Scotland and the other places
subject to his jurisdiction, who have adhered to Bartolomeo, former
archbishop of Bari [Urban vi], and to deprive them of their benefices
and offices, which may then be conferred upon persons whom the
nuncio judges worthy to receive them.
Avignon, 3 Id. Sept., anno 2.
CPL, iv, 242.

12 September, 1380   Reg Aven 221, 65v-66

To Dugall, bishop-elect of Dunblane. Provision to the bishopric of
Dunblane, vacant by the death of Bishop Andrew.
Avignon, 2 Id. Sept., anno 2.
Concurrent mandate to the chapter of Dunblane, the clergy, the
faithful, the vassals, and king Robert.

5 October, 1380   Reg Aven 221, 75-75v

To William de Angus, abbot of the abbey of St Mary de Lindores,
o.s.b., St Andrews diocese. Provision to the office of abbot of
Lindores, vacant by the death of Abbot Roger.
Avignon, 3 Non. Oct., anno 2.
Concurrent mandate to the convent of Lindores, the bishop of
St Andrews and to king Robert.

11 October, 1380   Reg Aven 221, 257v-8

To the abbot of Cambuskenneth, the archdeacon of Dunkeld, and
the official of St Andrews. Mandate to confer *in commendam* to
Dugall, bishop of Dunblane, a prebend of Dunblane, together with
the parish church of Kylmor in Loorn, Argyll diocese, annual value
not exceeding 24 marks sterling, on account of the poverty of his
diocese and the heavy burden of expenses to be met. Dugall had

possession of the parish church of Kilmore, which is subject to lay patronage, at the time of his promotion as bishop of Dunblane.
Avignon, 5 Id. Oct., anno 2.

11 October, 1380   Reg Aven 223, 542

To the chancellor of Aberdeen. Mandate to collate Alexander Trayl, B.LEG., clerk of Aberdeen diocese, to the parish church of Kynkel, same diocese, vacant by the death of the late John de Lothnyl, last rector.[1]
Avignon, 5 Id. Oct., anno 2.

13 October, 1380   Reg Aven 221, 281-1v

To the abbot of Kelso, the dean of St Agricola, Avignon, and the official of St Andrews. Mandate to collate William de Norberwik, rector of the parish church of Dawakindor, Aberdeen diocese, to the perpetual vicarage of the parish church of Norhberwik, St Andrews diocese, vacant by the free resignation of the late John Fabri, then vicar, made into the hands of bishop William at the papal court, on condition that he resign his parish church upon obtaining possession. Contrary to the statutes of the Lateran Council, William had been provided to the vicarage by ordinary authority, when provision was reserved to the pope.[2]
Avignon, 3 Id. Oct., anno 2.

15 October, 1380   Reg Aven 221, 72-73

To Adam, bishop-elect of Aberdeen. Provision to the bishopric of Aberdeen, vacant by the death of bishop Alexander.
Avignon, Id. Oct., anno 2.
Concurrent mandate to the chapter of Aberdeen, the clergy, the vassals, the faithful, and to king Robert.

14 November, 1380   Reg Aven 226, 157v

To Robert de Camera, priest of Aberdeen diocese. More ample

---

[1] See *CPP*, i, 551.   [2] See *CPP*, i, 551.

dispensation, having already been dispensed from illegitimacy of birth, being born out of wedlock, in order to receive holy orders, so that he may now hold any number of any kind of benefices, even if dignities, parsonages and offices, provided that they are not the greatest dignities of cathedrals or the principal ones of collegiate churches. Robert, who is said to be studying canon law, need not mention his defect of birth when petitioning for future graces. Avignon, 18 Kal. Dec., anno 3.

16 November, 1380   Reg Aven 226, 491v-2

To the dean of Aberdeen. Mandate to reserve to Gilbert de Camera, priest of St Andrews diocese, who holds no benefice, a benefice with cure usually assigned to the secular clergy in the gift of the abbot and convent of Holyrood, O.S.A., same diocese, together or separately, to the value of 25 marks sterling. Avignon, 16 Kal. Dec., anno 3.

17 November, 1380   Reg Aven 227, 1-1v

To Guy, cardinal priest of S. Croce in Gerusalemme, papal nuncio. Letter of credit for the sum of five thousand gold florins of the Camera (equal to 4,666 gold franks and 10 silver groats), to finance his mission to England, Scotland and elsewhere, which is to be paid to him annually by Armand Jaucerandi,[1] canon of Cambrai, papal collector, in four equal parts at Christmas, Easter, the feast of St John the Baptist [24 June], and the feast of All Saints [1 Nov.]. Avignon, 15 Kal. Dec., anno 3.

17 November, 1380   Reg Aven 227, 8

To Armand Jaucerandi, canon of Cambrai, papal collector in the province of Sens. Mandate to pay the sum of five thousand gold florins of the Camera annually to Guy, papal nuncio, during the period of his mission to England, Scotland and elsewhere. Avignon, 15 Kal. Dec., anno 3.

[1] Armand Jausserand, canon of Cambrai and papal collector, figures frequently in papal records during the second half of the fourteenth century. Cf. U. Berlière, *Suppliques d'Innocent VI*, Analecta Vaticano-Belgica, v (1911), 51, note 2.

18 November, 1380   Reg Aven 225, 33v-34

To the archdeacon of Dunkeld, the chanter of Aberdeen and the official of Dunkeld. Mandate to collate Thomas de Carguill, canon of Aberdeen, to the perpetual vicarage of the parish church of Loqnydornach, Aberdeen diocese, vacant by the death of the late Robert Manpeti, last vicar. This vicarage pertains to the convent of Londorys, O.S.B., St Andrews diocese, by ancient and approved custom, and the chapter of Aberdeen presented Thomas to the living, who having been peacefully installed by ordinary authority, now doubts that the provision might be reserved to the pope and has petitioned for confirmation.
Avignon, 14 Kal. Dec., anno 3.

18 November, 1380   Reg Aven 226, 53-53v

To Simon de Ketenys, LIC.U.J., M.A., dean of Aberdeen. Provision to the office of dean of Aberdeen, which is the greatest dignity of the cathedral, involving cure and elective, which is vacant by the promotion of Adam to the bishopric of Aberdeen, with dispensation to retain the parish church of Erollis, St Andrews diocese, provided the cure of souls is not neglected. During the vacancy of the bishopric Simon was elected as bishop by the chapter, but the pope provided *motu proprio* instead Adam, who was his honorary chaplain, collector, or sub-collector of the Apostolic Camera, and papal familiar.
Avignon, 14 Kal. Dec., anno 3.
Concurrent mandate to the bishop of Dunkeld, the dean of St Agricola, Avignon, and the official of Paris.

18 November, 1380   Reg Aven 227, 55-55v

To Simon de Ketenys, LIC.U.J., M.A., canon of Glasgow. Provision to a canonry and prebend of Glasgow, vacant by the promotion of Adam to the bishopric of Aberdeen, or through the free resignation of them by Jean, cardinal priest of S. Marcello.
Avignon, 14 Kal. Dec., anno 3.
Concurrent mandate to the bishop of Dunkeld, the dean of St Agricola, Avignon, and the official of Paris.

26 November, 1380   Reg Aven 227, 23-23v

To Armand Jaucerandi, canon of Cambrai, papal collector of the province of Sens. Mandate to give precedence to the payment of the sum of five thousand gold florins of the Camera, which is to be paid annually to the papal nuncio to England and Scotland, in four separate payments on the feasts of the Purification [2 Feb.], Easter, St John the Baptist [24 June] and All Saints [1 Nov.], from the revenues collected from the dioceses of Paris, Chartres and Orléans.
Avignon, 6 Kal. Dec., anno 3.

26 November, 1380   Reg Aven 227, 23v-24

To Guy, cardinal priest of S. Croce in Gerusalemme, papal nuncio. Letter of credit for the sum of five thousand gold florins of the Camera to finance his mission to England, Scotland and elsewhere.
Avignon, 6 Kal. Dec., anno 3.

27 November, 1380   Reg Aven 227, 106v

To the official of Glasgow. Mandate to reserve to David de Wardlau, clerk of St Andrews diocese, a canonry and prebend of Aberdeen, which are to be vacated by Simon de Kethenys upon obtaining peaceful possession of the deanship of Aberdeen, as is stipulated in the bull of provision.[1]
Avignon, 5 Kal. Dec., anno 3.

30 November, 1380   Reg Aven 226, 161-1v

To John de Aerd, priest, sub-chanter of Moray. Dispensation to retain the succentorship of Moray, which is a benefice with cure and the obligation of continuous residence, together with any other benefice with cure, even if a dignity, parsonage, or office, provided the cure of souls is not neglected. John is a scholar of canon law.
Avignon, 2 Kal. Dec., anno 3.

---

[1] See *CPP*, i, 555.

14 December, 1380   Reg Aven 226, 94-94v

To Thomas de Kilkonkar, B.DEC., priest, canon of Moray. Provision to a canonry of Moray with expectation of a prebend, and dignity with cure, or parsonage or office without cure, provided the dignity is not the greatest of the cathedral after that of the bishop, and on condition that he resign the perpetual vicarage of the parish church of Monymel, St Andrews diocese.
Avignon, 19 Kal. Jan., anno 3.
Concurrent mandate to the bishop of St Andrews, the dean of St Agricola, Avignon, and the official of St Andrews.

29 January, 1381   Reg Aven 225, 444-5

To Alexander de Gruchry, canon of Glasgow. Provision to a canonry of Glasgow with expectation of a prebend, notwithstanding that he holds the parish church of Kynel, St Andrews diocese; at the petition of king Robert, of whom he is a chaplain.[1]
Avignon, 4 Kal. Feb., anno 3.
Concurrent mandate to the bishop of St Andrews, the abbot of Lindores and the official of St Andrews.

31 January, 1381   Reg Aven 227, 22v-23

To Armand Jaucerandi, canon of Cambrai, papal collector of the province of Sens. Instructions regarding the provisions that must be made to ensure that the sum of five thousand gold florins of the Camera be paid in full each year to the papal nuncio to England, Scotland and elsewhere.
Avignon, 2 Kal. Feb., anno 3.

31 January, 1381   Reg Aven 227, 24-24v

To Guy, cardinal priest of S. Croce in Gerusalemme, papal nuncio. Regarding the payment of the money allotted to him from the revenues of the papal Camera to defray the expenses of his mission to England, Scotland and elsewhere.
Avignon, 2 Kal. Feb., anno 3.

[1] See CPP, i, 557.

20 February, 1381   Reg Aven 226, 400v-1v

To the official of St Andrews. Mandate to reserve to John de
Kynglassi, priest of St Andrews diocese, a benefice usually assigned
to the secular clergy in the gift of the abbot and convent of
Dunfermelin, o.s.b. same diocese, together or separately, to the
value of 25 marks sterling with cure, or 18 marks sterling without
cure.[1]
Avignon, 10 Kal. Mar., anno 3.

6 March, 1381   Reg Aven 227, 26v-28

To Guy, cardinal priest of S. Croce in Gerusalemme, papal nuncio.
Various faculties granted to the papal nuncio to England, Flanders
and elsewhere, which he may exercise in the city, diocese and
province of Rheims.
Avignon, 2 Non. Mar., anno 3.

10 March, 1381   Reg Aven 226, 234v

To the bishop of St Andrews. Faculty to dispense William Scot,
lord of Balweri, donzel, and Jeanette de Glen, damsel, of St Andrews
diocese, from the impediment to marriage arising from the third
and fourth degrees of consanguinity, in order that friendship may
be fostered between their families and feuds avoided.
Avignon, 6 Id. Mar., anno 3.
sro Vat. Trans., iv, no. 51.

16 March, 1381   Reg Aven 225, 123v-4

To the bishop of St Andrews, the dean of St Agricola, Avignon,
and the official of St Andrews. Mandate to collate *motu proprio*
Alexander de Caron, professor of canon and civil law, to the
canonry and prebend of Glasgow, vacant by the recent death of
the late John de Carryk.[2]
Avignon, 17 Kal. Apr., anno 3.

---

[1] See *CPP*, i, 558.   [2] See Reg Supp 61, 73.

23 April, 1381   Reg Aven 225, 588-8v;
                                                   Reg Vat 293, 121v-2

To the bishop of Glasgow. Mandate to ratify and confirm, at the
petition of Abbot John and the convent of Driburch, O.PREMON.,
St Andrews diocese, the grant made to the abbey by John, son of
the late John de Maxwell of Penteland, knight, of the rights of
patronage over the parish church of Penteland and the chapel of
Paston, St Andrews diocese, together with a gift of ten acres of
land by Sowthsyde, same diocese, and the subsequent appropriation
to the abbey of the said church and chapel by Bishop William of
St Andrews, when vacant by the resignation, or death, of Gilbert
de Gleir, then rector, which appropriation was confirmed unanimously by the chapter of St Andrews, as is contained in the
letters bearing the seals of the bishop, the chapter and the afore-
mentioned knight. Upon the death of Gilbert de Gleir, the abbot
and convent took possession and they have held the church and
chapel peacefully for over twenty years. The bishop of Glasgow has
to appoint a perpetual vicar, if one has not been appointed already,
assigning to him a suitable portion of the income for his maintenance.
Avignon, 9 Kal. Maii, anno 3.
CPL, iv, 243.

23 April, 1381   Reg Aven 225, 588v-9;
                                                   Reg Vat 293, 122-2v

To the bishop of Glasgow. Mandate to ratify and confirm, at the
petition of Abbot John and the convent of Driburch, O.PREMON.,
St Andrews diocese, the grant made to the abbey by Sir Walter,
seneschal of Scotland, of the right of patronage over the parish
church of Maxton, Glasgow diocese, together with a gift of four
acres of land at Lonccroffte, same diocese, and the subsequent
appropriation to the abbey of the said church by bishop John of
Glasgow, when vacant by the death of John de Goware, then rector,
which appropriation was confirmed unanimously by the chapter
of Glasgow, as is contained in the letters bearing the seals of the

bishop, the chapter and Sir Walter. Upon the death of John de Goware, the abbot and convent took possession and they have held the church peacefully for over thirty years. The bishop of Glasgow has to appoint a perpetual vicar, if one has not been appointed already, assigning to him a suitable portion of the income for his maintenance.
Avignon, 9 Kal. Maii, anno 3.
CPL, iv, 243.

4 May, 1381   Reg Aven 226, 233v

To John de Caron, LIC.U.J., rector of the parish church of Rathen, St Andrews diocese. Dispensation granted *motu proprio* to accept another benefice with cure, even if it be a dignity, parsonage, or office, and elective, but provided it is not the greatest dignity of a cathedral, or the principal one of a collegiate church, and retain it along with the parish church of Rathen, on condition that the cure of souls is not neglected.
Pont de Sorgues, Avignon diocese, 4 Non. Maii, anno 3.

7 May, 1381   Reg Aven 225, 234-4v

To the official of Aberdeen. Mandate to collate Roger de Butrwchyn, priest of Aberdeen diocese, to the perpetual vicarage of the parish church of Obyne, same diocese, vacant because Robert de Den, having been canonically collated and having obtained peaceful possession, neglected to be ordained priest within the prescribed limit of time. William de Fencon, donzel of Aberdeen diocese, who claims the right of presentation, presented Roger to the chapter of Aberdeen during the vacancy of the bishopric and the chapter instituted him to the living, but Roger now doubts the validity of his presentation and institution, on the grounds that on that occasion William de Fencon did not have the right of presentation, and so he seeks papal confirmation of them.
Pont de Sorgues, Avignon diocese, Non. Maii, anno 3.

18 May, 1381   Reg Aven 225, 593-3v;
Reg Vat 293, 126-6v

To the bishop and chapter of St Andrews, o.s.a. Concession, granted for the rebuilding of the cathedral of St Andrews which has been accidentally destroyed by fire almost to its very foundations, of the revenues of the first or second year, it being left to their own choice, of whatever benefices, with or without cure, fall vacant in the city and diocese of St Andrews during the coming ten years, provided, however, that a suitable portion is reserved for those who maintain the services in them.

Pont de Sorgues, Avignon diocese, 15 Kal. Jun., anno 3.

CPL, iv, 244; printed: *Moray Reg.* no. 266.

18 May, 1381   *Reg Aven* 226, 189-9v

Ad perpetuam rei memoriam. Reconfirmation, granted at the petition of bishop William and the chapter of St Andrews, o.s.a., of the union of the mensal church and lands of Inchechure, St Andrews diocese, and the annexed chapel of Kymard, same diocese, made by the said bishop and chapter to the cathedral church and approved by pope Gregory XI, on account of the exceedingly grave danger to the fabric of the cathedral from the incessant pounding of the sea, which has come well beyond its normal limits, against the rock upon which the cathedral is built, so that total destruction would have resulted unless a timely remedy had not been found by fortifying the foundations, but only at such a cost that the normal income for the fabric was insufficient, and so this additional income was approved for a period of twenty years, as is set out in the letters patent of the bishop and chapter, dated at St Andrews on 20 January, 1360, and witnessed by abbot John of Dunfermlyne, abbot William of Scona, abbot William of Lundores, William de Grenlaw, archdeacon of St Andrews, Walter de Wardlawe, archdeacon of Lothian, Master Henry Scirpy, official of St Andrews and rector of Kyngoryne, Thomas Hartas, rector of Dunbervy, John de Carnne, rector of Edvy, George de Abirnythy, David de Delwemy, sheriff of Fyff, and William de Dysigton, knights, William de Creychton, John de Creychton, William de Cressville and many others; all

of which is reconfirmed because the cathedral has been set on fire accidentally and almost destroyed to its foundations.
Pont de Sorgues, Avignon diocese, 15 Kal. Jun., anno 3.
SRO Vat. Trans., i, no. 45.

20 May, 1381   Reg Aven 226, 73-73v

To the bishop of Dunkeld, the abbot of St André, Avignon, and the official of St Andrews. Mandate to collate *motu proprio* David de Strevelyn, priest of St Andrews diocese, to the deanship of Dunblane, which is a dignity with cure, the greatest dignity of the cathedral after that of the bishop, and elective, together with the canonry and prebend attached to it, all of which are vacant by the death of the late Henry de Dunblan.[1]
Pont de Sorgues, Avignon diocese, 13 Kal. Jun., anno 3.

20 May, 1381   Reg Aven 225, 151v

To the official of Glasgow. Mandate to collate Gilbert Makcok, priest of Galloway diocese, to the perpetual vicarage of the parish church of Crosmichaell, same diocese, vacant by the death of the late John Willelmi.[2]
Pont de Sorgues, Avignon diocese, 13 Kal. Jun., anno 3.

20 May, 1381   Reg Aven 226, 402v-3v

To Robert de Monteos, priest, rector of the parish church of Quilt, St Andrews diocese. Reservation of a benefice with cure usually assigned to the secular clergy in the gift of the bishop, prior and chapter of St Andrews, O.S.A., together or separately, to the value of 25 marks sterling, on condition that he resigns the parish church, the annual value of which is stated to be 15 marks sterling, upon obtaining peaceful possession.[3]
Pont de Sorgues, Avignon diocese, 13 Kal. Jun., anno 3.
Concurrent mandate to the abbot of Lindores, the dean of St Agricola, Avignon, and the archdeacon of St Andrews.

[1] See *CPP*, i, 556.   [2] See *CPP*, i, 556.
[3] See Reg Supp 62, 163.

H

20 May, 1381   Reg Aven 226, 709v

To William, bishop of St Andrews. Indult for a plenary remission of his sins to be granted at the hour of death by a confessor of his own choice.
Pont de Sorgues, Avignon diocese, 13 Kal. Jun., anno 3.

31 May, 1381   Reg Aven 225, 154-4v

To the abbot of Dundrennan, the dean of St Agricola, Avignon, and the archdeacon of Galloway. Mandate to collate John Macbrenyn, priest, perpetual chaplain of the parish church of Donffris, Glasgow diocese, to the parish church of Botyl, Galloway diocese, vacant because the late Maurice Macmoran, onetime rector, having obtained canonical provision and peaceful possession, neglected to be ordained priest within the prescribed limit of time. John may retain his chaplaincy of Dumfries which does not involve cure of souls, founded by the late William Hawys, layman, the annual value of which does not exceed 20 gold florins.[1]
Avignon, 2 Kal. Jun., anno 3.

3 June, 1381   Reg Aven 225, 590v-1 ;
                                                  Reg Vat 293, 124

To William, bishop of St Andrews. Dispensation from the observance of the laws of fasting during Lent and on other prescribed days, on account of his advanced age. He may eat eggs and milk foods twice a day.
Avignon, 3 Non. Jun., anno 3.
CPL, iv, 243.

3 June, 1381   Reg Aven 225, 591 ;
                                                  Reg Vat 293, 124

To the same. Faculty to dispense six men and as many women

---

[1] See CPP, i, 556.

from the matrimonial impediment arising from the fourth degree
of consanguinity or affinity.
Avignon, 3 Non. Jun., anno 3.
CPL, iv, 243.

3 June, 1381   Reg Aven 225, 591;
                                      Reg Vat 293, 124

To the same. Dispensation from his vow to fast each Wednesday,
so that it may be commuted into some other work of piety by his
confessor, on account of his advanced age.
Avignon, 3 Non. Jun., anno 3.
CPL, iv, 243.

3 June, 1381   Reg Aven 225, 591;
                                      Reg Vat 293, 124v

To the same. Faculty to dispense ten persons of his diocese from the
impediment of defect of birth, so that they may be promoted to
holy orders, or may be eligible to accept benefices, even those with
cure.
Avignon, 3 Non. Jun., anno 3.
CPL, iv, 243

3 June, 1381   Reg Aven 225, 591-1v;
                                      Reg Vat 293, 124v

Ad perpetuam rei memoriam. Faculty, granted at the petition of the
bishop and chapter of St Andrews, that the claustral subprior, who
functions as diocesan penitentiary, may absolve penitents from all
their sins and irregularities, even those specially reserved to the
Apostolic See, on the feast of SS. Peter and Paul and during the
octave, in the same manner as minor papal penitentiaries.
Avignon, 3 Non. Jun., anno 3.
CPL, iv, 243.

3 June, 1381   Reg Aven 225, 593v-4;
                                      Reg Vat 293, 126v

To all Christ's faithful. Indulgence of four years and four quarantines is granted to all who visit the cathedral church of St Andrews and contribute towards the repair of the fabric on the principal feasts of the year, the feast of St Andrew and the feast of the Dedication, and one hundred days indulgence during the octaves of these feasts and the six days following Pentecost.

Avignon, 3 Non. Jun., anno 3.

CPL, iv, 244.

15 June, 1381   Reg. Aven. 226, 69v-70v, 72[1]

To the bishop of Dunblane. Whereas the pope provided Thomas Senescalli, canon of Glasgow, to the archdeaconry of St Andrews, o.s.a., which is an elective major dignity with cure, usually assigned to the secular clergy, vacant by the promotion of John to the bishopric of Dunkeld, and Thomas obtained possession of the archdeaconry in virtue of that papal provision [10 Feb., 1380] and holds it at present. It appears, however, that the archdeaconry was really vacant by the promotion by Gregory xi of the said John de Peebles to the bishopric of Dunkeld, not by the present pope, and provision to the archdeaconry passed to the pope, during Gregory xi's life, on account of the lapse of time between John's promotion and consecration. Moreover, Thomas was only in his twentieth year, or thereabouts, at the time of his provision and this was not mentioned in the letter of provision, nor was he dispensed from defect of age that he might accept the archdeaconry. He had been dispensed previously from defect of birth, being born of king Robert, then only seneschal of Scotland, and an unmarried woman, in order that he might be ordained to holy orders and accept any benefice with or without cure, even an elective dignity with cure, a parsonage, or office. Thomas, who must resign the archdeaconry, is hereby absolved from all incapacity or infamy, and at the petition of king Robert, the bishop is instructed to reassign the vacant archdeaconry to him, notwithstanding that he already holds a canonry and prebend of Glasgow [10 Feb., 1380].

Avignon, 17 Kal. Jul., anno 3.

---

[1] Folios disarranged as a result of faulty binding.

15 June, 1381   Reg Aven 226, 113-3v

To David de Strevelyn, canon of Glasgow. Provision to a canonry of Glasgow with expectation of a prebend, and dignity, parsonage, or office, provided it is not the greatest dignity of the cathedral after that of the bishop; at the petition of king Robert.[1] Avignon, 17 Kal. Jul., anno 3.

15 June, 1381   Reg Aven 226, 223v-4

To Thomas Senescalli, canon of Glasgow. Absolution, granted at the petition of king Robert, his natural father, from all irregularity and infamy incurred through accepting provision to the archdeaconry of St Andrews, when vacant by the promotion of John to the bishopric of Dunkeld by Gregory XI and the reservation to that pope of future provision to the archdeaconry on account of the lapse of time between John's provision and consecration, and not as was stated in the papal letters providing Thomas to the said archdeaconry [10 Feb., 1380], namely, that it was vacant by the promotion of John to the bishopric of Dunkeld by the reigning pope. Moreover, no mention was made in those same letters of the fact that Thomas was only in his twentieth year, or thereabouts, and he was not dispensed from defect of age in order to accept the archdeaconry, which he must now resign. Thomas was previously dispensed from defect of birth that he might be ordained to holy orders and accept any benefice with or without cure, and the pope extends that dispensation that he may now accept any number of benefices, provided they are mutually compatible, without having to mention his defect of birth when petitioning for future graces. Avignon, 17 Kal. Jul., anno 3.

15 June, 1381   Reg Aven 226, 443-4

To the official of Glasgow. Mandate to reserve to Adam Maclyn, clerk of Glasgow diocese, a benefice usually assigned to the secular clergy in the gift of the abbot and convent of Calcow, o.s.b., St

---

[1] See CPP, i, 559.

Andrews diocese, together or separately, value not exceeding 25 marks sterling with cure, or 18 marks sterling without cure. Avignon, 17 Kal. Jul., anno 3.

15 June, 1381   Reg Aven 227, 118

To Andrew Chaparial, canon of Brechin. Provision to a canonry of Brechin with expectation of a prebend; at the petition of king Robert. Andrew is said to have dwelt so long in Scotland that he has learned to speak the language well and intends to settle there for good.[1]
Avignon, 17 Kal. Jul., anno 3.
Concurrent mandate to the bishops of Dunkeld and Dunblane, and the dean of St Agricola, Avignon.

15 June, 1381   Reg Aven 227, 118v

To the official of St Andrews. Mandate to provide Thomas Fabri, clerk of St Andrews diocese, to a canonry of Dunblane with expectation of a prebend; at the petition of king Robert.[2]
Avignon, 17 Kal. Jul., anno 3.

16 June, 1381   Reg Aven 225, 480v-1;
                                Reg Vat 293, 27v

To Patrick Roberti, priest, rector of the parish church of Dalton Magna, Glasgow diocese. More ample dispensation, having already been dispensed from illegitimacy of birth, being born out of wedlock, in order to receive holy orders and hold a benefice even with cure, so that he may now hold three other compatible benefices, even if canonries and prebends, together with the parish church, and exchanges all four for similar, or dissimilar benefices, without mentioning his defect of birth when petitioning for future graces.
Avignon, 16 Kal. Jul., anno 3.
CPL, iv, 242.

[1] See CPP, i, 559.   [2] See CPP, i, 559.

9 July, 1381 Reg Aven 225, 609-9v;
Reg Vat 293, 139

To Robert de Montros, rector of the parish church of Quilt, St Andrews diocese. Dispensation to accept a second benefice, even one with cure, in the gift of the bishop, prior and chapter of St Andrews, O.S.A., together or separately, and hold it together with his parish, annual value not exceeding 15 marks sterling, but only for the period of one year, after which time he must exchange it for a compatible benefice, or resign the parish church.
Avignon, 7 Id. Jul., anno 3.
CPL, iv, 244.

11 July, 1381 Reg Aven 225, 343v-4v

To Master Walter Trayl, D.U.J., papal chaplain and judge of the papal palace. Reservation of a dignity, parsonage, or office, with or without cure, even if elective, of the cathedral of St Andrews, provided it is not the greatest dignity after that of the bishop, which he may hold together with the treasurership of Glasgow, which is a dignity without cure.
Avignon, 5 Id. Jul., anno 3.
Concurrent mandate to the abbot of Cambuskenneth, the archpriest of St Didier, Avignon, and the official of Glasgow.

13 July, 1381 Reg Aven 225, 682-3v

To the official of Glasgow. Whereas the abbot and convent of Passeleto, O.CLUN., Glasgow diocese, have petitioned for confirmation of the donation which the late bishop John of Glasgow made in perpetuity to them, with the consent of his chapter, of the parish church of Largyss in Cunyngham, said diocese, and the chapel of Cumbray, same diocese, with all the tithes, lands, fruits and rents pertaining to them, on account of the war between England and Scotland, which caused great damage to the monastery and the abbey church was burned down, as is all contained in the letters patent bearing the seals of the bishop and chapter. Since those letters patent cannot be sent with safety to the Roman Court, the official is herewith instructed to examine them and if they are found to

conform with the tenor of what is set forth above, he is authorized
to confirm the donation by apostolic authority, provided that the
cure of souls is not neglected in the parish church, but is excercised
by a suitable priest residing outside the monastic cloister.
Avignon, 3 Id. Jul., anno 3.
Printed : *Paisley. Registrum*, 241-2[1]

13 July, 1381　　　　　　　　　　　　　　Reg Aven 226, 330v-1

To John de Duglas, clerk of St Andrews diocese. Dispensation from
illegitimacy of birth, having been born out of wedlock, and also
from defect of age, being only about nineteen years old, in order
to receive holy orders and hold six benefices simultaneously, even
if they include a canonry and prebend, or if one of them is a dignity,
parsonage, or office, involving cure of souls and normally elective,
or the greatest dignity of a cathedral, or the principal one of a
collegiate church; at the petition of king Robert. John, who is
nobly born and studying at Paris, need not mention his defect of
birth when petitioning for future graces.
Avignon, 3 Id. Jul., anno 3.

24 August, 1381　　　　　　　　　　　　　Reg Aven 226, 447-7v

To the official of St Andrews. Mandate to reserve to John Wyld,
priest of Brechin diocese, a benefice usually assigned to the secular
clergy in the gift of the abbot and convent of Londorys, o.s.b.,
St Andrews diocese, together or separately, to the value of 25 marks
sterling with cure, or 18 marks sterling without cure.[2]
Avignon, 9 Kal. Sept., anno 3.

14 September, 1381　　　　　　　　　　　　Reg Aven 226, 284

To the bishop of Dunblane and the abbots of Dunfermline
and Holyrood. Mandate to provide John de Dersy, canon of
Cambuskeneth, o.s.a., St Andrews diocese, with an annual pension

[1] The text of this letter, with the sole exception of the date, is now quite illegible
as a result of extensive damage by water and so the text depends entirely on the
Paisley register.
[2] See *CPP*, i, 558.

of 10 marks sterling for five years from the revenues of Cambus-kenneth Abbey, so that he may pursue his studies at a university. John is said to be already introduced into the elementary sciences. Avignon, 18 Kal. Oct., anno 3.
SRO Vat. Trans., i, no. 46.

15 September, 1381   Reg Aven 226, 280

To the bishop of Glasgow. Faculty to dispense John de Honnyston and Edane de Roch, daughter of Sir Alexander de Rathe, of Glasgow diocese, from the impediment to marriage arising from the fourth degree of consanguinity. Avignon, 17 Kal. Oct., anno 3.
SRO Vat. Trans., iv, no. 52.

15 September, 1381   Reg Aven 226, 280

To the bishop of St Andrews. Faculty to dispense Alexander de Hamylton and Elizabeth Senescalli, of St Andrews diocese, from the impediment to marriage arising from the third and fourth degrees of consanguinity. Avignon, 17 Kal. Oct., anno 3.
SRO Vat. Trans. iv, no. 53.

14 October, 1381   Reg Aven 225, 240v-1

To the abbots of Holyrood and Tongland, and the dean of St Agricola, Avignon. Mandate to collate John Macbrenyn, perpetual chaplain of the parish church of Donfris, Glasgow diocese, to the parish church of Botyl, Galloway diocese, vacant by the death of the late Donald Makyldoli.[1] Avignon, 2 Id. Oct., anno 3.

18 October, 1381   Reg Aven 226, 296v-8v

Ad perpetuam rei memoriam. Confirmation of the transfer of the rights of patronage and presentation of a rector to the parish church of

---

[1] See *CPP*, i, 556.

St Colmanell de Botylle, Galloway diocese, made by the patron, William, earl of Dowglas and lord of the regality of the barony of Botylk, to the abbot and convent of St Mary de Dulcicorde, O.CIST., Glasgow diocese, for the good of his soul and the souls of his wife Margaret, his father and mother, his late uncle, Sir James Douglas, and those of his ancestors and heirs ; and of the union of the said parish church, vacant by the death of the late Donald McIndoli, last rector, to the monastery, made by bishop Thomas of Galloway, with the consent of his chapter, for the repair of the monastic church, hospice and other buildings, accidentally destroyed by fire, and for the support of the monks and the poor pilgrims who frequently visit the monastery, considering the great difficulty in those parts of collecting rents because of the depopulation along the borders between Scotland and England, with reservation of a suitable portion for a perpetual vicar.[1]

Avignon, 15 Kal. Nov., anno 3.

SRO Vat. Trans., i, no. 47.

21 October, 1381   Reg Aven 226, 38v-39

To Alexander, bishop-elect of Caithness. Provision of Alexander, priest, archdeacon of Ross, to the bishopric of Caithness, vacant by the death of bishop Malcolm. The diocese of Caithness is subject immediately to the Apostolic See.

Avignon, 12 Kal. Nov., anno 3.

Concurrent mandate to the chapter of Caithness and to king Robert.

23 October, 1381   Reg Aven 226, 338-8v

Ad perpetuam rei memoriam. Confirmation, granted at the petition of the abbot and convent of Sweetheart, O.CIST., Glasgow diocese,

---

[1] The letters of the earl of Douglas [undated], witnessed by abbot William of Melros, abbot William of Newbotill, abbot Giles of Dundraynane, William de Douglas, senior and William Bally, knights, John, son of William, constable de Douglas, and John McInqrigne, and those of bishop Thomas de Rossy, are sealed with his seal and that of the chapter of Whithorn, of abbot Thomas of Dudranan, abbot Gilbert of Tongland, prior Stephen of St Mary's Isle, official of Galloway, and abbot Adam of Glenlays, and dated *Hec acta et scripta sunt in choro parrochialis ecclesie de Kyrtuster, xvi^{mo} die mensis Julii anno Domini millesimo CCC^{mo} lxxx primo et consecrationis nostre anno secundo,* are inserted in the papal letter of confirmation.

of the annexation to the monastery of the parish church of Crosmichel, Galloway diocese, made some sixty years previously by Symon, bishop of Galloway, with the unanimous consent of his chapter, on account of the notorious poverty and evident poor state of the monastery, with the provision that a suitable portion of the income be set aside for the maintenance of a perpetual vicar, as is set out in the letters patent of the bishop, bearing his seal and that of the chapter, dated at his manor of Kyrcrist, the feast of St Matthew [21 Sept.] 1331, and witnessed by William, abbot of Dundynan, Walter, abbot of Tungland, Master Patrick, archdeacon of Galloway, John de Slekeburne, official, John Walays, vicar of Twman, dean of Desnes, Master Andrew, rector of Pacton, and many other clerks and laymen.

Avignon, 10 Kal. Nov., anno 3.

SRO Vat. Trans., i, no. 48; printed: Frazer, *Carlaverock*, ii, 408.

25 October, 1381   Reg Aven 227, 119v-20

To Alexander Trayl, D.U.J., rector of the parish church of Kinkell, Aberdeen diocese. Provision to the canonry and prebend of Moray, held by Alexander, bishop-elect of Caithness, and soon to be vacated by his consecration.[1]

Avignon, 8 Kal. Nov., anno 3.

Concurrent mandate to the archpriest of St Didier, Avignon, the precentor of Aberdeen, and to John de Ard, canon of Moray.

26 October, 1381   Reg Aven 226, 270v

To the archdeacon of Teviotdale, Glasgow diocese. Mandate to hear the dispute between Sir Archibald de Dowglas, Lord of Galloway, who claims to be the true patron of the parish church of Smalhame, Glasgow diocese, and Robert, the present rector, who has treated Sir Archibald with grave offence, injury and ingratitude.

Avignon, 7 Kal. Nov., anno 3.

SRO Vat. Trans., i, no. 49.

[1] Cf. *CPP*, i, 556 where it is wrongly dated as 8 Kal. Oct. (see Reg Supp 61, 169v).

29 October, 1381   Reg Aven 226, 287-7v

To Thomas, bishop of Galloway. Confirmation of the provision of
Thomas as rightful bishop of Galloway. As Thomas exposes in his
petition, after the death of the last bishop, Adam, which occurred
during a vacancy in the Apostolic See, the chapter elected unanimously Oswald, claustral prior of Glenluys, o.cist., same
diocese, who, having obtained the permission of his superior, consented to his election and sought papal provision from Urban vi.
In the meantime Clement vii had provided Ingeram, archdeacon
of Dunkeld, but he refused to accept his provision, and so the pope
then provided Thomas, having first commissioned the bishop of
Glasgow to enquire into Ingeram's refusal. By this time Oswald had
taken possession of the bishopric in virtue of the provision received
from Urban vi. Subsequently he brought his case before Clement
vii who entrusted the hearing to Nicola, cardinal priest of S. Maria
in Trastevere. The judgement has been given against Oswald and so
Thomas is confirmed as bishop.
Avignon, 4 Kal. Nov., anno 3.
sro Vat. Trans., i, no. 50.

29 October, 1381   Reg Aven 226, 287v-8

To the bishops of St Andrews and Dunkeld. Mandate to enquire
into the claim advanced by Oswald, claustral prior of Glenluys,
o.cist., Galloway diocese, to be the true bishop of Galloway in
virtue of his election by the chapter of Galloway and the subsequent
provision made by Urban vi. They are to impose silence upon him
and to put Thomas de Rossy, provided to the bishopric by Clement
vii and duly consecrated, into peaceful possession.
Avignon, 4 Kal. Nov., anno 3.

7 November, 1381   Reg Aven 229, 193v-4

To the official of Brechin. Mandate to inform himself regarding
the addition of a canonry to the cathedral of Dunkeld by the late
bishop John with the unanimous consent of the dean and chapter
of Dunkeld, and of the erection of the perpetual vicarage of the
parish church of Forgrund, same diocese, then vacant, into a
prebend and its annexation to the said canonry, as contained in the
petition of John Scalpi, M.A., B.U.J., canon of Dunkeld, and if these
facts be true, to confirm them.
Avignon, 7 Id. Nov., anno 4.

22 November, 1381   Reg Aven 230, 211

To the official of Brechin. Mandate to confirm the presentation of
William de Stramyglok, clerk of St Andrews diocese, to a canonry
of Aberdeen and the prebend of Mathelayk by Walter de Lesely,
knight, lord of Ross, the rightful patron, upon the death of the
previous canon, John de Edynhame, and the subsequent admission
and induction of William by the chapter of Aberdeen, while the
bishopric was vacant, on condition that the provision was not in
any way reserved to the Apostolic See. William himself has
petitioned for this confirmation.
Avignon, 10 Kal. Dec., anno 4.

2 December, 1381   Reg Aven 229, 519-19v

To the official of St Andrews. Mandate to provide Thomas de
Cornethon, perpetual vicar of the parish church of Strevyllyng,
St Andrews diocese, to a canonry of Glasgow with expectation of a

prebend, and dignity, parsonage, or office, with or without cure, even if normally elective, but provided it is not the greatest dignity of the cathedral after that of the bishop; at the petition of king Robert, to whom Thomas is a chaplain.[1]

Avignon, 4 Non. Dec., anno 4.

2 December, 1381   Reg Aven 229, 555v-6v

To the bishop of Ross. Mandate to provide Adam de Dundarlens, priest, canon of Ross, to a canonry of Moray with expectation of a prebend, and dignity, parsonage, or office, with or without cure, even if normally elective, but provided that the dignity is not the greatest of the cathedral after that of the bishop, notwithstanding that he has a canonry and prebend of Ross; but on condition that he resign the perpetual vicarage of the parish church of Dundurkus, Moray diocese; at the petition of king Robert.

Avignon, 4 Non. Dec., anno 4.

3 December, 1381   Reg Aven 228, 82v-83v

To Salomon Ra, B.DEC., priest, canon and dean of Dunkeld. Provision to a canonry and the deanship of Dunkeld, even if the latter be the greatest dignity of the cathedral after that of the bishop, or a parsonage with cure of souls, or elective, which were formerly held with papal dispensation by Jean, cardinal priest of San Marcello, and which Salomon now accepts in exchange for the canonry and prebend of Dunkeld and canonry and archdeaconry of Ross, all of which he freely resigns into the hands of Master Pierre Chambonis, dean of Langres, papal chaplain. Salomon must resign his canonry and chantership of Brechin.[2]

Avignon, 3 Non. Dec., anno 4.

Concurrent mandate to the archdeacon of Brechin, the chancellor of Ross and the treasurer of Glasgow.

3 December, 1381   Reg Aven 228, 107-8

To Jean, cardinal priest of San Marcello. Provision to a canonry and

---

[1] See *CPP*, i, 562.   [2] See Reg Supp 64, 24.

prebend of Dunkeld and canonry and office of archdeacon of Ross, even if the latter is a dignity, or parsonage with cure, or elective, which were formerly held by Salomon Ra, and which the cardinal now accepts in exchange for the canonry and deanship of Dunkeld, which he freely resigns into the hands of Master Pierre Chambonis, dean of Langres, papal chaplain, and notwithstanding that the cardinal is a professor of the Benedictine Order.[1]
Avignon, 3 Non. Dec., anno 4.
Concurrent mandate to the bishops of Mâcon, Galloway and Glasgow.

3 December, 1381   Reg Aven 229, 152v-3

To John de Montealto, priest of St Andrews diocese. More ample dispensation, having already been dispensed from illegitimacy of birth, being born out of wedlock, in order to receive holy orders and hold one benefice even with cure, so that he may now hold one or more benefices with or without cure, even if they include a canonry and prebend, dignity, parsonage, or office, of a cathedral or collegiate church, but provided the dignity is not the greatest of the cathedral after that of the bishop.
Avignon, 3 Non. Dec., anno 4.

19 January, 1382   Reg Aven 228, 126-6v

To the treasurer of Glasgow and the officials of Moray and St Andrews. Mandate to collate William de Spyny, M.A., D.DEC., priest, precentor of Moray, which is a dignity with a prebend, to a canonry of Ross and the prebend of Culycuden, to which he was provided by ordinary authority by Bishop Alexander of Ross, and of which he has peaceful possession; but since provision may have been specially reserved to the pope, doubts have arisen regarding the validity of his tenure, because the previous incumbent, John Crinidole, upon being collated by the bishop to a canonry and the prebend of Roskyn and Nolsthe, subsequently sought papal con-

---

[1] See Reg Supp 64, 24.

firmation of his collation. William also holds canonries of Aberdeen and Caithness in virtue of ordinary authority.
Avignon, 14 Kal. Feb., anno 4.

25 January, 1382   Reg Aven 228, 384-4v

To the official of Aberdeen. Mandate to reserve to John Cantoris, priest, perpetual chaplain of Moray diocese, a benefice usually assigned to the secular clergy in the gift of the abbot and convent of Londoris, o.s.b., St Andrews diocese, together or separately, to the value of 25 marks sterling with cure, or 18 marks sterling without cure, and notwithstanding his chaplaincy, the annual value of which does not exceed £5 sterling.[1]
Avignon, 8 Kal. Feb., anno 4.

25 January, 1382   Reg Aven 228, 394-5

To the official of Aberdeen. Mandate to reserve to William Forestarii, priest, archdeacon of Caithness, who has studied canon law for two years at Paris, a benefice usually assigned to the secular clergy in the gift of the bishop, prior and chapter of St Andrews, o.s.a., together or separately, to the value of 60 marks sterling with cure, or 18 marks sterling without cure, on condition that he resigns the archdeaconry upon obtaining peaceful possession. William is known to have been presented to a canonry of Moray and the prebend of Doffous by the lay patron, but this has not been confirmed by the bishop and so he intends to take legal action.[2]
Avignon, 8 Kal. Feb., anno 4.

2 February, 1382   Reg Aven 229, 188

To all Christ's faithful. Indulgence of one year and forty days is granted to all who visit the chapel of St Mary in the parish church of Moyboyl, Glasgow diocese, on certain feasts, and fifty days indulgence during their octaves, and contribute towards the completion of the fabric, which was canonically founded by Sir John

---

[1] Cf. CPP, i, 563.   [2] See CPP, i, 563.

Kenedy, **lord of** Donhon castle, and in great part has been completed. It has three chaplaincies attached to it, all of which are sufficiently endowed.
Avignon, 4 Non. Feb., anno 4.

2 February, 1382   Reg Aven 229, 188v

To the bishop of Glasgow. Mandate to confirm the erection of the chapel of St Mary in the parish church of Moyboyl, Glasgow diocese, made with the bishop's consent by Sir John Kenedy, lord of Donhower castle, who, together with his heirs, will excercise right of patronage over the chapel and over the three chaplaincies with which it is endowed, the chaplains to be presented by him. They may retain all the revenues of the chapel, due compensation being made to the perpetual vicar of the church.
Avignon, 4 Non. Feb., anno 4.

2 February, 1382   Reg Aven 229, 528v-9v

To the official of Aberdeen. Mandate to provide John de Abirkerdir, priest, perpetual vicar of the parish church of Banf, Aberdeen diocese, who is nobly born, to a canonry of Moray with expectation of a prebend, and parsonage, or office, without cure, on condition that he resigns the vicarage and the perpetual chaplaincy he holds in Moray diocese.
Avignon, 4 Non. Feb., anno 4.

9 February, 1382   Reg Aven 228, 122v-3v

To the bishop of Aberdeen, the archpriest of St Didier, Avignon, and the official of St Andrews. Mandate to collate *motu proprio* Walter Trayl, D.U.J., papal chaplain, treasurer of Glasgow, to the parish church of Fothiresthath, St Andrews diocese, vacant by the death of the late Findlay de Kechenis, last rector, or by the death at the Roman Court of the late Thomas Lang, with dispensation to retain it for three years together with the treasurership of Glasgow, which is a dignity, provided that the cure of souls is not neglected

I

and on condition that he resign one or other of them at the expiry
of that period of time.
Avignon, 5 Id. Feb., anno 4.

20 February, 1382   Reg Aven 228, 158-8v

To the chancellor and treasurer of Glasgow, and the official of St
Andrews. Mandate to collate William, called Wodcoli, priest,
perpetual chaplain of the chapel of St Mary of Moyboyl, Glasgow
diocese, to the parish church of St Michael of Monterduffy,
same diocese, vacant by the death of the late William Lorimer,
last rector, but which Gilbert, prior of Whithorn, has been
holding illicitly for over a year. William is dispensed to retain his
chaplaincy.
Avignon, 10 Kal. Mar., anno 4.

31 March, 1382   Reg Aven 229, 198-8v

To the bishop of Glasgow. Faculty to dispense Philip de Lindesay,
donzel, and Alice, widow of the late William Matland, both of his
diocese, from the impediment to marriage arising from the fourth
degree of consanguinity.
Avignon, 2 Kal. Apr., anno 4.
SRO Vat. Trans., iv, no. 54.

31 March, 1382   Reg Aven 229, 201-1v

To John de Merton, B.DEC., priest, perpetual vicar of the parish
church of Grenlaw, St Andrews diocese. More ample dispensation,
having already been dispensed from illegitimacy of birth, being born
out of wedlock, in order to receive holy orders and hold a benefice
even with cure, so that he may now hold a dignity, parsonage, or
office, with or without cure; even if the dignity be the greatest of
a cathedral or the principal one of a collegiate church and normally
elective, and retain them together with the vicarage, which he
obtained in virtue of the previous dispensation.
Avignon, 2 Kal. Apr., anno 4.

31 March, 1382   Reg Aven 229, 400v

To Hugh Ra, subdean of Glasgow. Indult, granted at the petition of
bishop Walter of Glasgow, to hold a second benefice with cure,
even if a dignity or parsonage, together with the subdeanship of
Glasgow.
Avignon, 2 Kal. Apr., anno 4.

14 April, 1382   Reg Aven 228, 458-9

To Master Walter Trayl, treasurer of Glasgow, professor of canon
and civil law, papal chaplain and judge of the papal palace.
Reservation of a benefice with or without cure, usually assigned to
the secular clergy, in the gift of the bishops of St Andrews or
Dunkeld, even if it be a canonry and prebend, dignity, parsonage,
or office, and even the greatest dignity of the cathedral after that of
the bishop.[1]
Avignon, 18 Kal. Maii, anno 4.
Concurrent mandate to the abbot of Paisley, the archpriest of St
Didier, Avignon, and the official of Glasgow.

29 April, 1382   Reg Aven 231, 167

To Master Walter Trayl, treasurer of Glasgow, professor of both
laws, papal chaplain, judge of the papal palace. Faculty to appoint
to the office of notary four suitable clerks, who are unmarried and
not in holy orders, after they have taken the prescribed oath.
Avignon, 3 Kal. Maii, anno 4.

30 April, 1382   Reg Aven 229, 502-3

To John Scalpy, M.A., B.U.J., priest, canon of Aberdeen. Provision
to a canonry of Aberdeen with expectation of a prebend, and
dignity, parsonage, or office, with or without cure, even if elective,
notwithstanding that he holds the parish church of Ffechirkem, St
Andrews diocese, a canonry and prebend of Dunkeld, and a canonry
of Brechin with expectation of a prebend, dignity, parsonage, or

[1] See *CPP*, i, 564.

office, with or without cure, which were obtained in virtue of an indult granted to king Robert to nominate suitable persons of his own choice to various cathedrals of the realm; all of which John may hold simultaneously for two years, after which time he must resign the parish church, or any other benefice incompatible with the cure of souls; at the petition of king Robert.

Avignon, 2 Kal. Maii, anno 4.

Concurrent mandate to the treasurer of Glasgow, the dean of St Pierre, Avignon, and the official of Brechin.

13 May, 1382   Reg Aven 230, 249

To Master Walter Trayl, D.U.J., treasurer of Glasgow, papal chaplain. Dispensation to accept another benefice, dignity, parsonage, or office, with or without cure, even if the dignity is the greatest of a cathedral or the principal one of a collegiate church, and retain it together with the treasurership of Glasgow, which is a dignity without cure, as well as the canonries and prebends of Aberdeen and Ross which he already holds.

Avignon, 3 Id. Maii, anno 4.

6 June, 1382   Reg Aven 229, 145v

To Ellen de Carrik, prioress of the priory of North Berwick, O.CIST., St Andrews diocese. Indult to choose her own confessor.

Avignon, 8 Id. Jun., anno 4.

17 June, 1382   Reg Aven 229, 146v

To James de Lyndesay, lord of Crawford castle, Glasgow diocese, nephew of king Robert. Indult to have a portable altar in his chapel and have Mass celebrated in his presence by a worthy priest.

Avignon, 15 Kal. Jul., anno 4.

17 June, 1382   Reg Aven 229, 146v

To the same. Indult to have Mass celebrated in his presence before dawn.

Avignon, 15 Kal. Jul., anno 4.

25 June, 1382   Reg Aven 230, 250-50v

To the bishop of Aberdeen. Faculty to dispense Alexander, son of king Robert, and Euphemia, countess of Ross, widow of the late Walter Lesli, from the impediment to marriage arising from the third and fourth degrees of consanguinity.
Avignon, 7 Kal. Jul., anno 4.
SRO Vat. Trans., iv, no. 55.

17 July, 1382   Reg Aven 230, 91

To all Christ's faithful. Indulgence of one year and forty days is granted to all who visit the chapel of St Columba in the parish church of St Congan, Sodor diocese, on certain feasts, and fifty days indulgence during their octaves and the six days following Pentecost, and contribute towards the repair of the chapel, which has fallen to the ground on account of its great antiquity.
Avignon, 16 Kal. Aug., anno 4.
SRO Vat. Trans., i, no. 51 ; printed : *Highland Papers*, iv, 140-2.

19 July, 1382   Reg Aven 231, 464-4v

To the prior of Oransay, Sodor diocese, and the treasurer and official of Glasgow. Mandate to collate Odo Macayd, deacon of Sodor diocese, to the parish church of St Colman, same diocese, vacant by the death of the late Dugald Macfinnhue, last rector. In his petition Odo stated how a certain Andrew, called Macheacerna, priest of Sodor diocese, in virtue of a dispensation from defect of birth, being born of a clerk and an unmarried woman, obtained collation to the parish church of St Kewan, Argyll diocese, which after many years possession he has resigned in exchange for the parish of St Colman, without obtaining a further dispensation, but which he has retained unlawfully now for several years and continues to detain on the pretext of collation made of him on the ordinary authority of the bishop. The pope orders that Andrew be removed from the living and Odo installed in his place.[1]
Avignon, 14 Kal. Aug., anno 4.

[1] See Reg Supp 64, 141v.

21 July, 1382   Reg Aven 229, 377v-8

Ad perpetuam rei memoriam. Confirmation, granted at the petition of king Robert, of the donation the king made to the abbot and convent of Cupro, O.CIST., St Andrews diocese, on account of the ruinous condition of the monastery as a result of the continual wars, of the church and almshouse of Turreff in Buchan, Aberdeen diocese, together with the right of patronage which the king has exercised for more than forty years, along with the right of presentation of the master of the almshouse to the local bishop for confirmation by ordinary authority.[1]

Avignon, 12 Kal. Aug., anno 4.

SRO Vat. Trans., i, no. 52.

24 July, 1382   Reg Aven 228, 434-4v

To the bishop of Dunblane. Mandate to reserve to Alan de Andyrston, priest, rector of the parish church of Dolar, Dunkeld diocese, a benefice usually assigned to the secular clergy in the gift of the bishop, prior and chapter of St Andrews, O.S.A., together or separately, to the value of 25 marks sterling with cure, or 18 marks sterling without cure, provided it is not a canonry and prebend, and on condition that he resigns his parish church upon obtaining possession of a benefice with cure.

Avignon, 9 Kal. Aug., anno 4.

24 July, 1382   Reg Aven 228, 329v-30

To the official of St Andrews. Mandate to collate Gilbert de Erth, priest of Aberdeen diocese, to the parish church of Dunnotyr, St Andrews diocese, vacant because Andrew, born of the late Adam Angousson, clerk of the same diocese, having been canonically

---

[1] The royal charter dated at the manor of Methfen on 17 October in King Robert's ninth regnal year [1379] is inserted, and witnessed by William, bishop of St Andrews, John, bishop of Dunkeld and royal chancellor, John, earl of Carrik and Athol, steward of Scotland, Robert, earl of Fyff and Menteth, his sons, William, earl of Douglas and Marr, James de Lyddesay and Alexander de Lyndesay, knights, and many others.

collated and having obtained peaceful possession, neglected to be ordained priest within the prescribed limit of time.[1]
Avignon, 9 Kal. Aug., anno 4.

24 July, 1382   Reg Aven 230, 201v-2

To the official of Dunblane. Mandate to confirm the provision of John Wernok, priest of St Andrews diocese, as perpetual chaplain of the chapel of St Ninian of Tybermaskot, same diocese, made by ordinary authority by bishop William of St Andrews upon the death of William Roux, on condition that the provision was not in any way reserved to the Apostolic See. John, who enjoys peaceful possession of the chaplaincy, which does not involve cure, has himself petitioned for confirmation, so that his tenure can not be attacked in the future.[2]
Avignon, 9 Kal. Aug., anno 4.

14 August, 1382   Reg Aven 230, 197v-8

To the bishops of Aberdeen and Dunkeld, and the dean of Aberdeen. Mandate to install abbot William, who was provided to the office by the pope upon the death of abbot Roger, as rightful abbot of the abbey of St Mary of Lindors, o.s.b., St Andrews diocese, and to remove John Steyl, monk of the same abbey, who has usurped the office on the pretext of his election by the convent and subsequent confirmation by the local ordinary, when provision was in fact reserved to the Apostolic See. If necessary, they are to invoke the help of the secular arm.
Pont de Sorgues, Avignon diocese, 19 Kal. Sept., anno 4.

14 August, 1382   Reg Aven 230, 304

To Laurence Kanth, perpetual vicar of the parish church of Longforgan, St Andrews diocese. Increase in the value of the benefice reserved to him in the gift of the bishop, prior and chapter of St Andrews, o.s.a., together or separately, which is usually

[1] See *CPP*, i, 565.   [2] See *CPP*, i, 565.

assigned to the secular clergy, the annual value of which, according to the terms of the original reservation, was not to exceed 50 marks sterling with cure, or 30 marks sterling without cure [6 March, 1379], but which is now augmented to 100 marks sterling with cure, or 60 marks sterling without cure, on condition that he resign the perpetual vicarage.

Pont de Sorgues, Avignon diocese, 19 Kal. Sept., anno 4.

14 August, 1382   Reg Aven 231, 138v

To James Bysech, canon of St Andrews, o.s.a. Permission to attend a university in order to study theology or canon law, while continuing to derive the revenues of the perpetual vicarage of the parish church of Forgrund, St Andrews diocese, for a period of seven years from the present date, provided the cure of souls is not neglected.

Pont de Sorgues, Avignon diocese, 19 Kal. Sept., anno 4.

Concurrent mandate to the bishops of Dunblane and Brechin, and Peter Bosquerii, canon of Thérouanne.

26 September, 1382   Reg Aven 230, 509v-10

To the bishop of Dunblane. Mandate to reserve to Thomas Mason, priest, professed canon of St Andrews, a benefice with or without cure, even if it be a priorship, administration, or office, which is usually assigned to these canons, in the gift of the bishop, prior and chapter of St Andrews, o.s.a., together or separately, to the value of 30 marks sterling; notwithstanding that similar letters have been issued today reserving a benefice to Thomas in the gift of the abbot and convent of Jedwort, o.s.a., but on condition that as soon as he obtains possession of one of these benefices, the letters reserving the other are invalidated.

Avignon, 6 Kal. Oct., anno 4.

26 September, 1382   Reg Aven 231, 581-1v

To the bishop of Dunblane. Mandate to reserve to Thomas Mason,

priest, canon of St Andrews, o.s.a., a benefice with or without cure usually assigned to those canons in the gift of the abbot and convent of Jedwort, o.s.a., Glasgow diocese, even if it be a priorship, administration, or office, to the value of 30 marks sterling, and provided that until 10 Kal. Dec., 1383 [22 November] no third party has an acquired right to it.
Avignon, 6 Kal. Oct., anno 4.[1]

6 October, 1382   Reg Aven 230, 132-2v

To Neil Obrolchan, priest of Sodor diocese. More ample dispensation, having already been dispensed from illegitimacy of birth, being born of a priest and a woman related to each other in the second and third degrees of affinity, in order to receive holy orders and hold one benefice even with cure, in virtue of which he obtained provision to the parish church of St Columba in Meol, Argyll diocese; that he may now accept a canonry of Argyll and retain the parish church, which has been raised to a prebend and attached to a canonry of the cathedral, along with the other nine, by Bishop Martin of Argyll with the unanimous consent of the chapter. Moreover, Neil was presented to the parish church of St Molrune, Sodor diocese, by John de Yle, lord of the Isles, the rightful patron, and has obtained peaceful possession and draws the revenues, but he must resign this parish forthwith.
Avignon, 2 Non. Oct., anno 4.

6 October, 1382   Reg Aven 230, 137

To Neil Obrolchan, priest of Sodor diocese. More ample dispensation to hold any other two compatible benefices, even if canonries and prebends, or a dignity, parsonage, administration, or office, with or without cure, even if normally elective, and even if the dignity be the greatest of a cathedral, or principal one of a collegiate church, together with the canonry and prebend of Argyll and the parish church of St Molruna, Sodor diocese, letters of provision to which

---

[1] Originally dated 'Fundis, 12 Kal. Dec., anno 1' [20 Nov, 1378], but this date is cancelled out.

are being issued this same day. In petitions for future graces no mention need be made of his defect of birth.
Avignon, 2 Non. Oct., anno 4.

6 October, 1382   Reg Aven 230, 137

To Neil Obrolchan, priest of Sodor diocese. Removal of all infamy that he may have incurred through accepting provision to a canonry and prebend on the bishop's authority, without first obtaining the required dispensation, on condition, however, that he herewith resigns the parish church of St Columba in Moll, Argyll diocese, which has been raised to a prebend of the cathedral.
Avignon, 2 Non. Oct., anno 4.

6 October, 1382   Reg Aven 231, 217-17v

To the abbot of the monastery of Iona, Sodor diocese, the dean of Argyll and the archdeacon of the Isles. Mandate to collate Neil Obrolchan, priest of Sodor diocese, to a canonry of Argyll and the prebend of St Columba in Mull, provided that Neil, who accepted collation on the ordinary authority of the bishop without first obtaining the required dispensation, resigns them both in order to be collated to them anew, and notwithstanding the collation made of Neil to the parish church of St Molruna, Sodor diocese.
Avignon, 2 Non. Oct., anno 4.

6 October, 1382   Reg Aven 231, 468v-9

To the abbot of the monastery of Iona, Sodor diocese, the dean of Argyll and the archdeacon of the Isles. Mandate to provide Neil Obrolcham, priest of Sodor diocese, to the parish church of St Molruna, same diocese, provided that Neil, who accepted provision on the ordinary authority of the bishop without first obtaining the required dispensation, resigns the parish in order to be provided anew.
Avignon, 2 Non. Oct., anno 4.

15 October, 1382   Reg Aven 230, 183v

To Maurice de Orwnsay, canon of the conventual priory of St Columba, O.S.A., on the island of Oronsay, Sodor diocese. Removal of all irregularity and infamy attached to the fact that Maurice, a priest and professed monk of St Columba's priory, although being born illegitimately of a canon regular and an unmarried woman, accepted his provision to the office of prior upon the death of Martin, last prior, made by the late Bishop William of Sodor, without having previously obtained the necessary dispensation. Maurice has had peaceful possession for over twenty years and has drawn the revenues, which do not exceed 160 gold francs annually. He must resign the priorship.
Avignon, Id. Oct., anno 4.

15 October, 1382   Reg Aven 228, 327-7v

To the bishop of Argyll. Mandate to collate Maurice de Orwansay, priest, canon of the conventual priory of St Columba, O.S.A., on the island of Orwonsay, Sodor diocese, to the office of prior, vacant by the death of Martin, last prior.[1]
Avignon, Id. Oct., anno 4.

10 November, 1382   Reg Aven 233, 476-6v

To Brice Mauricipauli, clerk of Sodor diocese. Reservation of a benefice, even of the cathedral, but provided it is not a canonry and prebend, in the gift of the bishop of Sodor, to the value of 25 marks sterling with cure, or 18 marks sterling without cure.
Avignon, 4 Id. Nov., anno 5.
Concurrent mandate to the bishop of Argyll, the prior of Oronsay, and the archdeacon of the Isles, Sodor diocese.

2 March, 1383   Reg Aven 233, 140v-1; 234, 315-15v;
                                       Reg Vat 294, 61v-62

To the bishops of Glasgow, Dunkeld and Aberdeen. Mandate to

---

[1] The details of the bull described immediately above, are repeated in this bull.

provide Abbot William of Lundors as abbot of Dunfermlin, o.s.b., St Andrews diocese, vacant by the resignation of John de Stramigloke into the hands of the bishop of St Andrews. William was provided firstly by the pope to the abbey of Lindores, but could not obtain possession; if the above named bishops now find that Dunfermline Abbey is not vacant, then they are to provide William as abbot of any other monastery of the Benedictine rule which is vacant, with the exception of Cistercian monasteries and the abbey of Kelso, but notwithstanding that the monastery be of another order, or the religious habit be of a different colour and form from that of Lindores, provided that Abbot William conform to the rule and habit of the monastery. Moreover, the bishops are to receive from him an oath of fealty in the form prescribed in the papal bull and they are to send it under seal to the pope.

Avignon, 6 Non. Mar., anno 5.

CPL, iv, 246-7.

29 March, 1383   Reg Aven 234, 261v;
                                   Reg Vat 294, 6-6v

To John de Daldowy, priest of Glasgow diocese. Appointment as an honorary chaplain of the pope.

Avignon, 4 Kal. Apr., anno 5.

CPL, iv, 244.

13 April, 1383   Reg Aven 234, 560-60v

To Laurence Kanth, perpetual vicar of the parish church of Longforgan, St Andrews diocese. Dispensation to retain the perpetual vicarage of Langforgrund, which entails cure, together with a benefice with or without cure usually assigned to the secular clergy in the gift of the bishop, prior and chapter of St Andrews, o.s.a., together or separately, for which Laurence originally received provision on condition that he resign the vicarage upon obtaining a benefice with cure [6 Mar., 1379]. Within three years from the present, however, he must exchange the vicarage for a benefice compatible with the second benefice involving cure, otherwise, upon the lapse of three years, he must in any case resign the vicarage.

Laurence has pleaded that the expense, his many labours and the dangers involved, have prevented him appearing personally at the papal Curia.

Avignon, Id. Apr., anno 5.

25 April, 1383   Reg Aven 234, 563

Ad futuram rei memoriam. Warrant, granted to Robert Grant, donzel of Moray diocese, recently appointed administrator of the master of the hospital of St John of Jerusalem, with consent of the convent of the Knights of Rhodes, to cite David de Marre, priest of St Andrews diocese, to appear before the executors, or sub-agents, conservators, or sub-conservators, and answer a charge of debt through non-payment of a cess due to the hospital from the land of Cultre; notwithstanding that David is an honorary chaplain of the pope, which must not be used as a pretext for not appearing before the court, where ecclesiastical penalties may be imposed on him, and even other remedies of the law.

Avignon, 7 Kal. Maii, anno 5.

SRO Vat. Trans., i, no. 53.

29 April, 1383   Reg Aven 233, 285-5v

To the bishop and chancellor of Aberdeen, and John Scalpy, canon of Dunkeld. Mandate to collate Robert Burnarde, clerk of St Andrews diocese, to the perpetual vicarage of the parish church of Monyeky, Brechin diocese, vacant because William de Leneryk, after having obtained peaceful possession, neglected to be ordained priest within the prescribed limit of time.

Avignon, 3 Kal. Maii, anno 5.

23 May, 1383   Reg Aven 234, 132-3

To Gilbert de Lyle, priest, canon of Glasgow. Provision to a canonry of Glasgow with expectation of a prebend, and dignity, office, or parsonage, provided that the dignity is not the greatest of the cathedral after that of the bishop, and notwithstanding that he already holds a canonry and prebend of Brechin and the parish church of St Mary de Foresta, Glasgow diocese.

Avignon, 10 Kal. Jun., anno 5.[1]

Concurrent mandate to the bishops of Brechin and Dunkeld, and the archpriest of St Didier, Avignon.

24 May, 1383   Reg Aven 233, 308v-9

To the abbot of Deer, the sub-chanter of Moray and the official of St Andrews. Mandate to collate William de Spyny, M.A., D.DEC., priest, precentor of Moray, to a canonry of Aberdeen and the prebend of Filorch, vacant by the free resignation of the late Hugh de Dunbar into the hands of Bishop Alexander of Aberdeen ; or vacant in the person of Robert Wys, priest of Moray diocese, or in whatsoever way vacant. William was provided by Bishop Alexander in virtue of letters issued by Guy, cardinal priest of S. Croce in Gerusalemme, but he doubts the legality of his provision on account of the letters having been issued at Paris, before the papal legate had arrived in Scotland, and so he seeks papal confirmation. William also holds the precentorship of Moray, which is a dignity of the cathedral, and canonries and prebends of Ross and Orkney, the income from which, however, is very meagre.

Avignon, 9 Kal. Jun., anno 5.

30 May, 1383   Reg Aven 234, 265-5v;
                                      Reg Vat 294, 10

To Gilbert de Lyle, rector of the parish church of Forest, Glasgow diocese. Dispensation to accept another benefice with cure, even if it be a dignity, parsonage, or office, and elective, but provided that it is not the greatest dignity of a cathedral, or the principal one of a collegiate church, and on condition that the cure of souls is not

---

[1] Owing to extensive water staining the date is illegible, but in Index 623, 214v the date is given quite clearly as ' 10 Kal. Jun., anno 5 ', copied from the register in the eighteenth century presumably while the text was still legible.

neglected; notwithstanding that he holds a canonry and prebends of Brechin.

Avignon, 3 Kal. Jun., anno 5.

CPL, iv, 244.

30 May, 1383   Reg Aven 234, 350-50v;
Reg Vat 294, 98v-99

To William, abbot of the monastery of Lindores, o.s.b., St Andrews diocese. Grant of an annual pension of £20 to be paid in equal portions at Christmas and Candlemas from the abbatial *mensa* of Dunfermilin Abbey, until he obtains possession of Lindores, or some other monastery.

Avignon, 3 Kal. Jun., anno 5.

Concurrent mandate to the bishop of Glasgow and the provosts of Avignon and of the free Chapel Royal of St Andrews.

CPL, iv, 247.

31 May, 1383   Reg Aven 232, 119-19v

To Stephen, bishop-elect of Brechin. Provision to the bishopric of Brechin, vacant by the free resignation of bishop Patrick, submitted by Stephen personally at the papal court, acting as the bishop's proxy, into the hands of Pierre d'Ameil, cardinal priest of S. Marco. Stephen is a priest and archdeacon of Brechin.

Avignon, 2 Kal. Jun., anno 5.

Concurrent mandate to the chapter of Brechin, the clergy of the diocese, the faithful, and king Robert.

31 May, 1383   Reg Aven 234, 357;
Reg Vat 294, 105v

To Duncan Petit, provost of St Andrews. Faculty to dispense twelve persons of the realm of Scotland from the impediment of illegitimacy of birth, irrespective of whether their parents were married or unmarried, acolytes, or in priest's orders, or nuns, that they may be ordained to holy orders and accept benefices, even those involving cure of souls.

Avignon, 2 Kal. Jun., anno 5.

CPL, iv, 247.

4 June, 1383   Reg Aven 234, 357-7v;
                                           Reg Vat 294, 105v

To Duncan Petit, provost of St Andrews. Faculty to dispense six men
and as many women of the realm of Scotland, who are related to one
another in the third or fourth degrees of consanguinity or affinity,
that they may marry, or having already married in ignorance of
an impediment, that they may remain in their marriage, with
legitimation of their past and future offspring.
Avignon, 2 Non. Jun., anno 5.
CPL, iv, 247.

4 June, 1383   Reg Aven 234, 266v;
                                           Reg Vat 294, 11

To Gilbert de Lile, rector of the parish church of St Mary de Forest,
Glasgow diocese. Indult to choose his own confessor.
Avignon, 2 Non. Jun., anno 5.
CPL, iv, 245.

4 June, 1383   Reg Aven 234, 364;
                                           Reg Vat 294, 112v-13

To the bishop of St Andrews. Faculty to dispense Patrick de
Sandilandis, donzel, and Isabelle, widow of Sir John de Lyndissen,
to marry in spite of the fact that John was related to Patrick in the
third degree of consanguinity.
Avignon, 2 Non. Jun., anno 5.
CPL, iv, 247.

4 June, 1383   Reg Aven 234, 365-7;
                                           Reg Vat 294, 114-16

Ad perpetuam rei memoriam. Confirmation, granted at the petition
of the abbot and convent of Dunferynlyne, o.s.b., St Andrews
diocese, of the feu of all the lands belonging to the abbey and to its
dependency, the prior and convent of Coldinghame, within the

domain of Swynton Magna, granted by them to John de Swynton, knight, lord of Swynton Parva, and to his heirs, in return for an annual rent or cess of 20 marks sterling, to be paid to the prior and convent of Coldingham.[1]
Avignon, 2 Non. Jun., anno 5.
CPL, iv, 247-8.

4 June, 1383   Reg Aven 234, 593v

To Gilbert de Lile, rector of the parish church of St Mary de Forest, Glasgow diocese. Dispensation to accept another benefice with cure, even if it be the major dignity of a cathedral or the principal one of a collegiate church, or a parsonage, or office, and retain it along with the parish church and the canonry and prebend he holds of Brechin, on condition that the cure of souls be not neglected. Within three years from the present date Gilbert must exchange it for a benefice compatible with the rectory, or upon the lapse of three years he must resign the parish of Forest.
Avignon, 2 Non. Jun., anno 5.

9 June, 1383   Reg Aven 234, 265v;
                                                         Reg Vat 294, 10

To Euphemia, consort of Robert, king of Scots. Indult to choose her own confessor.
Avignon, 5 Id. Jun., anno 5.
CPL, iv, 245.

[1] The letter of abbot John and the convent of Dunfermline is inserted, sealed with the conventual seal and witnessed by William, bishop of St Andrews, John de Carrik, seneschal of Scotland, Robert, earl of Ffyf and Menteth, William, earl of Douglas and Marr, George, earl of March, lord of Annandale and Man, John, earl of Murrawe, James de Douglas, lord of Liddlesdale, Archibald de Douglas, lord of Galloway, and many others; together with the confirmatory letter of king Robert, dated at Methfen, 20 May of his tenth regnal year [1380], witnessed by William, bishop of St Andrews, John, bishop of Dunkeld and chancellor of Scotland, John, earl of Carryk, eldest son of the king and seneschal of Scotland, Robert, earl of Fif and Menteth, also the king's son, William, earl of Douglas and Mar, the king's cousin, James de Lyndessay, the king's nephew, and Alexander de Lyndessay, the king's cousin, both knights, and the writ of approbation of bishop William of St Andrews, sealed with his seal and the common seal of the chapter, dated at St Andrews. 2 November 1382.

K

9 June, 1383   Reg Aven 234, 357v ;
                                              Reg Vat 294, 105v-6

To Euphemia, consort of Robert, king of Scots. Indult that all
members of her household, while in her service, may choose a
confessor with faculties equal to those enjoyed by the minor
penitentiaries at the papal court.
Avignon, 5 Id. Jun., anno 5.
CPL, iv, 247.

9 June, 1383   Reg Aven 234, 593-3v

To John Rollock, priest and canon of Bethlehem, o.s.a. More ample
dispensation, granted at the petition of queen Euphemia of Scotland,
to whom John is secretary and household chaplain, that having
previously been dispensed from defect of birth, being born out of
wedlock to people related in the third and fourth degrees of consanguinity, that he might be ordained priest and accept a benefice,
even with cure ; that he may now accept a second benefice with cure
and exchange it, if necessary, without making mention of his defect,
or dispensation, in future petitions.
Avignon, 5 Id. Jun., anno 5.

12 June, 1383   Reg Aven 233, 680v-1

To Henry Alani and Margaret his wife, Brechin diocese. Indult for a
plenary remission of their sins to be granted at the hour of death by
a confessor of their own choice.
Avignon, 2 Id. Jun., anno 5.

13 June, 1383   Reg Aven 233, 305-5v

To the official of Brechin. Mandate to collate Hugh Henrici, subdeacon of Dunkeld diocese, to the parish church of Adel, St Andrews
diocese, vacant because Cuthbert Fernarial, former rector, having
obtained peaceful possession for more than a year, neglected to be
ordained priest within the prescribed limit of time. Bishop William

of St Andrews provided Hugh to the living on his own authority, but after more than four months of taking possession Hugh has sought confirmation from the pope on the grounds that doubts may be raised against the legality of his tenure because an unnamed third party has already obtained illicit possession of the parish. Avignon, Id. Jun., anno 5.

13 June, 1383   Reg Aven 234, 399;
                                                Reg Vat 294, 145-5v

To Alan de Lorgis, priest, rector of the parish church of Methven, St Andrews diocese. Dispensation to accept another benefice with cure, even if a dignity of a collegiate church that normally is elective, and retain it along with the parish, at the pleasure of the Apostolic See. Alan is clerk of the audit of the household of king Robert and also holds a canonry and prebend of Dunkeld.
Avignon, Id. Jun., anno 5.
CPL, iv, 248.

13 June, 1383   Reg Aven 234, 399-9v;
                                                Reg Vat 294, 145v

To Duncan Petyt, B.U.J., provost of St Mary's, St Andrews diocese. Extension of a previous dispensation [29 Feb., 1380] allowing him to accept a benefice with cure, even if a dignity, parsonage, or office, and hold it together with the archdeaconry of Galloway, which is a dignity with cure, or having resigned the archdeaconry in exchange for another benefice with cure, to retain the former benefice with the second one, on condition that within a time stated in the original dispensation [three years], he would have exchanged either the archdeaconry or the other benefice for a benefice compatible with the remainder, otherwise, upon the expiry of that period, the archdeaconry was to be considered vacant; so that Duncan, upon the lapse of the three years, may retain the archdeaconry of Galloway together with the provostship of St Mary's, which is a dignity with cure, obtained in virtue of the original dispensation, or if he must exchange or resign either of them at some future date, may accept

in its place and hold along with the other, any benefice with cure, even if it be a dignity, parsonage, or office.
Avignon, Id. Jun., anno 5.
CPL, iv, 248.

20 June, 1383   Reg Aven 234, 233

To Patrick, formerly bishop of Brechin. Indult for a plenary remission of his sins to be granted at the hour of death by a confessor of his own choice.
Avignon, 12 Kal. Jul., anno 5.

20 June, 1383   Reg Aven 234, 596v-7

To Patrick, formerly bishop of Brechin. Grant of an annual pension of 100 marks sterling to be paid in equal portions on the feast of All Saints and at Easter from the *mensa* of the bishop of Brechin. Mention is made of Patrick's resignation of the bishopric on account of his advanced age and infirmity, made into the hands of Pierre d'Ameil, cardinal priest of S. Marco, at the papal court by the bishop's special proxy.
Avignon, 12 Kal. Jul., anno 5.
Concurrent mandate to the bishop of St Andrews, and the dean and archdeacon of Aberdeen.

20 June, 1383   Reg Aven 234, 598-8v

To Patrick, formerly bishop of Brechin. Indult to continue to wear his episcopal vesture and also to be interred so vested.
Avignon, 12 Kal. Jul., anno 5.
SRO Vat. Trans., i, no. 54.

25 June, 1383   Reg Aven 232, 145-5v

To Cuthbert Henrici, archdeacon of Brechin, in subdeacon's orders. Provision to the archdeaconry of Brechin, vacant by the free resignation of Stephen de Sellario, made personally at the papal court into the hands of Master Walter Trayl, treasurer of Glasgow and papal chaplain, on condition that Cuthbert resigns the perpetual

vicarage of the parish church of Guronyy, Aberdeen diocese, upon obtaining peaceful possession.
Avignon, 7 Kal. Jul., anno 5.
Concurrent mandate to the abbot of St Taurin, Evreux, the provost of St Andrews, and the archpriest of St Didier, Avignon.

26 June, 1383   Reg Aven 234, 233

To Euphemia, consort of Robert, king of Scots. Indult for a plenary remission of her sins to be granted at the hour of death by a confessor of her own choice.
Avignon, 6 Kal. Jul., anno 5.

26 June, 1383   Reg Aven 234, 593v

To Master John Rollok, priest and canon of Bethlehem, O.S.A. Appointment as an honorary chaplain of the pope.
Avignon, 6 Kal. Jul., anno 5.

27 June, 1383   Reg Aven 232, 260v-1

To the official of St Andrews. Mandate to reserve to Thomas Senestri, archdeacon of St Andrews, the canonry and prebend of Dunkeld presently held by Stephen, bishop-elect of Brechin, but soon to be vacant through his promotion and consecration, notwithstanding that Thomas holds the archdeaconry of St Andrews and a canonry and prebend of Glasgow.
Avignon, 5 Kal. Jul., anno 5.

27 June, 1383   Reg Aven 232, 417

To the bishop of Glasgow. Mandate to reserve to James, called son of Walter, M.A., clerk of Glasgow diocese, a benefice usually assigned to the secular clergy in the gift of the abbot and convent of Kalcon, O.S.B., St Andrews diocese, together or separately, to the value of 25 marks sterling with cure, or 18 marks sterling without cure.
Avignon, 5 Kal. Jul., anno 5.

27 June, 1383   Reg Aven 232, 429v-30

To the official of Glasgow. Mandate to reserve to Symon, called
'de Keth', priest of St Andrews diocese, a benefice usually assigned
to the secular clergy in the gift of the bishop, prior and chapter of
St Andrews, O.S.A., together or separately, to the value of 25 marks
sterling with cure, or 18 marks sterling without cure.
Avignon, 5 Kal. Jul., anno 5.

27 June, 1383   Reg Aven 232, 451v-2

To the official of Aberdeen. Mandate to reserve to Gilbert Bell,
priest of St Andrews diocese, a benefice usually assigned to the
secular clergy in the gift of the bishop, prior and chapter of St
Andrews, O.S.A., together or separately, to the value of 25 marks
sterling with cure, or 18 marks sterling without cure.
Avignon, 5 Kal. Jul., anno 5.

27 June, 1383   Reg Aven 233, 571v

To the official of Glasgow. Mandate to reserve to Andrew de Blari,
priest of Glasgow diocese, said to be nobly born, a benefice usually
assigned to the secular clergy in the gift of the abbot and convent
of Kylwyny, O.S.B., same diocese, together or separately, to the
value of 25 marks sterling with cure, or 18 marks sterling without
cure.
Avignon, 5 Kal. Jul., anno 5.

4 July, 1383   Reg Aven 232, 331v

To the official of Glasgow. Mandate to collate William Petit,
priest of Sodor diocese, to the perpetual vicarage of the parish church
of Dalry, Glasgow diocese, vacant because Duncan Petit, clerk of
the same diocese, having been collated by ordinary authority and
obtained peaceful possession for more than a year, neglected to be
ordained priest within the prescribed limit of time.
Avignon, 4 Non. Jul., anno 5.

4 July, 1383   Reg Aven 233, 586v-7

To the official of Aberdeen. Mandate to reserve to Richard Cornel, priest of St Andrews diocese, a benefice usually assigned to the secular clergy in the gift of the bishop, prior, chapter, individual canons and parsons of St Andrews, O.S.A., together or separately, to the value of 25 marks sterling with cure, or 18 marks sterling without cure; at the petition of queen Euphemia, to whom he is chaplain and continual commensal familiar.
Avignon, 4 Non. Jul., anno 5.

5 July, 1383   Reg Aven 234, 623-3v

To the official of Glasgow. Mandate to confirm the provision of John Wischard, priest of Glasgow diocese, to the canonry and prebend of Glasgow, which he exchanged with Maurice de Inees for the parish church of Kyrcmichel, same diocese, both resigning their respective benefices into the hands of bishop Walter of Glasgow. This exchange took place over a year ago and both have enjoyed peaceful possession since, but John doubts the legality of his provision on the grounds that provision to the canonry and prebend may have been reserved to the pope, or that Maurice was exceedingly old at the time of the exchange, or because the annual value of the canonry exceeds that of the parish church, and so he has petitioned for papal confirmation.
Avignon, 3 Non. Jul., anno 5.

11 July, 1383   Reg Aven 232, 429-9v

To Thomas Herny, priest of Argyll diocese. Reservation of a benefice usually assigned to the secular clergy in the gift of the abbot and convent of Passeleto, O.CLUN., Glasgow diocese, together or separately, to the value of 25 marks sterling with cure, or 18 marks sterling without cure.
Pont de Sorgues, Avignon diocese, 5 Id. Jul., anno 5.
Concurrent mandate to the archdeacon of Sodor and the treasurer and official of Glasgow.

1 August, 1383   Reg Aven 234, 157v-8

To Thomas Herny, priest, canon of Dunblane. Provision to a canonry of Dunblane with expectation of a prebend, notwithstanding that letters were issued recently [11 July, 1383] reserving to him a benefice in the gift of the abbot and convent of Passeleto, with or without cure, or that similar letters have been issued today granting a like grace in Dunblane.

Pont de Sorgues, Avignon diocese, Kal. Aug., anno 5.

Concurrent mandate to the abbot of Cambuskenneth and the treasurer and official of Glasgow.

3 August, 1383   Reg Aven 232, 339v-40

To the chancellor of Paris. Mandate to collate Thomas Trayl, LIC.ART., clerk of Aberdeen diocese, studying at Paris, to the parish church of Fechiressach, St Andrews diocese, vacant by the free resignation of Master Walter Trayl, papal chaplain, made into the hands of Guy, archbishop of Tours, at the papal court, notwithstanding that Thomas has a canonry of Moray with expectation of a prebend, or that he is under age, being only in his twenty-second year.

Pont de Sorgues, Avignon diocese, 3 Non. Aug., anno 5.

9 September, 1383   Reg Aven 229, 455

To the abbot of Holywood, Glasgow diocese. Mandate to enquire into the case of Thomas Ewer, priest of Glasgow diocese, who has petitioned the pope regarding his presentation by the rightful patron to a canonry of Glasgow and the prebend of Moffet, vacant by the death of John de Carrik, to which bishop Walter of Glasgow, against all justice, refuses to admit him. Having ascertained the facts of the case, the abbot is to expel any unjust intruder and put Thomas in possession.

Pont de Sorgues, Avignon diocese, 5 Id. Sept., anno 5.

1 October, 1383   Reg Aven 233, 368v-9

To Thomas de Edinham, M.A., B.U.J., rector of the parish church of

Aberbuthnott, St Andrews diocese. Provision to the parish church of Abirbochnot, St Andrews diocese, vacant by the recent death at the papal court of Robert de Camera, last rector, and notwithstanding that Thomas already holds canonries and prebends of Aberdeen and Caithness.

Châteauneuf-du-Pape, Avignon diocese, Kal. Oct., anno 5.

Concurrent mandate to the archpriest of St Didier, Avignon, and the officials of St Andrews and Aberdeen.

1 October, 1383   Reg Aven 234, 448v-9 ;
                                   Reg Vat 294, 187v-8

To the bishop of Brechin and the officials of St Andrews and Dunkeld. Warrant to summon those concerned and if the facts be as reported by abbot William of Lundors and his friends to restore order to the monastery of Lindores, o.s.b., St Andrews diocese, where one of the monks, John Steil, has intruded himself, and on account of which abbot William, Hugh Liel, Simon de Dunde and John de Angusia, all monks of that house, having refused to obey and comply with the said John, or associate with him and the other excommunicate monks, have been forced to leave the monastery for fear of arrest, or other vexations and ill treatment. John Steele and his accomplices are accused of taking a topaz, valued at £20 sterling, which the late abbot Roger entrusted for safe-keeping to Hugh [Liel], as well as books, vestments, copes, cloths and other gear, so that the aforesaid abbot and monks have had to beg for two years from their friends, thereby bringing religious life into disrepute and causing scandal to many. Steele and his adherents have been publicly excommunicated by abbot William for their refusal to show him obedience, or obey the papal injunction, yet they continue to celebrate and assist at Mass, while two of them, John de Stramigloke and Donald de Echlyn, have even dared to have themselves ordained as priests. The properties are to be restored to the abbot and provision is to be made from the revenue of the monastery for food and clothing until he reobtains possession. Sentences of excommunication are to be solemnly published and John de Stramygloke and Donald de Echlyn are to be suspended from the excercise of their priestly orders until they come to the pope for absolution.

Châteauneuf-du-Pape, Avignon diocese, Kal. Oct., anno 5.

CPL, iv, 248-9.

28 November, 1383   Reg Aven 238, 13-13v

To the dean of Ross, the chancellor of Aberdeen, and the archpriest of St Didier, Avignon. Mandate to collate Master Walter Trayl, D.U.J., treasurer of Glasgow, papal chaplain, to the deanship of Moray, which is an elective dignity with cure and the greatest of the cathedral after that of the bishop, when vacated by the consecration of Robert de Sanctoclaro as bishop of Orkney, the canons of Orkney having elected him unanimously to fill the vacant bishopric. The collation of Walter is made *motu proprio* and he is hereby dispensed to retain the treasurership of Glasgow, which is a dignity without cure, along with the deanship, provided the cure of souls is not neglected.[1]

Avignon, 4 Kal. Dec., anno 6.

28 November, 1383   Reg Aven 238, 61-61v

To Master Walter Trayl, D.U.J., canon of Moray, papal chaplain. Provision to a canonry of Moray with expectation of a prebend, together with the office of dean of Moray, whenever vacated by the consecration of Robert de Sanctoclaro, who has been elected unanimously as bishop of Orkney by the chapter of canons. Walter is dispensed to retain the deanship of Moray along with the treasurership of Glasgow.

Avignon, 4 Kal. Dec., anno 6.

Concurrent mandate to the dean of Ross, the chancellor of Aberdeen, and the archpriest of St Didier, Avignon.

23 December, 1383   Reg Aven 235, 63-64

To Walter, cardinal priest of Holy Roman Church. Grant made to

---

[1] See *CPP*, i, 566.

him *in commendam* of the bishopric of Glasgow, considered as vacant by his elevation to the cardinalate, that he may continue to derive the revenues thereof for his maintenance.

Avignon, 10 Kal. Jan., anno 6.

Concurrent mandate to the chapter of Glasgow, the clergy, the faithful, the vassals, and to king Robert.

11 January, 1384   Reg Aven 236, 34v-35v

To Walter, cardinal priest of Holy Roman Church. Reservation of one benefice in each cathedral and another in each city or diocese of all the bishoprics of Scotland, with or without cure, whether secular or regular, even if a priorship, dignity, parsonage, or office, or canonry and prebend, but provided that they are not parish churches, or the major dignities of cathedrals, or principal dignities of collegiate churches, or a priory consisting of more than eight monks, belonging to the gift of whomsoever, the aggregate annual revenues from which must not exceed one thousand marks sterling ; with dispensation for the cardinal to hold these multiple benefices as a means of defraying his expenses. This reservation is valid for a period of two years from the present date, after which time he must not accept any further benefice, or new provision to one.

Avignon, 3 Id. Jan., anno 6.

Concurrent mandate to the patriarch of Antioch, the abbot of Kilwinning and the provost of St Mary's, St Andrews.

27 January, 1384   Reg Aven 235, 167v-8

To Robert, bishop-elect of Orkney. Provision to the bishopric of Orkney, vacant by the death of bishop William, during whose lifetime the provision of a successor was specially reserved to the pope. Robert is described as a bachelor of laws, in priest's orders, and dean of Moray.

Avignon, 6 Kal. Feb., anno 6.

Concurrent mandate to the chapter of Orkney, the clergy, and the faithful.

30 January, 1384   Reg Aven 236, 406

To Robert, bishop-elect of Orkney. Permission to receive episcopal consecration from any bishop in communion with the Apostolic See, with two or three co-consecrators. The officiating prelate is to receive the oath of fidelity from bishop Robert and transmit it, duly sealed, to the pope. The rights of the archbishop of Nidaros must not be prejudiced in any way.
Avignon, 3 Kal. Feb., anno 6.

10 February, 1384   Reg Aven 236, 406v

To Robert, bishop-elect of Orkney. Dispensation to retain the deanship of Moray, which he held at the time of his promotion to the bishopric of Moray, and still holds, along with the bishopric, provided the cure of souls is not neglected. The deanship is the greatest dignity of the cathedral after that of the bishop, involves cure and is normally elective.
Avignon, 4 Id. Feb., anno 6.

18 February, 1384   Reg Aven 238, 568-8v ;
                                              Reg Vat 295, 155

Ad perpetuam rei memoriam. Confirmation of the grant made by William, bishop of St Andrews, with the consent of his chapter, to the abbess and convent of Northberwyk, o.s.b., same diocese, of the perpetual vicarage of the parish church of North Berwick, vacant by the free resignation of John Fabri into the hands of the said bishop. The nuns have now held it for over twenty-three years[1] and have presented to the bishop, in accordance with the conditions of the grant, a chaplain to serve the church, assigning to him an annual pension. If this pension is not sufficient, then a suitable portion of the revenues of the vicarage has to be allotted to the chaplain.
Avignon, 12 Kal. Mar., anno 6.
CPL, iv, 249

---

[1] Cf. Cowan, *Parishes*, 157.

9 March, 1384   Reg Aven 236, 408v

To Thomas de Lothorwart, priest of St Andrews diocese. Appointment as an honorary chaplain of the pope.
Avignon, 7 Id. Mar., anno 6.

21 April, 1384   Reg Aven 236, 507

To Robert Wysse, canon of Moray. Dispensation to retain the parish church of Fordown, St Andrews diocese, which in those parts is called a vicarage, together with the canonry of Moray and prebend, dignity, parsonage, or office, with or without cure, which were reserved to him by the pope [20 Nov., 1378], but of which as yet he has not obtained possession; on condition that within two years from the present he will exchange the parish for a benefice compatible with the other, otherwise upon the lapse of this period of time he must resign the parish, which will be considered vacant.
Avignon, 11 Kal. Maii, anno 6.

16 October, 1384   Reg Aven 238, 547v-8;
                                       Reg Vat 295, 139v

To all Christ's faithful. Indulgence of one year and forty days is granted to all who contribute towards the rebuilding of the bridge across the river Newdach in Cowal, Argyll diocese, which was swept away by floodwaters, causing those who now have to cross the river to be completely submerged and in great danger.
Châteauneuf-du-Pape, Avignon diocese, 17 Kal. Nov., anno 6.
CPL, iv, 249.

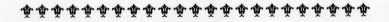

24 November, 1384   Reg Aven 240, 83v-84

To Walter, cardinal priest of Holy Roman Church. Faculty to confer on worthy persons within the realms of Scotland and Ireland forty benefices with or without cure, even if dignities, parsonages, or offices of collegiate churches, provided that the dignities are not the principal ones, if vacant at present, or upon becoming vacant, the annual value of each must not exceed 20 marks sterling. He may confer two, or even three, of these benefices upon the same person.
Avignon, 8 Kal. Dec., anno 7.

24 November, 1384   Reg Vat 300, 283v; 296, 36v-37

To Walter, cardinal priest of Holy Roman Church. Indult for the duration of two years to perform the pastoral visitation of the diocese of Glasgow by proxy, including the churches, monasteries and other ecclesiastical places and persons within the city and diocese, and to accept moderate procurations in ready money.
Avignon, 8 Kal. Dec., anno 7.
CPL, iv, 250.

24 November, 1384   Reg Vat 300, 285v-6; 296, 38

To the abbot of Kilwinning, the provost of St Andrews and the subdean of Glasgow. Injunction, which recapitulates the two-year indult granted to Cardinal Walter de Wardlaw, to allow any deputy of his to be admitted for the visitation of the city and diocese of Glasgow and payment to be made to the cardinal or his deputy of the procurations due to him.

Avignon, 8 Kal. Dec., anno 7.
CPL, iv, 251.

24 November, 1384 Reg Vat 300, 283 ; 296, 36-36v

To the dean and chapter of Glasgow. Injunction bidding them assist
and obey Walter, cardinal priest of Holy Roman Church, whom the
pope, in order to honour the church of Glasgow and the kingdom
of Scotland, has raised to the cardinalate, granting him for a certain
fixed time the administration of the spiritualities and temporalities
of that diocese, just as before his elevation.
Avignon, 8 Kal. Dec., anno 7.
CPL, iv, 250.

24 November, 1384 Reg Vat 300, 283-3v ; 296, 36v

To Robert, king of Scots. Commendation of Walter, cardinal priest
of Holy Roman Church, to the king's favour.
Avignon, 8 Kal. Dec., anno 7.
CPL, iv, 250.

24 November, 1384 Reg Vat 300, 283v-4 ; 296, 37

To Walter, cardinal priest of Holy Roman Church. Faculty to
dispense fifty men and a like number of women within the realms
of Scotland and Ireland from the impediments to marriage arising
from the fourth degrees of consanguinity and affinity.
Avignon, 8 Kal. Dec., anno 7.
CPL, iv, 250.

24 November, 1384 Reg Vat 300, 284 ; 296, 37

To Walter, cardinal priest of Holy Roman Church. Faculty to
dispense ten men and a like number of women within the realms
of Scotland and Ireland from the impediments to marriage arising
from the fourth degrees of consanguinity and affinity, when in
ignorance of the impediment they have already attempted to

contract marriage, with permission for them to remain in the marriage so contracted and legitimation of their past and future offspring.

Avignon, 8 Kal. Dec., anno 7.

CPL, iv, 250-1.

24 November, 1384   Reg Vat 300, 284-4v ; 296, 37-37v

To Walter, cardinal priest of Holy Roman Church. Faculty to visit in person, or by proxy, the houses of exempt religious of both sexes and also of those immediately subject to the Apostolic See, within the realms of Scotland and Ireland, where there is said to be grave need of reform, and to correct and reform the abuses found in them. His procurators are permitted to accept moderate emoluments.

Avignon, 8 Kal. Dec., anno 7.

CPL, iv, 251.

24 November, 1384   Reg Vat 300, 284v-5 ; 296, 37v

To Walter, cardinal priest of Holy Roman Church. Faculty valid for the duration of two years for any bishop in communion with the Apostolic See to confer first tonsure, the minor and major orders, to consecrate bishops, basilicas, churches and altars, bless abbots and abbesses, reconcile churches and other holy places after sacrilege, bless the chrism and oil of the sick, and perform all other ceremonies pertaining to bishops, within the city and diocese of Glasgow.

Avignon, 8 Kal. Dec., anno 7.

CPL, iv, 251.

24 November, 1384   Reg Vat 300, 285 ; 296, 37v

To Walter, cardinal priest of Holy Roman Church. Faculty to dispense one hundred persons within the realms of Scotland and Ireland from defect of birth, whether they were born through fornication, adultery, or from some sacriligious union, that they may be ordained to the priesthood and accept as many as three benefices,

one of which may be with cure of souls, which they may exchange as often as they please for similar, or dissimilar benefices.
Avignon, 8 Kal. Dec., anno 7.
CPL, iv, 251.

24 November, 1384 Reg Vat 300, 285-5v; 296, 37v-38

To Walter, cardinal priest of Holy Roman Church. Nomination by the pope as his legate *a latere*, with jurisdiction over even exempt religious.
Avignon, 8 Kal. Dec., anno 7.
CPL, iv, 251.

24 November, 1384 Reg Vat 300, 599-9v

To Walter, cardinal priest of Holy Roman Church. Faculty to admit twenty persons to the office of notary.
Avignon, 8 Kal. Dec., anno 7.

28 November, 1384 Reg Aven 240, 23

To Walter, cardinal priest of Holy Roman Church. Mandate to enquire into the circumstances surrounding the resignation of abbot John of Abubronthoch Abbey, o.s.b., St Andrews diocese, for reasons of advanced old age, made into the hands of Pierre, cardinal priest of S. Marco, by Simon de Creych of St Andrews diocese, the abbot's proxy, after several witnesses had been heard on the matter at the papal Curia. If the reasons are found to be valid, the cardinal is to confirm this resignation and to provide John Gedy, priest and professed monk of the said monastery, to the office of abbot, as was desired by abbot John himself, with permission for the solemn blessing to be imparted on the new abbot by any bishop in communion with the Apostolic See, to whom the oath of fidelity must be made, and then, duly sealed, transmitted with all care to the pope.
Avignon, 4 Kal. Dec., anno 7.

L

28 November, 1384   Reg Vat 300, 372-2v; 296, 99v-100

To John de Spiny, scholar of Moray diocese. More ample dispensation, having already been dispensed from illegitimacy of birth, being born of a priest and an unmarried woman, in order to receive holy orders and hold one benefice even with cure, so that he may now accept a canonry and prebend of the cathedral, with permission to resign, or exchange, them, or the original benefice, for similar or dissimilar benefices which are compatible, without having to mention his defect of birth, or dispensation, when petitioning for future graces.
Avignon, 4 Kal. Dec., anno 7.
CPL, iv, 252.

13 December, 1384   Reg Aven 245, 339

To Walter, cardinal priest of Holy Roman Church. Mandate, granted at the petition of William, bishop of St Andrews, to dispense his kinsman, Alexander de Crychcon, clerk of St Andrews diocese, said to be nobly born, from defect of age, he being only in his seventeenth year, so that he may accept a benefice with cure, provided that the cure of souls is not neglected.
Avignon, Id. Dec., anno 7.

25 January, 1385   Reg Vat 300, 263v; 296, 10

To Thomas de Kirkcubrich, monk of Sweetheart Abbey, O.CIST., Glasgow diocese. Appointment as an honorary chaplain of the pope.[1]
Avignon, 8 Kal. Feb., anno 7.
CPL, iv, 250.

28 March, 1385   Reg Aven 242, 129v-30

To Richard de Cornell, priest of St Andrews diocese. Provision to a canonry of Dunkeld with expectation of a prebend, notwithstanding that he holds the perpetual vicarage of the parish church of Muschulburgh, St Andrews diocese.

---

[1] In Reg Aven 262, 31 it is recorded that Thomas de Kirkcudbright was received as an honorary papal chaplain and took the customary oath on 11 July, 1385.

Avignon, 5 Kal. Apr., anno 7.
Concurrent mandate to . . . the treasurer of Glasgow . . .[1]

4 April, 1385   Reg Aven 240, 170 *bis verso*[2] - 171

To the abbot of Holyrood de Edinburgh, St Andrews diocese. Whereas it appears that upon the death of Thomas de Torrech the perpetual vicarage of the parish church of Mouschilburg, St Andrews diocese, fell vacant, whereupon the abbot and convent of Donfirmelyn, o.s.b., said diocese, the true patron, presented Richard de Cornell, priest of St Andrews diocese, to the living and he received institution to it from the bishop of St Andrews. At the same time, a certain Bartholomew de Kylconkar, who says he is a priest of St Andrews diocese, claimed the vicarage in virtue of certain papal letters of provision and immediately cited Richard before the official of St Andrews, the executor of the said provision, who without observing the due course of law pronounced sentence against Richard. The pope, having been informed that neither has a right to the vicarage, commissions the abbot to summon both to appear before him, and if the facts be as stated, to award the vicarage to Richard, in consideration of the fact that he is a chaplain of Queen Euphemia of Scotland.
Avignon, 2 Non. Apr., anno 7.

4 April, 1385   Reg Vat 300, 262v ; 296, 9

To Euphemia, queen of Scots. Indult to choose her own confessor.
Avignon, 2 Non. Apr., anno 7.
CPL, iv, 250.

4 April, 1385   Reg Vat 300, 595v

To Henry de Douglas, knight, and his wife Marion, St Andrews diocese. Indult for a plenary remission of their sins to be granted at the hour of death by a confessor of their own choice.
Avignon, 2 Non. Apr., anno 7.

[1] The text is completely illegible, but on fo. 476 this letter is entered in the rubric as: *de canonicatu sub expectatione prebende.* See *CPP*, i, 566.
[2] Folio 170 occurs twice in this register.

13 April, 1385   Reg Vat 300, 339v-40; 296, 76

To the archdeacon of Galloway, the chancellor of Glasgow and the official of Glasgow. Mandate to provide Thomas de Kyrcubrych, monk of Sweetheart Abbey, O.CIST., Glasgow diocese, papal chaplain, with an annual pension of £10 sterling, to be paid by the abbot and convent for a period of five years, so that Thomas may pursue his studies at a university, notwithstanding that he holds the perpetual vicarage of Loch Kendelok, which pertains to his monastery, the revenues of which, however, he claims are insufficient for his needs.
Avignon, Id. Apr., anno 7.
CPL, iv, 251.

19 August, 1385   Reg Vat 300, 249v-50

To Hugh de Dalmehoy, subdeacon, canon of Moray. Provision to a benefice with or without cure usually assigned to the secular clergy in the gift of the bishop, prior and chapter of St Andrews, O.S.A., together or separately, notwithstanding that he holds a canonry of Moray and the prebend of Cromdole and Atuy, the revenues of which are very poor, and for a long time [15 Nov., 1378] has had hope of a provision to a canonry of Glasgow with expectation of a prebend. Hugh is described as a scholar of civil law, formerly the notary of Pierre, cardinal deacon of S. Eustacio. Avignon, 14 Kal. Sept., anno 7; expedited, 2 Kal. Jul., anno 16 [30 June, 1394]; consigned, 4 Kal. Aug., anno 16 [29 July, 1394].
Concurrent mandate to the bishop of Dunkeld, the abbot of Holyrood de Edinburgh, and the dean of St Pierre, Avignon.

15 November, 1385   Reg Aven 243, 546

To James Douglas, knight, lord of Dalkeith, and Egidia his wife. Indult for a plenary remission of their sins to be granted at the hour of death by a confessor of their own choice.
Avignon, 17 Kal. Dec., anno 8.

29 November, 1385   Reg Aven 245, 56v-57v

To Walter, bishop-elect of St Andrews. Provision to the bishopric of St Andrews, vacant by the death of bishop William. Walter is a priest, treasurer of Glasgow, papal chaplain and doctor of both canon and civil law.
Avignon, 3 Kal. Dec., anno 8.
Concurrent mandate to the chapter of St Andrews, the clergy, the faithful, the vassals, and to king Robert.

23 December, 1385   Reg Aven 245, 225v-6

To John de Melros, priest, canon of Holyrood, o.s.a., St Andrews diocese. Reservation of a benefice with or without cure, usually held by the canons of Holyrood, in the gift of the abbot and convent of Holyrood, together or separately, to the value of 40 marks sterling.
Avignon, 10 Kal. Jan., anno 8.
Concurrent mandate to the prior of St Mary's Isle, the dean of St Pierre, Avignon, and the official of St Andrews.

6 January, 1386   Reg Aven 245, 557-7v

To John Melios, canon of Holyrood Abbey, o.s.a., of Edinburgh, St Andrews diocese. Indult for a plenary remission of his sins to be granted at the hour of death by a confessor of his own choice.
Avignon, 8 Id. Jan., anno 8.

13 January, 1386   Reg Aven 244, 85;
                                      Reg Vat 297, 44

To Abbot David and the convent of Holyrood de Edinburgh, o.s.a., St Andrews diocese. Indult for the abbot and his successors to ordain any of the canons, present and future, to the four minor orders, and they may consecrate chalices and bless corporals, altar linens and vestments destined for use in the abbey and in other places subject to it, without requiring the permission of the local ordinaries.
Avignon, Id. Jan., anno 8.
CPL, iv, 253.

13 January, 1386   Reg Aven 244, 85-85v;
                                           Reg Vat 297, 44-44v

To all Christ's faithful. Indulgence of one year and forty days is granted to all who visit the church of St Mary de Qwytkyrk, St Andrews diocese, which is situated at a day's journey from the English border and is renowned for the miracles worked at it, on certain principal feasts of the year, and an indulgence of three years and three quarantines if the visit takes place on the four principal feasts of the Blessed Virgin Mary, her Nativity [8 Sept.], the Annunciation [25 Mar.], her Purification [2 Feb.], and her Assumption [15 Aug.], and of fifty days during the octaves of these feasts and the six days after Pentecost, and contribute towards its maintenance.
Avignon, Id. Jan., anno 8.
CPL, iv, 253.

14 January, 1386   Reg Aven 244, 127v-8;
                                           Reg Vat 297, 80-80v

To the bishop of Dunkeld and the archdeacons of St Andrews and Brechin. Mandate to commend, at the petition of king Robert, his clerk and familiar, David de Strevelyne, canon of Glasgow, to the parish church of Ketnes, St Andrews diocese, said to pertain to the minister and friars of the Trinitarian priory of the Bridge of Berwyc, who must be removed on account of their submission to Bartolomeo, onetime archbishop of Bari; notwithstanding that the pope has recently provided David to a canonry of Glasgow with expectation of a prebend, and dignity, parsonage, or office.
Avignon, 19 Kal. Feb., anno 8.
CPL, iv, 253.

14 January, 1386   Reg Aven 245, 345-5v

To the abbot of Holyrood de Edinburgh, St Andrews diocese. Mandate to absolve James de Valence, knight, lord of Inchegall, and Christine, daughter of Sir Thomas de Erskyn, St Andrews diocese, from the excommunication incurred when they unlawfully contracted marriage and to dispense them from the matrimonial impediment of public honesty. In their petition to the pope it is explained that James had carnal relations with a serving girl, related to Christine in the third degree of common kindred, after which he contracted marriage with Christine *per verba de presenti* in the presence of friends, and having consummated their marriage, they have remained in the union for a year without obtaining a dispensation. Avignon, 19 Kal. Feb., anno 8.

21 January, 1386   Reg Aven 244, 432v-3

To the official of Orléans. Mandate to reserve to Alexander Trayl, B.LEG., canon of Aberdeen, a benefice with or without cure and of whatsoever value, usually assigned to the secular clergy, in the gift of the bishop, prior and chapter of St Andrews, O.S.A., together or separately, even if a dignity, parsonage, or office, notwithstanding, that he holds canonries and prebends of Aberdeen and Moray. Avignon, 12 Kal. Feb., anno 8.

24 January, 1386   Reg Aven 244, 34v ;
                                                     Reg Vat 297, 1v

To David Falconer, LIC. LEG., perpetual vicar of the parish church of Montrose, Brechin diocese. Appointment as an honorary chaplain of the pope.[1]
Avignon, 9 Kal. Feb., anno 8.
CPL, iv, 252.

24 January, 1386   Reg Aven 245, 397

To the abbots of Paisley and Kilwinning, Glasgow diocese, and the dean of St Agricola, Avignon. Mandate, granted at the petition of king Robert, to erect the provostship of the Chapel Royal at St Andrews, which is a dignity with cure usually assigned to the secular clergy, into the third dignity of the cathedral of St Andrews

---

[1] In Reg Aven 262, 32v it is recorded that David Falconer was received as an honorary papal chaplain and took the customary oath on 12 Feb., 1386.

along with the two archdeaconries, which are also dignities usually held by seculars. The present provost and his successors are to have a stall in choir and a place in the chapter, with a voice in all elections to the bishopric, or to any other office, and in all other capitular acts and negotiations, with equal weight as that of the two archdeacons. The provost, like the archdeacons, remains subject to the bishop, who has the authority to correct him, and if necessary even deprive him of office. The mandatories are to conduct the provost to his stall in choir.
Avignon, 9 Kal. Feb., anno 8.

24 January, 1386   Reg Aven 245, 397v-8

Ad perpetuam rei memoriam. At the petition of king Robert, the pope hereby constitutes as a secular dignity with cure of the cathedral of St Andrews, that dignity of the Chapel Royal of St Andrews, immediately subject to the Apostolic See, which is commonly known as the provostship of St Andrews, assigning to the provost and his successors a stall in choir and a place in the chapter, with a voice in the election of the bishop, or of any other office, and in all capitular acts and negotiations, the said provost nevertheless remaining subject to the authority of the bishop, who has the power to correct him, and if necessary even deprive him of office. Although in the cathedral there are no dignities, there are two archdeaconries which are reckoned as dignities, and the seculars holding them have stalls in the choir and places in the chapter, with a voice in all capitular matters.
Avignon, 9 Kal. Feb., anno 8.
SRO Vat. Trans., i, no. 55.

24 January, 1386   Reg Aven 245, 398v

To Alexander Senescalli, scholar of Dunblane diocese. Dispensation from defect of birth, granted at the petition of king Robert, he being the king's natural son by an unmarried woman, and from defect of age, being only in his twelfth year, that he may be promoted to all grades of holy orders and accept one, two, or three benefices with or without cure, or even more, provided that they be conferred

upon him canonically, even if they are canonries and prebends of cathedral or collegiate churches, but not the major or principal dignities thereof, and provided that they are compatible. In petitions for future graces no mention need be made of his defects, or of this dispensation from them.
Avignon, 9 Kal. Feb., anno 8.

27 January, 1386   Reg Aven 243, 118-18v

To David Falconer, LIC.JUR.CIV., M.A., canon of Glasgow. Provision to a canonry of Glasgow and a prebend and the treasurership of Glasgow, which is a dignity with cure, but not elective, with all the annexed rights and privileges, whenever vacant by the consecration of Walter, bishop-elect of St Andrews, who holds them at present, notwithstanding that David holds the perpetual vicarages of the parish church of Monros, and the chapel of the Holy Cross, Brechin diocese, but provided the cure of souls is not neglected.
Avignon, 6 Kal. Feb., anno 8.
Concurrent mandate to the dean of St Pierre, Avignon, and the archdeacon and precentor of Brechin.

27 January, 1386   Reg Aven 244, 266v-7

To David de Strevelyn, priest, canon of Moray. Provision made *motu proprio* to the canonry and prebend of Moray, vacant by the death of David de Marr, honorary chaplain of the pope.
Avignon, 6 Kal. Feb., anno 8.
Concurrent mandate to the bishop of St Andrews and the chanters of Le Mans and Aberdeen.

27 January, 1386   Reg Aven 245, 218-18v

To Gilbert de Muffald, B.DEC., priest, canon of Glasgow. Provision to a canonry of Glasgow with reservation of a prebend, and dignity, parsonage, or office, even if the dignity is with cure and the greatest after that of the bishop, provided he resigns the perpetual vicarage of

the parish church of Drumfres, same diocese, upon obtaining possession of a benefice with cure.
Avignon, 6 Kal. Feb., anno 8.
Concurrent mandate to the bishops of St Andrews and Dunkeld,
and the dean of St Agricola, Avignon.

1 February, 1386   Reg Aven 244, 253-3v

To Duncan Petyt, B.U.J., canon of Glasgow and secretary of king
Robert. Provision made *motu proprio* to the canonry of Glasgow
and prebend of Are, vacant by the death of John More, honorary
chaplain of the pope.
Avignon, Kal. Feb., anno 8.
Concurrent mandate to the abbots of Paisley and Kilwinning, and
the archdeacon of Brechin.

15 February, 1386   Reg Aven 244, 73v;
                                           Reg Vat 297, 33v-34

To Walter, bishop of St Andrews. Faculty, granted at the bishop's
own petition, to hear and decide without further appeal, seeing that
all the bishops of Scotland are subject immediately to the Apostolic
See and appeals must go to it from them, whatever cases of first
appeal are lodged at the Apostolic See, and to enforce his decisions,
invoking if necessary the aid of the secular arm, on account of the
number of appeals made to the pope against the decisions of the
bishops and other ordinaries, as well as from delegate and sub-
delegate judges. These appeals are then attended by such delay of
justice, that the appellants take their cases to the civil court, to the
prejudice and loss of ecclesiastical liberty.
Avignon, 15 Kal. Mar., anno 8.
CPL, iv, 252-3.

15 February, 1386   Reg Aven 244, 73v;
                                           Reg Vat 297, 34

To Walter, bishop of St Andrews. Indult to visit by deputy, when
prevented from doing so in person by sickness or other necessity,

all churches, monasteries and other ecclesiastical places within his diocese, and the persons belonging to them, and to receive his procurations in ready money. Those, however, who cannot pay in full, are to pay according to their means, and those who cannot pay at all are not to be compelled.
Avignon, 15 Kal. Mar., anno 8.
CPL, iv, 253.

19 February, 1386   Reg Aven 243, 345v-6v

To Walter, bishop of St Andrews. Faculty to reserve for twenty suitable persons an equal number of benefices, with or without cure, and of whatsoever value, if conferred upon persons having a degree in theology, or in civil or canon law, and for non-graduates valued at 25 marks sterling with cure, or 18 marks sterling without cure, all being in the gift of the bishop of St Andrews himself, with permission for the beneficiaries to hold one, two, or even three benefices.
Avignon, 11 Kal. Mar., anno 8.

24 February, 1386   Reg Aven 243, 190-90v

To Walter, bishop of St Andrews. Faculty to reserve to a suitable person one, two, or even three benefices of the cathedral of St Andrews, even if one benefice is with cure, or a dignity with cure, but provided it is not the greatest dignity after that of the bishop.
Avignon, 6 Kal. Mar., anno 8.

24 February, 1386   Reg Aven 244, 435v-6

To the official of St Andrews. Mandate to reserve to Fergus Brune, priest of St Andrews diocese, a benefice usually assigned to the secular clergy in the gift of the abbot and convent of Dunfermeclyn, o.s.b., same diocese, together or separately, to the value of 25 marks sterling with cure, or 18 marks sterling without cure.
Avignon, 6 Kal. Mar., anno 8.

24 March, 1386   Reg Aven 243, 125v-6

To Richard de Cornel, priest, canon of Moray. Provision to a canonry of Moray and the prebend of Speny, vacant by the death of David de Marr, papal chaplain, with dispensation to retain the perpetual vicarage with cure of the parish church of Muschilburgh and the chaplaincy of the hospital of St Mary Magdalene at Musselburgh, St Andrews diocese, notwithstanding that he also has a canonry of Dunkeld with expectation of a prebend : granted at the petition of queen Euphemia, of whom Richard is familiar, chaplain and continual commensal.

Avignon, 9 Kal. Apr., anno 8.

Concurrent mandate to the bishop of St Andrews, and the deans of Aberdeen and of St Pierre, Avignon.

24 March, 1386   Reg Aven 244, 260-60v

To John Forster, M.A., priest, canon of Aberdeen. Provision, granted at the petition of Pierre, cardinal priest of S. Marco, to a canonry of Aberdeen and the prebend of Onin, vacant by the death of David de Mar, papal chaplain, notwithstanding that he holds the parish church of Strabrot, St Andrews diocese. John is said to be proficient in decreets.

Avignon, 9 Kal. Apr., anno 8.

Concurrent mandate to the bishop of Dunkeld, the dean of St Agricola, Avignon, and the chanter of Moray.

25 March, 1386   Reg Aven 244, 72v-73 ;
                                            Reg Vat 297, 33v

Universis presentes litteras inspecturis. Indulgence of one year and forty days is granted to all who visit the chapel of the hospital of St Mary Magdalene de Muschilburgh, St Andrews diocese, on certain principal feasts of the year and the feast of St Mary Magdalene [22 July] and the Dedication of the chapel, and fifty days indulgence during their octaves and the six days after Pentecost, and contribute towards the repair of the fabric, which has been so destroyed during the wars which have been waged in those parts, that the poor, the

infirm and the lepers, who sought refuge there in great numbers, cannot now be received and lodged.
Avignon, 8 Kal. Apr., anno 8.
CPL, iv, 252.

6 June, 1386   Reg Aven 245, 146

To Walter, cardinal priest of Holy Roman Church. Nomination as administrator of the spiritualities and temporalities of his former bishopric of Glasgow, which is considered to be vacant through his elevation to the cardinalate, with permission to derive for three years all the revenues of the said diocese for his support as cardinal, with a further extension of three years when the first period has expired.
Avignon, 8 Id. Jun., anno 8.
Concurrent mandate to the chapter of Glasgow, the clergy, the vassals, and to king Robert.

6 June, 1386   Reg Aven 245, 146v

To Walter, cardinal priest of Holy Roman Church. Faculty to dispense twenty-five persons of the realms of Scotland and Ireland, where the cardinal has many important matters to transact on behalf of the Apostolic See, who have attained their twenty-second year, that they may accept a parish church, provided it is canonically conferred upon them, and the cure of souls is not neglected.
Avignon, 8 Id. Jun., anno 8.

6 June, 1386   Reg Aven 245, 146v-7v

To Walter, cardinal priest of Holy Roman Church. Extension of the original reservation of two benefices in each diocese of Scotland [11 Jan., 1384], considering the fact that the first period of two years has already elapsed without the cardinal being able to obtain full advantage of the concession, that he may enjoy it for another two years under the same terms, with the exception that in the dioceses of St Andrews, Glasgow and Aberdeen the reservation may include parish churches, provided their annual value does not exceed 200 gold francs. After the expiry of this second two-year period the cardinal must not accept other benefices.

Avignon, 8 Id. Jun., anno 8.

Concurrent mandate to the abbot of Kilwinning, the dean of Aberdeen and the official of St Andrews.

18 July, 1386   Reg Aven 244, 143v ;
Reg Vat 297, 94v-95

Ad futuram rei memoriam. Declaration that the nomination of the late John More, canon of Glasgow, as an honorary chaplain of the pope, made on 17 Kal. Jul., anno 7 [15 June, 1385], was effective from that date, even although it is alleged that this appointment was never made known to him.

Avignon, 15 Kal. Aug., anno 8.

CPL, iv, 253-4.

24 July, 1386   Reg Aven 243, 360-60v

To the official of St Andrews. Mandate to reserve to John, son of the late William de Cupro, priest of St Andrews diocese, a benefice usually assigned to the secular clergy in the gift of the prioress and convent of Northberwik, O.CIST., same diocese, together or separately, to the value of 25 marks sterling with cure, or 18 marks sterling without cure.

Avignon, 9 Kal. Aug., anno 8.

24 July, 1386   Reg Aven 243, 360v-1

To the official of St Andrews. Mandate to reserve to Robert, son of the late William de Cupro, clerk of St Andrews diocese, a benefice usually assigned to the secular clergy in the gift of the abbot and convent of Londoris, O.S.B., same diocese, together or separately, to the value of 25 marks sterling with cure, or 18 marks sterling without cure.

Avignon, 9 Kal. Aug., anno 8.

24 July, 1386   Reg Aven 243, 361-1v

To the official of Glasgow. Mandate to reserve to John de Langlandis, priest, rector of the parish church of Langlandis, Glasgow diocese, a benefice usually assigned to the secular clergy in the gift of the abbot and convent of Kalcaw, o.s.b., St Andrews diocese, together or separately, to the value of 25 marks sterling with cure, or 18 marks sterling without cure.
Avignon, 9 Kal. Aug., anno 8.

6 August, 1386   Reg Aven 244, 540v-1

To the bishop of Dunblane. Mandate to reserve to Thomas Marascalli, priest of St Andrews diocese, a benefice usually assigned to the secular clergy in the gift of the abbot and convent of Passeleto, o.clun., Glasgow diocese, together or separately, to the value of 25 marks sterling with cure, or 18 marks sterling without cure.
Châteauneuf-du-Pape, Avignon diocese, 8 Id. Aug., anno 8; expedited, Id. Jan., anno 12 [13 Jan., 1390]; consigned, Kal. Feb., anno 12 [1 Feb., 1390].

6 October, 1386   Reg Aven 243, 303v-4

To the abbot of Scone, St Andrews diocese. Mandate to collate John Bel, priest of St Andrews diocese, to the parish church of Culasse, same diocese, vacant because Simon de Creffe, after having peaceful possession for more than a year, neglected to be ordained priest within the prescribed limit of time.
Avignon, 2 Non. Oct., anno 8; expedited, 2 Non. Jun., anno 12 [4 June, 1390].

20 November, 1386   Reg Aven 253, 503v;
                                        Reg Vat 299, 115

To Walter, bishop of St Andrews. Injunction, if he wishes to avoid the displeasure of the pope and the Apostolic See, to procure the revocation of all unlawful alienations arising from concessions granted by his predecessors for the payment of fixed sums, or annual feus, to clerks and laymen, to some for life, to others for short terms, and to others in perpetuity, of tithes, rents, lands, possessions, houses, cottages, meadows, pastures, granges, woods, mills, rights, jurisdictions and certain other goods of the episcopal *mensa*, notwithstanding all public writs, oaths, or confirmations to the contrary.

Avignon, 12 Kal. Dec., anno 9.

CPL, iv, 256.

19 April, 1387   Reg Aven 251, 223-3v

To the bishop of Brechin. Mandate to collate Robert de Monres, priest and professed canon of St Andrews, O.S.A., to the office of prior of St Andrews, vacant by the death of Stephen Pey, last prior, after whose death the chapter elected Robert, unaware that provision to this office was specially reserved to the pope. The election was confirmed by Cardinal Walter, papal legate, and the blessing was given by Bishop Walter of St Andrews. The priorship is the greatest dignity of the cathedral after that of the bishop, involves cure of souls and is normally elective.

Avignon, 13 Kal. Maii, anno 9; expedited, 5 Kal. Dec., anno 12 [27 Nov., 1389]; consigned, Kal. Dec., anno 12 [1 Dec., 1389].

26 April, 1387   Reg Aven 251, 39-40v

To John, bishop-elect of Argyll. Provision to the bishopric of Argyll, vacant by the death of bishop Martin, during whose lifetime provision to the bishopric was specially reserved to the pope. After his death, the chapter, unaware of the reservation, proceeded to elect John Dugaldi, B.DEC., priest and archdeacon of Argyll, but since his election is invalid on account of the previous reservation, he has submitted his case to the consistory.

Avignon, 6 Kal. Maii, anno 9; expedited, 2 Non. Jul., anno 12 [6 July, 1390].

Concurrent mandate to the chapter of Argyll, the clergy, the faithful, the vassals, and to king Robert.

10 May, 1387   Reg Aven 248, 69v-70

To Walter, cardinal priest of Holy Roman Church. Prorogation for
a further period of three years of the grant *in commendam* of the
administration of the spiritualities and temporalities of his former
bishopric of Glasgow, with dispensation for him to accumulate as
many benefices, until their aggregate annual value equals 3000 gold
florins, as a means of defraying his expenses as a cardinal.
Avignon, 6 Id. Maii, anno 9.
Concurrent mandate to the chapter of Glasgow.

10 May, 1387   Reg Aven 251, 392v

To John de Merton, B.DEC., rector of the parish church of
Cambuslang, Glasgow diocese. Confirmation of the gift made to
him by abbot John de Pasleto of all the tithes, sheaves, revenues
and fruits belonging to the abbot and convent of Paisley, O.CLUN.,
Glasgow diocese, within the boundaries of the parish of Ruchglen,
same diocese, to be enjoyed during his lifetime as a reward for the
many useful services rendered to the abbey both in Scotland and
elsewhere, as is contained in the public writ, bearing the abbot's seal.
Avignon, 6 Id. Maii, anno 9.

10 May, 1387   Reg Aven 251, 475v-6

To John de Merton B.DEC., rector of the parish church of
Cambuslang, Glasgow diocese. More ample dispensation, having
already been dispensed from illegitimacy of birth, being born out of
wedlock, in order to receive holy orders and accept one benefice
even with cure, in virtue of which he obtained the perpetual vicarage
of the parish church of Grenaldo, St Andrews diocese; and later
having received a further dispensation to accept a dignity or parsonage with or without cure, or an office with cure, even if the dignity
was the greatest of a cathedral, or principal dignity of a collegiate
church, or elective, with permission to exchange them for similar
or dissimilar benefices [31 Mar., 1382]. In time he did resign the
vicarage in order to accept canonical provision to the parish church
of Cambuslang, Glasgow diocese, and is now dispensed to accept
any benefice, even a canonry and prebend, dignity, parsonage, or

M

office, of a cathedral or collegiate church, and may even accept a bishopric, without making mention of his defect or of the dispensation when petitioning for future graces.
Avignon, 6 Id. Maii, anno 9.

28 May, 1387   Reg Aven 247, 72-72v

To the official of Glasgow. Mandate to reserve to Thomas Marschall, priest, rector of the parish church of Colbanton, Glasgow diocese, a benefice usually assigned to the secular clergy in the gift of the abbot and convent of Pasleto, O.CLUN., same diocese, together or separately, to the value of 25 marks sterling with cure, or 18 marks sterling without cure, on condition that he resigns his parish.
Avignon, 5 Kal. Jun., anno 9; expedited, 3 Non. Aug., anno 9 [3 Aug., 1387]; consigned, 8 Id. Aug., anno 9 [6 Aug., 1387].

28 May, 1387   Reg Aven 249, 370v-1

To Patrick de Huyston, clerk of Glasgow diocese. Reservation of a benefice in the gift of the bishop, dean and chapter of Glasgow, together or separately, to the value of 25 marks sterling with cure, or 18 marks sterling without cure, provided it is not a canonry and prebend.
Avignon, 5 Kal. Jun., anno 9; expedited, 6 Kal. Aug., anno 9 [27 July, 1387]; consigned, 3 Kal. Aug., anno 9 [30 July, 1387].
Concurrent mandate to the abbot of Paisley, the dean of St Pierre, Avignon, and the official of Glasgow.

28 May, 1387   Reg Aven 250, 242-2v

To the official of Glasgow. Mandate to provide Patrick de Spaldyng, clerk of Brechin diocese, to a canonry of Dunkeld with expectation of a prebend. Patrick is described as having studied for three years in the faculty of Arts at Paris and to still be pursuing his studies.[1]
Avignon, 5 Kal. Jun., anno 9; expedited, 6 Kal. Aug., anno 9 [27 July, 1387]; consigned, 2 Kal. Aug., anno 9 [31 July, 1387].

[1] Cf. Reg Aven 243, 420v where an identical letter has been cancelled out, with the note in the margin: *Cassata quia de anno nono est et ideo scripta in suo loco.*

30 May, 1387   Reg Aven 248, 332–2v

To Walter, cardinal priest of Holy Roman Church. Reservation to him of the archdeaconry of Argyll, to be vacated by the promotion of John to the bishopric of Argyll, granted at the cardinal's own request, as a means of defraying his many expenses.[1] Avignon, 3 Kal. Jun., anno 9; expedited, 16 Kal. Sept., anno 9 [17 Aug., 1387]; consigned, 10 Kal. Sept., anno 9 [23 Aug., 1387]. Concurrent mandate to the abbots of Paisley and Kilwinning and the dean of St Pierre, Avignon.

3 June, 1387   Reg Aven 248, 69

To Walter, cardinal priest of Holy Roman Church. Faculty to dispense as many as twelve canons regular or monks of whatsoever order, within the realms of Scotland and Ireland, from the impediment of defect of birth, that they may accept, or be elected to benefices and offices of their order.
Avignon, 3 Non. Jun., anno 9.

3 June, 1387   Reg Aven 248, 69

To Walter, cardinal priest of Holy Roman Church. Faculty to dispense one hundred persons, within the realms of Scotland and Ireland, from the impediment of defect of birth, that they may enter the clerical state and be promoted to holy orders, and may accept one, or two benefices, even if one of them involves cure of souls, or is a dignity, parsonage, or office, provided they are mutually compatible.
Avignon, 3 Non. Jun., anno 9.

3 June, 1387   Reg Aven 248, 69v

To Walter, cardinal priest of Holy Roman Church. Faculty to dispense forty regulars of whatsoever order, within the realms of Scotland and Ireland, who have completed their twentieth year, to be ordained priest and accept a benefice with cure.
Avignon, 3 Non. Jun., anno 9.

[1] See *CPP*, i, 568.

11 June, 1387   Reg Aven 250, 241v-2

To the bishop of Brechin. Mandate, granted at the petition of Adam, bishop of Aberdeen, to reserve to his kinsman, Thomas de Tynynghame, perpetual vicar of the parish church of Tarlan, Aberdeen diocese, the canonry of Aberdeen and prebend of Syrlorch, which have been held for a long time by William de Spyny, who is obliged to resign them upon obtaining provision to the deanship of Aberdeen, whenever they become vacant in this way, or in any other, except by the death of the same William de Spyny, with dispensation for Thomas to retain his vicarage.[1]
Avignon, 3 Id. Jun., anno 9; expedited, 10 Kal. Aug., anno 9 [23 July, 1387]; consigned, 4 Non. Aug., anno 9 [2 Aug., 1387].

13 June, 1387   Reg Aven 250, 44-44v

To the bishop of Dunkeld, the abbot of Lindores and the dean of St Pierre, Avignon. Mandate, granted at the petition of cardinal Walter, to collate his familiar, John de Mertone, B.DEC., official of Glasgow and rector of the parish church of Cambuslang, same diocese, to the canonry of Glasgow and prebend of Barlanark, vacant by the death of the late Simon de Kethins.[2]
Avignon, Id. Jun., anno 9; expedited, 15 Kal. Aug., anno 9 [18 July, 1387]; consigned, 14 Kal. Aug., anno 9 [19 July, 1387].

20 June, 1387   Reg Aven 251, 480v

To David Bell, canon of Holyrood de Edinburgh, O.S.A., St Andrews diocese. Appointment as an honorary chaplain of the pope.
Avignon, 12 Kal. Jul., anno 9.
SRO Vat. Trans., i, no. 57.

20 June, 1387   Reg Aven 251, 480v-1v

To David Bell, canon of Holyrood de Edinburgh, O.S.A., St Andrews diocese. Confirmation, granted at his own petition, of the

---

[1] See Reg Supp 70, 147v-8.   [2] See *CPP*, i, 568.

grant made to him when he resigned as abbot of Holyrood by cardinal Walter, papal legate, with the consent of all the canons, of certain tithes and lands belonging to the abbey as a means of support, with dispensation from the obligation of residing in the cloister and assisting in choir, but on condition that he forfeit the grant upon obtaining provision to a bishopric, an abbey, or a priory.[1]
Avignon, 12 Kal. Jul., anno 9.
SRO Vat. Trans., i, no. 58.

21 June, 1387   Reg Aven 251, 38-39

To Abbot John of Holyrood de Edinburgh, O.S.A., St Andrews diocese. Confirmation of his election as abbot of Holyrood, when the office became vacant by the free resignation, made into the hands of cardinal Walter, papal legate, by David, last abbot, during whose lifetime provision to the office was specially reserved to the pope. Unaware of this reservation the convent elected John, a professed monk of the abbey in priest's orders, and the abbatial blessing was given by bishop Walter of St Andrews. John came

---

[1] The letters patent of the cardinal are inserted, dated: *Acta fuerunt hec apud monasterium predictum* [*Sancte Crucis*] *in loco capitulari eiusdem anno Domini MºCCCº octuagesimo sexto, mensis Junii die ultimo, indictione nona, pontificatus sanctissimi in Christo patris ac domini nostri, domini Clementis divina providentia pape septimi anno octavo.* The lands granted to him are listed as follows: the tithes and sheaves from the churches of Varia Capella, St Andrews diocese, and Melkynthe, Dunkeld diocese; the lands of Redehugh, within the domains of Delkers in the county of Strivelyn, and the lands of Bondyncton and Hillouse in the barony of Brochton in the county of Edynburgh; one hospice belonging to John Gray, clerk, at Leth; and the new hospice, which the late abbot John founded in the grounds of the Abbey, where David Bell resides at present, with its upper and lower storeys and kitchen, and garden on its east and west sides. The canons consenting to the grant are listed as follows: John Wichtschank, sub-prior, Thomas de Bolden, John de Balloyn, William Bell, William de Hadyngton, David, vicar of the church of Craufford, John de Leth, John de Qwhyukyrstanys, John de Melros, John de Mundavilla, John de Edynburgh, Richard de Cupro, William Wricht, William de Brade, John de Crale, John de Scallis and John Marschell. The donation was granted at the petition of John, eldest son of king Robert, earl of Carrik and seneschal of Scotland, and the letters patent were sealed with the seal of the cardinal and the common seal of the chapter. The following witnessed the document: Master Walter Forstar, archdeacon of Lothian, John de Merton, official of Glasgow, Andrew de Trebrun, rector of the church of Kynoule, Adam Forstar, lord of Corstorfyns and many others. The notaries public were: Thomas de Bonavilla, clerk of St Andrews diocese, and Robert de Glenesk, priest.

to know of the irregularity of his election only after taking possession and he has submitted his case to the consistory. He is hereby instructed to take his oath of fidelity in the prescribed form in the presence of the bishop of Glasgow within one month of receiving these letters.

Avignon, 11 Kal. Jul., anno 9; expedited, 2 Kal. Jun., anno 11 [31 May, 1389]; consigned, 4 Non. Jun., anno 11 [2 June, 1389].

Concurrent mandate to the convent of Holyrood and to Walter, bishop of St Andrews.

23 June, 1387   Reg Aven 251, 54-54v

To William de Spyny, D.DEC., M.A., dean of Aberdeen. Provision to the deanship of Aberdeen, vacant by the death of Simon de Ketenis, whereupon the chanter and chapter elected William, canon of Aberdeen, by way of inspiration of the Holy Spirit. Since provision to the deanship was specially reserved to the pope and this election is invalid, William, together with bishop Adam of Aberdeen, and the chanter and chapter, have petitioned that William be provided to the office. Moreover, he is dispensed to retain the precentorship of Moray, a dignity with cure, for a period of three years and draw its revenues along with those of the deanship of Aberdeen, which is the greatest dignity after that of the bishop and involves cure of souls, but the revenues of which are so meagre that it would be impossible for him to maintain the status proper to the dean and fulfil the many obligations on these revenues alone. The cure of souls must not be neglected. William may also retain his canonries and prebends of Moray and Ross, but must resign his other canonry and prebend of Aberdeen. He is said to be proficient in laws.[1]

Avignon, 9 Kal. Jul., anno 9; expedited, 10 Kal. Aug., anno 9 [23 July, 1387]; consigned, 7 Kal. Aug., anno 9 [26 July, 1387].

Concurrent mandate to the bishop of Brechin, the abbot of Kinloss and the prior of Monymusk.

---

[1] The corresponding petition is dated 3 Id. Jun., anno 9 [11 June, 1387] (Reg Supp 70, 147v).

6 July, 1387   Reg Aven 251, 183-3v

To David Bell, canon of Holyrood de Edinburgh, o.s.a., St
Andrews diocese. Reservation to him of the priory of Portmohok,
o.s.a., St Andrews diocese, a dependency of St Andrews priory,
which is usually governed by one of the canons, even if the priorship
is a dignity, or parsonage, involving cure, whenever vacant by the
provision of prior Robert de Munros as prior of St Andrews, with
obligation of resigning the priorship of Portmoak [19 Apr., 1387],
but not if vacant by the death of Robert.[1]
Avignon, 2 Non. Jul., anno 9; expedited, 10 Kal. Aug., anno 9
[23 July, 1387]; consigned, 7 Kal. Aug., anno 9 [26 July, 1387].
Concurrent mandate to the bishop of Dunkeld, the provost of
Avignon and the chancellor of Glasgow.

7 July, 1387   Reg Aven 251, 487v

To David Bell, canon of Holyrood de Edinburgh, o.s.a., St Andrews
diocese. Dispensation to retain all the lands and revenues [as above
p 127], which he received upon his resignation as abbot of Holyrood,
together with the priorship of Portmohok, notwithstanding the
clause to the contrary in the letters of the papal legate.[2]
Avignon, Non. Jul., anno 9.

9 July, 1387   Reg Aven 249, 413-13v

To John de Merton, B.DEC., rector of the parish church of
Cambuslang, Glasgow diocese. Reservation of a benefice with or
without cure usually assigned to the secular clergy, even if a
canonry and prebend, dignity, parsonage, or office, but not the
major dignity of a cathedral, or principal one of a collegiate church,
in the cathedrals or cities and dioceses of either Glasgow or St
Andrews, with dispensation to retain the parish church and notwithstanding that he has papal provision to a canonry of Glasgow with
expectation of a prebend [13 June, 1387], but of which he has not
yet gained possession. This is granted at the petition of cardinal

---

[1] See Reg Supp 70, 196v.   [2] Cf. 20 June, 1387, p 126 above.

Walter, of whom John is a familiar and ecclesiastical judge, as well as being the official of the diocese of Glasgow.

Avignon, 7 Id. Jul., anno 9; expedited, 6 Kal. Aug., anno 9 [27 July, 1387]; consigned 4 Kal. Aug., anno 9 [29 July, 1387].

Concurrent mandate to the bishop of Dunkeld, the abbot of Lindores and the dean of St Pierre, Avignon.

13 July, 1387   Reg Aven 247, 257v-8v

To the bishop of Dunblane. Mandate to reserve to Nigel Wyschard, priest of Glasgow diocese, a benefice in the gift of the bishop, dean and chapter of Glasgow, together or separately, provided it is not a canonry and prebend, to the value of 25 marks sterling with cure, or 18 marks sterling without cure.[1]

Avignon, 3 Id. Jul., anno 9; expedited, 7 Kal. Sept., anno 15 [26 Aug., 1393]; consigned, 6 Kal. Sept., anno 15 [27 Aug., 1393].

15 July, 1387   Reg Aven 248, 153v-4

To Michael, bishop of Sodor. Provision to the bishopric of Sodor, vacant by the removal of bishop John on account of his adherence to Bartolomeo Prignano [Urban VI]. Until now Michael has been archbishop of Cashel in Ireland.

Avignon, Id. Jul., anno 9.

Concurrent mandate to the chapter of Sodor, the clergy, the faithful, the vassals, and to king Robert.

19 July, 1387   Reg Aven 251, 22

To the bishop of Dunkeld. Mandate to provide William de Culros, priest and professed monk of his order, canon of Inchaffray, as abbot of Inchaffray, O.S.A., Dunblane diocese, vacant by the death of abbot John, whereupon the prior and convent elected William as abbot, unaware that during the lifetime of the last abbot provision was specially reserved to the pope. When William became conscious of the reservation and the consequent invalidity of his election, he brought the matter to the pope, who decrees that he is to be

[1] See *CPP*, i, 567.

blessed as abbot and to take the oath of fidelity in the prescribed form, which duly signed and sealed is to be sent to the Apostolic See. The rights of the bishop of Dunblane must be respected.
Avignon, 14 Kal. Aug., anno 9; expedited, 4 Kal. Aug., anno 9 [29 July, 1387]; consigned, 3 Kal. Aug., anno 9 [30 July, 1387]; corrected letter expedited, 4 Id. Dec., anno 10 [10 Dec., 1387]; corrected letter resealed and consigned, 19 Kal. Jan., anno 10 [14 Dec., 1387].
SRO Vat. Trans., i, no. 59; printed *Inchaffray Chrs.*, no. 141.

20 September, 1387   Reg Aven 250, 60v-61

To John de Merton, B.DEC., canon of Glasgow. Confirmation of his collation to the canonry of Glasgow and prebend of Barlanark, vacant by the death of Simon de Kethins [13 June, 1387], although collation was reserved to the pope on account of the death of cardinal Walter, to whom John was chaplain and a member of his household, notwithstanding that he holds the parish church of Cambuslang, same diocese, and has an expectative grace of a benefice, parsonage, or office, in the dioceses of either Glasgow or St Andrews [9 July, 1387].
Roquemaure, Avignon diocese, 12 Kal. Oct., anno 9; expedited, 2 Kal. Oct., anno 9 [30 Sept, 1387]; consigned, 6 Non. Oct., anno 9 [2 Oct., 1387].
Concurrent mandate to the abbots of Kilwinning and Paisley, and the dean of St Pierre, Avignon.

3 October, 1387   Reg Aven 247, 496v;
         Reg Vat 298, 143

To John Barber, archdeacon of Aberdeen. Dispensation, granted at the petition of king Robert, to visit the churches, monasteries and other ecclesiastical places in his archdeaconry by deputy, when hindered from doing so personally because he is engaged in the king's service, or prevented by age or infirmity, and to receive the procurations due to him in ready money to the amount of thirty silver Tournois daily, twelve silver Tournois being equal to one gold florin of the Camera.

Avignon, 5 Non. Oct., anno 9.
Concurrent mandate to the prior of St Andrews, the treasurer of
Glasgow, and the official of St Andrews.
CPL, iv, 254-5.

3 October, 1387   Reg Aven 247, 497;
                                                   Reg Vat 298, 143-3v

To the bishop of Glasgow. Mandate to dispense Robert de
Benachtyn, donzel, and Egidia Senescalli, damsel, of Glasgow
diocese, from the impediment to marriage arising from spiritual
affinity. Several years previously they desired to contract marriage
in order to foster peace between their friends, but they were prevented by the fact that the natural father of Egidia was also the
godfather of Robert. King Robert has petitioned for this dispensation.
Avignon, 5 Non. Oct., anno 9.
CPL, iv, 255.

4 October, 1387   Reg Aven 251, 582v-3

To the bishop of Brechin. Whereas the bishop of St Andrews has
informed the pope that on account of wars, raids, and many other
reasons, the revenues of his episcopal *mensa* have become so reduced
as to be quite inadequate to meet the calls upon his hospitality and
charity, and moreover the two manors of Dorvesin and Lyston,
within his diocese, which pertain to the *mensa*, and which in times
past were magnificently constructed, but are now dilapidated and
in a collapsed condition and their revenues are not sufficient to
repair them, therefore the said bishop has petitioned that the parish
church of Lyston, which is near Lyston manor, and the parish church
of Kylmanin, which is near Dorevesin manor, be incorporated to
the episcopal *mensa*. Wherefore the pope, who is ignorant of the
facts of the matter, commissions the bishop of Brechin to ascertain
the truth, especially about the reduction of revenue and the value
of the parishes, and to report back to the pope, who can then decide
what should be done in this case.
Avignon, 4 Non. Oct., anno 9.
SRO Vat. Trans., i, no. 60.

5 October, 1387   Reg Aven 248, 452-2v

To Henry de Wardlau, LIC.ART., canon of Moray. Provision to the canonry of Moray and prebend of Kynnor, vacant by the death of cardinal Walter, notwithstanding that he holds a canonry and prebend of Glasgow [22 Sept, 1379] and has been provided by the pope to the precentorship of Glasgow, then vacant in a certain way, but without yet obtaining possession. Henry, who was the late cardinal's nephew, has studied civil law for two years.[1]
Avignon, 3 Non. Oct., anno 9; expedited, 7 Id. Dec., anno 10 [7 Dec., 1387]; consigned, 5 Id. Dec., anno 10 [9 Dec., 1387]. Concurrent mandate to the dean of St Agricola, Avignon, and the officials of St Andrews and Glasgow.

5 October, 1387   Reg Aven 247, 525-5v;
                                             Reg Vat 298, 166v-7

To Henry de Wardlau, canon of Moray. Permission to retain the canonry of Moray and prebend of Kynnor, vacant by the death of cardinal Walter, to which Henry has been provided by the pope. The office of sacrist is attached to the prebend, which does not involve cure, but is elective, and about which no mention is made in the letters of provision. Henry, who has petitioned for confirmation so as not to be molested over his provision, is described as LIC.ART., scholar of civil law for two years, nephew of the late cardinal, and is said to hold a canonry and prebend of Glasgow [22 Sept., 1379].
Avignon, 3 Non. Oct., anno 9.
CPL, iv, 255.

9 October, 1387   Reg Aven 247, 349

To Patrick de Innerpefyr, layman resident in Dundee, Brechin diocese. Indult for a plenary remission of his sins to be granted at the hour of death by a confessor of his own choice.
Avignon, 7 Id. Oct., anno 9.

[1] See Reg Supp 70, 235.

19 October, 1387   Reg Aven 248, 471v-2

To the officials of St Andrews, Dunkeld and Brechin. Mandate to
collate to John Oggistoune, priest of Ross diocese, the parish church
of Neuet, St Andrews diocese, to which he received provision from
the late cardinal Walter, papal legate *a latere* in Scotland, when it
became vacant by the transfer of John de Grahame to the parish
church of Erol, same diocese, by authority of the ordinary; or
vacant because the said John, having had possession of the parish
for more than a year, neglected to be ordained priest within the
prescribed limit of time. Oggistoune now doubts that these are the
true reasons for the vacancy and asserts that the parish became vacant
by the death at the Roman Curia of Godfrey de Sanctoclaro, after
the election of Clement VII as pope; or because John de Grahame,
who then held the parish of Neuet, received collation to the parish
church of Aberbuchnor, St Andrews diocese. Whatever the true
reason for the vacancy, Oggistoune is to be confirmed in his possession, provided no third party has a legitimate right.
Avignon, 14 Kal. Nov., anno 9; expedited, 9 Kal. Jan., anno 10
[24 Dec., 1387]; consigned, 5 Kal. Jan., anno 10 [28 Dec., 1387].

26 October, 1387   Reg Aven 251, 401v

To all Christ's faithful. Indulgence of one hundred days is granted
to all who visit the altar of the Holy Rude in the church of St Mary
de Dunde, Brechin diocese, which has been refounded canonically
and endowed, on certain principal feasts of the year and on the
feasts of the Holy Cross [3 May or 14 Sept.] and of the Dedication
of the altar, and fifty days indulgence during their octaves and the
six days after Pentecost.
Avignon, 7 Kal. Nov., anno 9.
SRO Vat. Trans., i, no. 61.

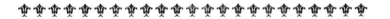

10—13 CLEMENT VII

22 November, 1387   Reg Aven 252, 217-17v

To the official of Glasgow. Mandate to collate Alexander de Wardlau, B.A., canon of Glasgow and nephew of the late cardinal Walter, to the archdeaconry of Argyll, which is a dignity with cure, vacant by the promotion of John to the bishopric of Argyll and by his consecration at the Roman Curia by special mandate of the pope; or vacant by the death of the said cardinal, and notwithstanding that Alexander holds a canonry and prebend of Glasgow.
Avignon, 10 Kal. Dec., anno 10; expedited, 19 Kal. Jan., anno 10 [14 Dec., 1387]; consigned, 15 Kal. Jan., anno 10 [18 Dec., 1387].

30 November, 1387   Reg Aven 252, 197v-8v

To Henry de Wardlau, LIC.ART., canon and precentor of Glasgow. Provision to a canonry of Glasgow and the office of precentor, together with the prebend of Kybride, which are canonically annexed to one another, vacant by the death of William de Wardlau, brother of the late cardinal Walter. Henry, who was himself a nephew of the late cardinal, has studied civil law at Orléans for two years. He must resign his other canonry and prebend of Glasgow upon obtaining possession of the present canonry, prebend and precentorship, but he may retain his canonry of Moray with expectation of a prebend [5 Oct., 1387], of which he has not yet gained possession.
Avignon, 2 Kal. Dec., anno 10; expedited, 19 Kal. Jan., anno 10 [14 Dec., 1387]; 17 Kal. Jan., anno 10 [16 Dec., 1387].
Concurrent mandate to the dean of St Pierre, Avignon, and the officials of St Andrews and Glasgow.

7 December, 1387   Reg Aven 253, 63-63v

To Gilbert de Podelwyk, clerk of Tournai diocese. Reservation of
a benefice usually assigned to the secular clergy in the gift of the
abbot and convent of Abberbrochoc, o.s.b., St Andrews diocese,
together or separately, to the value of 25 marks sterling with cure,
or 18 marks sterling without cure. Gilbert is said to have lived
continuously in Scotland since his tenth year.[1]
Avignon, 7 Id. Dec., anno 10; expedited, 15 Kal. Feb., anno 10
[18 Jan., 1388]; consigned, 11 Kal. Feb., anno 10 [22 Jan., 1388].
Concurrent mandate to the bishop of Dunkeld, the dean of St
Agricola, Avignon, and the official of St Andrews.

21 December, 1387   Reg Aven 252, 602-2v

To William Ramsay, b.dec., priest, canon of Dunkeld. Provision
to a canonry of Dunkeld with expectation of a prebend, and dignity,
parsonage, or office, provided the dignity is not the greatest after that
of the bishop, notwithstanding that he holds the parish church of
Tanadas, St Andrews diocese, which he must resign, however, upon
obtaining a benefice with cure.[2]
Avignon, 12 Kal. Jan., anno 10; expedited, 9 Kal. Jul., anno 13
[23 June, 1391]; consigned, 5 Kal. Jul., anno 13 [27 June, 1391].
Concurrent mandate to the provost of St Andrews, the dean of
St Pierre, Avignon, and the official of Brechin.

21 December, 1387   Reg Aven 252, 43v-44

To the official of Glasgow. Mandate to collate Hugh Raa, subdean
of Glasgow, kinsman of John, eldest son of king Robert, to the
parish church of Cavers, Glasgow diocese, vacant by the promotion
of Matthew to the bishopric of Glasgow. Hugh is already dispensed
to accept a benefice with cure, even if a dignity or parsonage, and
retain it together with the office of subdean, which also involves
cure.
Avignon, 12 Kal. Jan., anno 10; expedited, 3 Non. Mar., anno 10
[5 Mar., 1388]; consigned, Non. Mar., anno 10 [7 Mar., 1388].

[1] See *CPP*, i, 569.   [2] See *CPP*, i, 569.

2 January, 1388   Reg Aven 254, 409-9v

To Thomas de Barry, priest of St Andrews diocese. Reservation of a benefice with or without cure in the gift of whomsoever and of whatsoever value, even if it is a canonry and prebend, dignity, parsonage, or office, but provided it is not the greatest dignity of a cathedral after that of the bishop, or the principal dignity of a collegiate church, granted to him as a reward for the hardship he suffered when captured and imprisoned while coming from Scotland to the papal court on official business, and the large ransom he had to pay his captors before being released. He is to have precedence over all others in obtaining execution of this reservation, with the exception of cardinals, papal familiars and judges of the papal palace, masters in theology and doctors of canon and civil law.
Avignon, 4 Non. Jan., anno 10; expedited, 2 Kal. Mar., anno 10 [2 Feb., 1388].
Concurrent mandate to the dean of St Pierre, Avignon, and the officials of St Andrews and Glasgow.

4 January, 1388   Reg Aven 253, 403v
                                                   Reg Vat 299, 35v

To Henry de Wardlau, LIC.ART., canon and precentor of Glasgow. Dispensation to hold a parish church, or other benefice with cure, together with the precentorship of Glasgow, which is a dignity with cure, to which he was provided recently by the pope [30 Nov., 1387], or to hold it along with some other dignity, or another benefice with cure, if he does not obtain possession of the precentorship; either of which benefices he may freely exchange for another compatible with the remaining one, provided that the cure of souls is not neglected. Henry was the nephew of the late cardinal Walter.
Avignon, 2 Non. Jan., anno 10.
CPL, iv, 255-6.

8 January, 1388   Reg Aven 253, 401v-2;
                                                   Reg Vat 299, 34

To Jean, bishop of Tusculum. Indult, valid for five years, to visit by deputy, even on the same day, two churches, monasteries, or other ecclesiastical places, and the persons thereof, in the archdeaconry of Glasgow, and to receive the procurations due to him in ready money to the amount of thirty silver Tournois, twelve being equal to one gold florin of Florence. Those, however, who cannot pay in full, are to pay according to their means, and those who cannot pay at all are not to be compelled.

Avignon, 6 Id. Jan., anno 10.

Concurrent mandate to the bishops of Dunkeld and Ross, and the dean of St Agricola, Avignon.

CPL, iv, 255.

8 January, 1388   Reg Aven 253, 402-2v ;
                                              Reg Vat 299, 34-34v

To Jean, bishop of Tusculum. Similar indult regarding the archdeaconry of Ross.

Avignon, 6 Id. Jan., anno 10.

Concurrent mandate to the bishops of Dunkeld and Glasgow, and the dean of St Agricola, Avignon.

CPL, iv, 255.

18 January, 1388   Reg Aven 252, 49v-50

To Thomas de Barry, M.A., priest, perpetual vicar of the parish church of Montrose, Brechin diocese. Provision, made *motu proprio*, to the perpetual vicarage of the parish church of Monros, Brechin diocese, vacant by the death of the late David Fauconier, papal honorary chaplain.

Avignon, 15 Kal. Feb., anno 10; expedited, 14 Kal. Apr., anno 10 [19 Mar., 1388]; consigned, 9 Kal. Apr., anno 10 [24 Mar., 1388]. Concurrent mandate to the dean of St Pierre, Avignon, and the officials of St Andrews and Glasgow.

18 January, 1388   Reg Aven 252, 366-7v

To John de Vaus, priest, rector of the parish church of Libberton, Glasgow diocese. Reservation of the canonry of Glasgow and pre-

bend of Auld Roxburgh, presently held by Henry de Wardlau, but to become vacant whenever he obtains possession of another canonry of Glasgow and the annexed prebend of Kylbride, as stipulated in letters recently issued providing him to them [30 Nov., 1387], notwithstanding that John holds the parish church of Lyberton, but on condition that he resigns the other canonry and prebend of Glasgow which he holds. He is said to have studied canon law for four years and to have been a commensal chaplain of the late cardinal Walter.
Avignon, 15 Kal. Feb., anno 10; expedited, 5 Id. Jun., anno 10 [9 June, 1388]; consigned, 2 Id. Jun., anno 10 [12 June, 1388].
Concurrent mandate to the dean of St Pierre, Avignon, and the officials of Paris and Glasgow.

1 February, 1388   Reg Aven 254, 377v-8

To the official of Glasgow. Mandate to reserve to Thomas de Butyll, priest, perpetual vicar of the parish church of Loychruten, Glasgow diocese, a benefice usually assigned to the secular clergy in the gift of the prioress and convent of Nortberwyk, O.CIST., St Andrews diocese, together or separately, to the value of 25 marks sterling with cure, or 18 marks sterling without cure, notwithstanding that he holds the provostship of the chapel of St Mary de Mayboyl, Glasgow diocese, which is a simple benefice without cure, but on condition that he resigns the vicarage upon obtaining execution of these letters. Thomas is said to have studied canon law at the university of Oxford for five years.
Avignon, Kal. Feb., anno 10; expedited, 14 Kal. Maii, anno 10 [18 Apr., 1388]; consigned, 9 Kal. Maii, anno 10 [23 Apr., 1388].

1 February, 1388   Reg Aven 254, 412-13

To the official of Glasgow. Mandate to reserve to John de Struchem, priest, perpetual vicar of the parish church of Casteltarris, Glasgow diocese, a benefice usually assigned to the secular clergy in the gift of the abbot and convent of Pasleto, O.CLUN., same diocese, together or separately, to the value of 25 marks sterling with cure, or 18

N

marks sterling without cure, on condition that he resigns his vicarage upon obtaining possession of a benefice with cure.[1]
Avignon, Kal. Feb., anno 10; expedited, 5 Id. Apr., anno 10 [9 Apr., 1388]; consigned, 9 Kal. Maii, anno 10 [23 Apr., 1388].

1 February, 1388   Reg Aven 253, 421v-3;
                                                  Reg Vat 299, 47-48

To Jean, bishop of Tusculum. Convalidation of his provision to the canonry, prebend and archdeaconry of Glasgow, originally made by Gregory XI, with exemplification from the register of the papal chancery of the original letters, dated 3 Id. Sept., anno 6 [11 Sept., 1376], which have been lost. This bull, entitled *Dum ad personam*, provided him to the archdeaconry, when he was cardinal priest of S. Marcello, the provision having been reserved to the pope on 7 Kal. Mar., anno 6 [23 Feb., 1376], during the lifetime of the previous archdeacon, Guido Quieret, who subsequently died shortly before 11 September 1376. The concurrent mandate was given to the deans of St Agricola and St Pierre, Avignon, and the official of Glasgow.
Avignon, Kal. Feb., anno 10.
CPL, iv, 256.

12 May, 1388   Reg Aven 252, 177-7v

To the bishop of Brechin. Mandate to collate John Archier, priest of Brechin diocese, to the perpetual vicarage of the parish church of Carale, St Andrews diocese, vacant by the death of the late Robert Belle. Bishop Walter of St Andrews provided John to the living on his own authority and he obtained peaceful possession, but he has petitioned the pope for confirmation.
Avignon, 4 Id. Maii, anno 10; expedited, 14 Kal. Oct., anno 11 [18 Sept., 1389]; consigned, 8 Kal. Oct., anno 11 [24 Sept., 1389].

30 May, 1388   Reg Aven 253, 541v-2

To Walter, bishop of St Andrews. Faculty to make a pastoral

---

[1] See *CPP*, i, 570.

visitation of all exempt and non-exempt monasteries in the realm of Scotland, either personally or by his deputy, and to reform any abuses he finds in them, whether in spiritualities or temporalities, in head or in members.
Avignon, 3 Kal. Jun., anno 10.

26 August, 1388   Reg Aven 255, 482v-3

To the official of Glasgow. Mandate to provide Thomas de Arthurle, priest, rector of the parish church of Eglisham, Glasgow diocese, to a canonry of Glasgow with expectation of a prebend, provided he resigns the parish upon obtaining possession of the prebend.[1]
Châteauneuf-du-Pape, Avignon diocese, 7 Kal. Sept., anno 10; expedited, 2 Kal. Jun., anno 12 [31 May, 1390]; consigned, 8 Id. Jun., anno 12 [6 June, 1390].

22 September, 1388   Reg Aven 252, 491v-2

To Malcolm de Aula, canon of Glasgow. Provision to a canonry of Glasgow and the prebend of Edilston, vacant by the death of Alexander de Wardlaw, who was a nephew of the late cardinal Walter, being a son of the cardinal's brother, notwithstanding that Malcolm holds the perpetual vicarage of the parish church of Kilquonkar, St Andrews diocese.[2]
Châteauneuf-du-Pape, Avignon diocese, 10 Kal. Oct., anno 10; expedited, 2 Kal. Nov., anno 10[3] [31 Oct., 1388]; consigned, 2 Non. Nov., anno 11 [4 Nov., 1388].
Concurrent mandate to the abbot of Cambuskenneth, the dean of St Pierre, Avignon, and the official of St Andrews.

25 September, 1388   Reg Aven 253, 256-6v

To Richard de Gourlay, priest of Glasgow diocese. Reservation of a benefice, even if only a simple office, in the gift of the bishop, dean

---

[1] See *CPP*, i, 571.
[2] The corresponding petition appears in Vatican Library, Barb. Lat 2101, 198v.
[3] More correctly this should have been dated *anno 11*, which began precisely on that day.

and chapter of Brechin, together or separately, provided it is not a canonry and prebend, to the value of 25 marks sterling with cure, or 18 marks sterling without cure. Richard is said to be of noble birth.[1]

Avignon, 7 Kal. Oct., anno 10; expedited, 9 Kal. Oct., anno 13 [23 Sept., 1391]; consigned, 4 Kal. Oct., anno 13 [28 Oct., 1391]. Concurrent mandate to the dean of St Pierre, Avignon, John de Caron, canon of Moray, and the official of Aberdeen.

3 November, 1388   Reg Aven 258, 424-4v

To the bishop of Glasgow. Faculty to dispense John Cambel, lord of Glaston, donzel, and Marjory Stewart, damsel, Glasgow diocese, from the impediment to marriage arising from the third and fourth degrees of consanguinity.

Avignon, 3 Non. Nov., anno 11.
SRO Vat. Trans., iv, no. 56.

14 November, 1388   Reg Aven 258, 36v-37

To John Lethe, archdeacon of Argyll. Provision to the archdeaconry of Argyll, which is a dignity with cure and normally elective, but not the greatest dignity of the cathedral, value not exceeding 40 marks sterling, vacant by the death of Alexander de Wardlau, nephew of the late cardinal Walter, whom the pope provided to the archdeaconry when it was vacated by the promotion of John to the bishopric of Argyll [22 Nov., 1387].

Avignon, 18 Kal. Dec., anno 11; expedited, 8 Id. Maii, anno 11 [8 May, 1389]; consigned, 16 Kal. Jul., anno 11 [16 June, 1389]. Concurrent mandate to the bishop of Dunkeld, the dean of St Pierre, Avignon, and William Ade, canon of Dunkeld.

23 December, 1388   Reg Aven 256, 104-4v

To John, abbot of Dunfermline, O.S.B., St Andrews diocese. Provision as abbot of Dunfermline, vacant by the death of abbot

---

[1] See Reg Supp 74, 227.

John, last abbot, during whose lifetime provision of a successor was specially reserved to the pope. Unaware of this reservation, the prior and convent proceeded to elect John, a professed monk of their order and a priest, who accepted the election, but upon becoming aware of the reservation has brought his case before the consistory. Avignon, 10 Kal. Jan., anno 11 ; expedited, 5 Non. Maii, anno 12 [3 May, 1390] ; consigned, 4 Non. Maii, anno 12 [4 May, 1390]. Concurrent mandate to the convent of Dunfermline, the vassals, the bishop of St Andrews, and to king Robert.

18 January, 1389   Reg Aven 258, 32v-33

To the abbot of Iona, Sodor diocese. Mandate to collate Bean Johannis Andree, priest, nobly born, rector of the parish church of St Monewog, Lismore diocese, to the deanery of Lismore, which is the major dignity of the cathedral and involves cure of souls, but is not elective and the annual value of which, together with that of the parish church, does not exceed £12 sterling. The deanery is vacant either because the late Lochan Lochani, having received canonical provision to the living, continued to hold it together with the parish church of St Columba in Glosros, Lismore diocese, without obtaining the requisite dispensation, or because provision was specially reserved to the pope. Bean must resign the parish church.[1]
Avignon, 15 Kal. Feb., anno 11 ; expedited, 2 Non. Jan., anno 14 [4 Jan., 1392] ; consigned, 2 Non. Jan., anno 14 [4 Jan., 1392].[2]

4 April, 1389   Reg Aven 257, 322v-3

To the bishop of Brechin. Mandate to collate Henry de Drumbrek, clerk of Aberdeen diocese, to the perpetual vicarage of the parish church of Kerimar, St Andrews diocese, vacant by the death of John Alves. Henry was provided to the living by bishop Walter of St Andrews, but he doubts the validity of this provision and

---

[1] See *CPP*, i, 573.
[2] The following dates have been cancelled out in the register and substituted with what is given above: expedited 6 Kal Apr., anno 11 [27 Mar., 1389]; consigned 4 Kal. Apr., anno 11 [29 Mar., 1389].

since the vicarage is still considered to be vacant, he has petitioned the pope for confirmation. He is a familiar of the said bishop.
Avignon, 2 Non. Apr., anno 11; expedited, 7 Kal. Oct., anno 11 [25 Sept., 1389]; consigned, 2 Kal. Oct., anno 11 [30 Sept., 1389].

9 April, 1389   Reg Aven 256, 433v-4

To the abbots of Balmerino and Lindores, and the prior of Pittenweem, St Andrews diocese. Mandate to enquire into the case of William de Nortberwyk, priest of St Andrews diocese, who has petitioned the pope regarding his presentation to the perpetual vicarage of the parish church of Carale, same diocese, by prioress Alice and the convent of Hadyngton, o.s.b., the rightful patron, when it fell vacant by the death of Robert Bel. Although this presentation was made within the legal limit of time, bishop Walter of St Andrews rejected it and refused to institute William, despite his suitability, and instead has instituted John Archier, priest of St Andrews diocese, who still occupies the vicarage unlawfully. Having ascertained the facts, they are to expel any unjust intruder and put William in possession.
Avignon, 5 Id. Apr., anno 11; expedited, Non. Jun., anno 11 [5 June, 1389]; consigned, 5 Non. Jul., anno 11 [3 July, 1389].

10 April, 1389   Reg Aven 257, 267v-8

To Henry de Wardlau, LIC.ART., rector of the parish church of Cavers, Glasgow diocese. Provision made *motu proprio* to the parish church of Caveris, vacant either by the promotion of Matthew to the bishopric of Glasgow, or by the transfer of Hugh Raa to the parish church of Strathaven, same diocese, by the bishop's ordinary authority. Henry was a nephew of the late cardinal Walter.[1]
Avignon, 4 Id. Apr., anno 11; expedited, 8 Id. Maii, anno 11 [8 May, 1389]; consigned, 4 Id. Maii, anno 11 [12 May, 1389].
Concurrent mandate to the dean of Limoges, and the officials of Glasgow and St Andrews.

---

[1] See *CPP*, i, 573.

7 May, 1389   Reg Aven 259, 471-2v

To the bishop of Glasgow. Whereas, as is contained in the petition of Archibald de Douglas, lord of Galloway, his predecessors founded and built the monastery of Lyncludan, O.CLUN., Glasgow diocese, to the glory of God and of the blessed Virgin Mary, for the good of their souls and the souls of their ancestors, and endowed it sufficiently for the maintenance of eight or nine nuns, to be ruled by a prioress, while right of patronage remained with the lords of Galloway; these women have now taken to living dissolute and scandalous lives, allowing the beautiful monastic buildings to fall into disrepair and ruin through their neglect, while they dress their daughters, born in incest, in sumptuous clothes with gold ornaments and pearls. The number of nuns, including the prioress, is reduced to four, and they neglect the observance of the day and night divine office, devoting their time to the making of wool. Mass is celebrated only once a week. Cardinal Walter, when bishop of Glasgow, tried to put a stop to these abuses and reform the convent. The local neighbours, who are very evil men, repair to the monastery in order to defend themselves from the enemies of Scotland, the monastery being situated on the borders, or to a house about a mile distant from it, where they hold a market and even commit incest. Moreover, there is a poorhouse, also about a mile away from the monastery, called Holywood, which is governed by a secular priest and was bountifully endowed by Archibald's predecessors for the maintenance of eighteen poor men. Archibald wishes to transfer the nuns to some other nunnery, so that he may re-endow the monastery and establish it as a provostship with eight secular priests, who will live in community, and unite the hospice, augmented for twenty-four poor men, to the church and the provost of the church will excercise the functions of master of the hospice. Presentation of the provost and the priests will remain the right of the lord of Galloway. Wherefore, the bishop is commissioned to ascertain that these facts be true and having transferred the nuns to a house of the Cluniac or Benedictine order, to erect the collegiate church and hospice in accordance with the conditions stated above.

Avignon, Non. Maii, anno 11.

SRO Vat. Trans., i, no. 62.

8 May, 1389   Reg Aven 259, 583v-4

To John de Merton, B.DEC., rector of the parish church of Cambuslang, Glasgow diocese. In order that the reservation made to him on 7 Id. Jul., anno 9 [9 July, 1387] of a benefice, with or without cure, even if a canonry and prebend, dignity, parsonage, or office, of whatsoever value and in the gift of whomsoever, in the cathedrals, cities, or dioceses of St Andrews or Glasgow, might have speedier effect, the pope grants him precedence over all others, from the original date, with the exception of cardinals and papal familiars.
Avignon, 8 Id. Maii, anno 11; expedited, 19 [Kal] Feb., anno 13 [14 Jan., 1391]; consigned, 16 Kal. Feb., anno 13 [17 Jan., 1391].

16 May, 1389   Reg Aven 259, 410v-11

To abbot John of Holyrood de Edinburgh, O.S.A., St Andrews diocese. Absolution, granted at the abbot's own petition, from all irregularity and infamy incurred through taking possession of the monastery without having received the papal letters of provision [21 June, 1387], and for having administered the abbey in this fashion for several years, deriving the revenues thereof, contrary to the decree of Boniface VIII declaring null all that is performed in the meantime, with ratification of all the acts of his administration during that period.
Avignon, 17 Kal. Jun., anno 11.
SRO Vat. Trans., i, no. 63.

19 May, 1389   Reg Aven 259, 410v

To the bishops of St Andrews and Glasgow. Mandate to receive the oath of fidelity to the Apostolic See from abbot John of Holyrood O.S.A., St Andrews diocese, who was provided to the office by the pope, according to the prescribed form included with the present letter and to return it, properly sealed, to the pope as soon as possible, in order to save the abbot the fatigue and expense of coming personally to the papal court.
Avignon, 14 Kal. Jun., anno 11.

26 June, 1389   Reg Aven 259, 413v-14

To John de Merton, B.DEC., rector of the parish church of
Cambuslang, Glasgow diocese. In order that the reservation made
to him on 7 Id. Jul., anno 9 [9 July, 1387] of a benefice with or
without cure, even if a canonry and prebend, dignity, parsonage, or
office, of whatsoever value and in the gift of whomsoever, in the
cathedrals, cities, or dioceses of St Andrews or Glasgow, might have
speedier effect, even over those who have also received graces with
the prerogative of precedence over others, the pope now grants
him absolute precedence, even over those whose expectative graces
have the clause *anteferri*, with the sole exception of cardinals, the
servants of cardinals, and judges of the papal palace, notwithstanding
that he has the parish church of Cambuslang and has been provided
by the pope to a canonry and prebend of Glasgow [13 June, 1387].
Avignon, 6 Kal. Jul., anno 11 ; expedited, 6 Id. Jul., anno 11 [10
July, 1389] ; consigned, 3 Id. Jul., anno 11 [13 July, 1389].

14 July, 1389   Reg Aven 256, 20v

To the bishop of Dunkeld, the abbot of Inchaffray, and the dean of
St Pierre, Avignon. Mandate to have William Colitar admitted as a
monk of the monastery of Dunfermelyn, O.S.B., St Andrews
diocese. William, who is a professor of the Carmelite order, studied
as a youth in England and at the suggestion of certain friars, but
against the wishes of all his friends, entered and was professed in
the Carmelite order. He has petitioned the pope to allow him to
join the Benedictine convent of Dunfermline on account of his
special devotion for that church.
Avignon, 18 Kal. Jul., anno 11.

26 July, 1389   Reg Aven 259, 457

Ad perpetuam rei memoriam. Union of the parish church of Torref,
Aberdeen diocese, value not exceeding £100 sterling, to the
monastery of Cupro, O.CIST., St Andrews diocese, at the petition
of the abbot and convent, to whom belonged the right of presentation of a secular priest ; on account of the serious reduction in

the revenues of the monastery as a result of the wars, which for many years have been waged in those parts, reducing the monastery to ruins, and also on account of the expenses incurred in providing hospitality to guests, more of whom are entertained there than in any other monastery in Scotland. Upon the death, or resignation, of the present rector, the abbot and convent are to obtain full possession, but a suitable portion must be set aside for a perpetual vicar, so that the cure of souls will not be neglected.

Avignon, 7 Kal. Aug., anno 11.

SRO Vat. Trans., i, no. 64; printed: *Coupar Angus Chrs.*, no. 119.

4 September, 1389   Reg Aven 258, 45v-46

To Thomas Senescalli,[1] dean of Dunkeld. Provision to the deanship of Dunkeld, which is the greatest dignity of the cathedral after that of the bishop, and to which are attached a canonry and prebend, vacant by the death of the late Salomon Raa, with dispensation to hold it together with the archdeaconry of St Andrews, provided the cure of souls is not neglected. Thomas is said to be born of king Robert.

Avignon, 2 Non. Sept., anno 11; expedited, 15 Kal. Oct., anno 11 [17 Sept., 1389]; consigned, 13 Kal. Oct., anno 11 [19 Sept., 1389]. Concurrent mandate to the abbot of Scone, and the officials of Paris and St Andrews.

26 November, 1389   Reg Aven 263, 330v-1v

To Henry de Arthouroley, B.LEG., canon of Glasgow. Previously, on 15 Kal. Dec., anno 1 [17 Nov., 1378], a mandate was issued to the official of Glasgow to reserve to Henry a benefice in the gift of the bishop of St Andrews, value not exceeding 30 marks sterling with cure, or 18 marks sterling without cure; but Henry has never obtained execution of this expectative grace, although many others have, the grace is now increased to a benefice with cure, the annual value of which may be as much as 50 marks sterling, and Henry is to

[1] Cf *CPP*, i, 574; the version given there, 'Thomas B Steward', is derived from a marginal correction, where the name 'Thome', omitted in the body of the text, has been added in the margin accompanied by the initial of the corrector – 'B'!

have precedence over all others, notwithstanding that he holds a canonry and prebend of Glasgow.

Avignon, 6 Kal. Dec., anno 12; expedited, 3 Id. Jan., anno 12 [11 Jan., 1390]; consigned, 18 Kal. Feb., anno 12 [15 Jan., 1390].

29 November, 1389   Reg Aven 264, 53-53v

To John Gerland, priest of St Andrews diocese. Reservation of a benefice usually assigned to the secular clergy in the gift of the abbot and convent of Kilwinun, O.S.B., Glasgow diocese, together or separately, to the value of 25 marks sterling with cure, or 18 marks sterling without cure.[1]

Avignon, 3 Kal. Dec., anno 12; expedited, 2 Non. Jan., anno 12 [4 Jan., 1390]; consigned, Non. Jan., anno 12 [5 Jan., 1390].

Concurrent mandate to the deans of Dunkeld and St Agricola, Avignon, and the official of Glasgow.

8 January, 1390   Reg Aven 259, 578-8v

To Thomas Senescalli, archdeacon of St Andrews. Indult, granted at the petition of king Robert, for the duration of five years from the present date, to visit his archdeaconry by deputy, so that he may pursue the study of letters at a university, and to receive in ready money the procurations due to him.

Avignon, 6 Id. Jan., anno 12; expedited, Kal. Feb., anno 12 [1 Feb., 1390].

Concurrent mandate to John de Caron, canon of Aberdeen, and the officials of St Andrews and Aberdeen.

14 January, 1390   Reg Aven 263, 310-10v

Ad perpetuam rei memoriam. Declaration that the clause *non obstante quibuscumque reservationibus et constitutionibus ac ordinationibus aposto-licis per nos factis,* contained in the letters reserving a canonry and prebend of Glasgow to Gilbert Muffald, B.DEC., [27 Jan., 1386], was inserted contrary to the intention of the pope. In virtue of this provision Gilbert obtained the canonry and prebend of Edilston,

---

[1] See Reg Supp 77, 31v.

vacant by the death of Alexander de Wardlaw, but his tenure was disputed by Malcolm de Aula, the petitioner in this case, who also had letters providing him to the same canonry and prebend [22 Sept., 1388]. The case was submitted to Master Wilderic de Mitra, papal chaplain and judge of the papal palace, and subsequently, when he was absent from the papal court, it was handled by Master John Fayditi, also a papal chaplain and judge, and the above sentence was given.

Avignon, 19 Kal. Feb., anno 12 ; expedited, 6 Kal. Feb., anno 12 [27 Jan., 1390] ; consigned, 5 Kal. Feb., anno 12 [28 Jan., 1390].

19 January, 1390   Reg Aven 261, 77-78

To Gilbert, bishop-elect of Aberdeen. Provision to the bishopric of Aberdeen, which is immediately subject to the Apostolic See, vacant by the death of bishop Adam, during whose lifetime provision of a successor was specially reserved to the pope. Unaware of this reservation, the chapter of Aberdeen elected Gilbert, LIC.ART., priest and canon of Aberdeen, and he accepted the election, but on becoming conscious of the reservation, he has brought his case before the consistory. Although, in fact, his election was invalid, the pope now provides him to the bishopric.

Avignon, 14 Kal. Feb., anno 12 ; expedited, 4 Id. Feb., anno 12 [10 Feb., 1390] ; consigned, 2 Id. Feb., anno 12 [12 Feb., 1390].

Concurrent mandate to the chapter of Aberdeen, the clergy, the faithful, [the vassals], and to king Robert.

19 February, 1390   Reg Aven 263, 342

To David de Strevelin, priest, canon of Glasgow. Special concession that he may now take precedence over all others, with the exception, of cardinals, papal servants and judges of the papal palace, in obtaining execution of his provision to a canonry of Glasgow with expectation of a prebend, and dignity, parsonage, or office, which was granted on 17 Kal. Jul., anno 3 [15 June, 1381], but so far has remained ineffective.

Avignon, 11 Kal. Mar., anno 12 ; expedited, 16 Kal. Apr., anno 12 [17 Mar., 1390] ; consigned, 12 Kal. Apr., anno 12 [21 Apr., 1390].

23 February, 1390   Reg Aven 262, 438-9

To David de Seton, priest, canon of Dunkeld. Provision to a canonry and prebend of Dunkeld, vacant by the resignation of Jean, bishop of Tusculum, made freely into the pope's own hands. Avignon, 7 Kal. Mar., anno 12; expedited, 6 Id. Mar., anno 12 [10 Mar., 1390]; consigned, 2 Id. Mar., anno 12 [14 Mar., 1390].
Concurrent mandate to the abbot of Scone, the dean of St Agricola, Avignon, and the official of Aberdeen.

12 March, 1390   Reg Aven 262, 420-20v

To Cristin Cromdoll, B.DEC., canon of Moray. Provision to a canonry and prebend of Moray, vacant by the promotion of Gilbert to the bishopric of Aberdeen [19 Jan., 1390], with dispensation to retain the parish church of Hawiyk, Glasgow diocese, and the poor hospital, called the Red Spittal, St Andrews diocese, in the foundation statutes of which it is laid down that it is a perpetual benefice to be assigned to the secular clergy.
Avignon, 4 Id. Mar., anno 12; expedited, 5 Kal. Apr., anno 12 [28 Mar., 1390]; consigned, 3 Kal. Apr., anno 12 [30 Mar., 1390].
Concurrent mandate to the bishop of Aberdeen, the abbot of Kinloss and the dean of St Pierre, Avignon.

12 March, 1390   Reg Aven 263, 109v-10

To the bishop of Dunkeld, the dean of St Pierre, Avignon, and the official of St Andrews. Mandate to collate Patrick Davidis, clerk of St Andrews diocese, to the parish church of Culas, same diocese, vacant by the transfer of Malcolm de Urwell to the parish church of Fortevyot, said diocese, in virtue of his provision by Gregory XI. Originally Patrick declared the value of the parish to be £30 Tournois, whereas it is really £20 sterling, and on this account he has petitioned for confirmation.
Avignon, 4 Id. Mar., anno 12; expedited, 5 Kal. Apr., anno 12 [28 Mar., 1390]; consigned, 4 Kal. Apr., anno 12 [29 Mar., 1390].

18 April, 1390   Reg Aven 264, 124-4v

To Thomas de Butyl, B.DEC., priest, provost of the chapel of St
Mary de Maybole, Glasgow diocese. Reservation of a benefice with
or without cure in the gift of the prior and chapter of Whithorn,
O.PREMON., together or separately, usually assigned to the secular
clergy, to the value of 30 marks sterling, notwithstanding that he
holds the provostship of St Mary's, Mayboil, which is a simple
office, but on condition that upon obtaining execution of these
letters or of the other expectative grace of a benefice with or without
cure in the gift of the prioress and convent of Nortberwik, O.CIST.,
St Andrews diocese, [1 Feb., 1388], he resigns the perpetual vicarage
of the parish church of Lochruten, Glasgow diocese, and the
remaining expectation ceases to be valid.[1]
Avignon, 14 Kal. Maii, anno 12; expedited, 3 Non. Jan., anno 13
[3 Jan., 1391]; consigned, 7 Id. Jan., anno 13 [7 Jan., 1391].
Concurrent mandate to the deans of Aberdeen and St Pierre,
Avignon, and the official of Glasgow.

2 July, 1390   Reg Aven 260, 248v-9

To the official of Paris. Mandate to collate John de Hawic, priest,
perpetual vicar of the parish church of Donlop, Glasgow diocese,
to a canonry of Glasgow and the prebend of Casteltarris, to the
value of 8 marks sterling, vacant by the provision by the pope of
John Vaus to another canonry of Glasgow and the prebend of
Veteriroxburg [18 Jan., 1388]. John, who is said to have studied
canon law for five years at Oxford and Paris and to have been a
chaplain of the late cardinal Walter, is dispensed to retain the perpetual vicarage.
Avignon, 6 Non. Jul., anno 12; expedited, 3 Kal. Sept., anno 12
[30 Aug., 1390]; consigned, 4 Non. Sept., anno 12 [3 Sept., 1390].

9 July, 1390   Reg Aven 264, 115-15v

To the official of Glasgow. Mandate to reserve to Patrick Coll,
priest of Glasgow diocese, a benefice usually assigned to the secular

---

[1] See *CPP*, i, 574.

clergy in the gift of the abbot and convent of Passeleto, O.CLUN., same diocese, together or separately, to the value of 25 marks sterling with cure, or 18 marks sterling without cure.[1] Avignon, 7 Id. Jul., anno 12; expedited, 8 Kal. Oct., anno 12 [24 Sept., 1390]; consigned, 2 Kal. Oct., anno 12 [30 Sept., 1390].

2 August, 1390   Reg Aven 261, 376

To Elizeus Adougan, rector of the parish church of Kirkmahoe, Glasgow diocese. Dispensation to accept the presentation made of him to the provostship of the church of Lyncludan, which was raised to collegiate status recently [7 May, 1389] at the petition of Archibald, earl of Douglas, to whom the rights of patronage and presentation belong, and to hold it together with the parish church, even although the provostship also involves cure of souls, but provided that cure is not neglected in either. At the end of two years, however, he must exchange one or the other for a benefice compatible with the remainder, or resign the parish, or the provostship.[2] Avignon, 4 Non. Aug., anno 12; expedited, 13 Kal. Sept., anno 12 [20 Aug., 1390]; consigned, 6 Kal. Sept., anno 12 [27 Aug., 1390].

30 August, 1390   Reg Aven 261, 405v-6

To James de Borthwik, archdeacon of Lothian, St Andrews diocese. Indult for the duration of four years to visit his archdeaconry by deputy and receive in ready money the procurations due to him, to the amount of 30 silver Tournois daily, twelve being equal to one gold florin of Florence. James is said to be studying at Paris. Beaucaire, Arles diocese, 3 Kal. Sept., anno 12; expedited, 8 Kal. Nov., anno 12 [25 Oct., 1390]. Concurrent mandate to the bishops of Dunkeld and Aberdeen, and John de Caron, canon of Aberdeen.

---

[1] See Reg Supp 77, 117v.
[2] This letter is repeated on 25 November, 1390, see p. 158 below.

11 September, 1390   Reg Aven 261, 386v

To John Senescalli, clerk of Glasgow diocese. Dispensation from
defect of birth, being born out of wedlock, granted at the petition
of his kinsman, king Robert, so that he may be ordained to the
priesthood and may accept as many benefices with or without cure
as are conferred upon him canonically, even if a canonry and
prebend, dignity, parsonage, or office, and even when the dignity
is the major one of a cathedral, or principal one of a collegiate
church, but provided that they are all compatible.
Beaucaire, Arles diocese, 3 Id. Sept., anno 12; expedited, 8 Id.
Oct., anno 12 [8 Oct., 1390].

17 September, 1390   Reg Aven 261, 386v-7

To John Barber, priest of Aberdeen diocese. Confirmation, granted
at his own petition, of his provision to the perpetual vicarage of the
parish church of Tarnas, Aberdeen diocese, effected by bishop
Gilbert of Aberdeen, when vacated by the free resignation of Thomas
Umfridi, made into the hands of William de Calabre, canon of
Aberdeen, in exchange for a canonry and prebend of the chapel,
situated within the city of St Andrews, which John had held, but
freely resigned into the hands of king Robert, to whom provision
belonged through a special privilege granted him by the pope.
This is confirmed, provided Thomas was not a member of the
papal household, and in spite of the fact that the provision this time
should have been made by the pope on account of the length of
time the vicarage was kept vacant.
Beaucaire, Arles diocese, 15 Kal. Oct., anno 12; expedited, 8 Id.
Oct., anno 12 [8 Oct., 1390]; consigned, 6 Id. Oct., anno 12 [10
Oct., 1390].

24 September, 1390   Reg Aven 261, 387-7v

To the dean of St Pierre, Avignon, and the chancellor and official
of Glasgow. Mandate to collate John Gardenar, priest of Glasgow
diocese, after due examination of the facts, to the perpetual vicarage
of the parish church of Morins, same diocese, at the petition of king

Robert, to whom John is a chaplain. From the petition it appears that John Gardenar and John Gerland, priest of St Andrews diocese, wishing to effect an exchange of benefices, freely resigned into the hands of cardinal Walter, papal legate, the parish church of Lundi, St Andrews diocese, and the vicarage of Mearns, Glasgow diocese, and were provided by him to the respective benefices. John Gardenar has had peaceful possession for four years, but doubts have been raised about his tenure and so he has petitioned the pope for confirmation. The vicarage can be considered vacant, either for the reason stated above, or because John has neglected to be ordained to the priesthood within the required limit of time, without obtaining a dispensation, or because Nicholas de Irwyn, was collated by the pope from the said vicarage to the parish church of Lohwortanth, St Andrews diocese.

Beaucaire, Arles diocese, 8 Kal. Oct., anno 12; expedited, 5 Id. Oct., anno 12 [11 Oct., 1390]; consigned, 4 Id. Oct., anno 12 [12 Oct., 1390].

27 October, 1390   Reg Aven 263, 497

Universis presentes litteras inspecturis. Declaration to put an end to all doubt in the matter, that William de Camera, senior, M.A., clerk of Aberdeen diocese, who is of noble birth and studied canon law at Paris for several years, was a member of the pope's household at the time of his provision to a canonry of Dunkeld with expectation of a prebend, which was made to him *motu proprio* on 8 Id. Nov., anno 1 [6 Nov., 1378].

Aramon, Uzès diocese, 6 Kal. Nov., anno 12; expedited, 10 Kal. Dec., anno 13 [22 Nov., 1390]; consigned, 9 Kal. Dec., anno 12 [23 Nov., 1390].

28 October, 1390   Reg Aven 263, 489v-90

To the abbot and convent of Holyrood de Edinburgh, o.s.a., St Andrews diocese. Concession that the presentation and institution of John de Ballochm, canon of Holyrood, to the perpetual vicarage of the parish church of Tranerent, St Andrews diocese, which is

o

usually served by canons from the abbey, be regarded as valid, notwithstanding the fact that he is a papal honorary chaplain. Aramon, Uzès diocese, 5 Kal. Nov., anno 12; expedited, 6 Id. Nov., anno 13 [8 Nov., 1390]; consigned, 2 Id. Nov., anno 13 [12 Nov., 1390].

28 October, 1390   Reg Aven 263, 490

To the bishop of St Andrews. Faculty to dispense Henry de Balloym from defect of birth, being born of an Augustinian friar in priest's orders and an unmarried woman, that he may be ordained to holy orders and accept a benefice, even if it is a canonry and prebend, dignity, parsonage, or office, with cure and elective, but not a major dignity of a cathedral, or the principal one of a collegiate church.[1] Aramon, Uzès diocese, 5 Kal. Nov., anno 12; expedited, 6 Id. Nov., anno 13 [8 Nov., 1390]; consigned, 2 Id. Nov., anno 13 [12 Nov., 1390].

28 October, 1390   Reg Aven 263, 490v

To John de Belochm, canon of Holyrood de Edinburgh, O.S.A., St Andrews diocese. Concession that he may hold *in commendam* the perpetual vicarage of the parish church of Tranerent, St Andrews diocese, which is a dependency of Holyrood Abbey and is usually served by one of the canons. Aramon, Uzès diocese, 5 Kal. Nov., anno 12; expedited 6 Id. Nov., anno 13 [8 Nov., 1390]; consigned, 2 Id. Nov., anno 13 [12 Nov., 1390].

28 October, 1390   Reg Aven 263, 502

To Henry de Balloym, scholar of St Andrews diocese. Dispensation from defect of birth, having been born of an Augustinian friar in priest's orders and an unmarried woman, that he may be ordained to holy orders and accept a benefice, even if it is a canonry and prebend, dignity, parsonage, or office, even with cure and normally

[1] This letter has been cancelled out with a note in the margin to this effect: *Cassata de mandato Iohannis de Neapoli et albi gratiose scripta.*

elective, but provided it is not a major dignity of a cathedral, or the principal dignity of a collegiate church.
Aramon, Uzès diocese, 5 Kal. Nov., anno 12.

12 November, 1390   Reg Aven 265, 364-4v

To the official of St Andrews. Mandate to collate Gilbert de Bothwyle, perpetual vicar of the parish church of Caldore, St Andrews diocese, to a canonry of Glasgow and the prebend of Askyrk, vacant by the free resignation of William de Bothwyle, made at the Roman Curia by his proxy, John Trich, into the hands of Master Giles de Curtibus, canon of Carpentras, papal chaplain.[1]
Avignon, 2 Id. Nov., anno 13; expedited, 7 Id. Jan., anno 13 [7 Jan., 1391]; consigned, 3 Id. Jan., anno 13 [11 Jan., 1391].

12 November, 1390   Reg Aven 265, 242-2v

To the prior of Oransay, Sodor diocese. Mandate to collate Nigel Ymari, priest of Argyll diocese, rector of the parish church of St Symioge, same diocese, who has studied canon law for three years, to the archdeaconry of the Isles, which is a dignity with cure, vacant because Bean Johannis, priest of Sodor diocese, retained the archdeaconry together with the parish church of St Mary de Aran, which he already held, without obtaining the necessary dispensation.[2]
Avignon, 2 Id. Nov., anno 13; expedited, 14 Kal. Feb., anno 13 [19 Jan., 1391]; consigned, 13 Kal. Feb., anno 13 [20 Jan., 1391].

23 November, 1390   Reg Aven 268, 184v

To James de Borthwik, archdeacon of Lothian, St Andrews diocese. Permission for a period of three years to study civil law at a university, provided that cure of souls is not neglected in the archdeaconry in the meantime.
Avignon, 9 Kal. Dec., anno 13.

---

[1] See *CPP*, i, 574.   [2] See Reg Supp 78, 2v.

25 November, 1390   Reg Aven 268, 211v-12

To Elizeus Adougan, rector of the parish church of Kirkmahoe, Glasgow diocese. Dispensation to accept the presentation made of him to the provostship of the church of Lyncludan, which was raised to collegiate status recently [7 May, 1389] at the petition of Archibald, earl of Douglas, to whom the rights of patronage and presentation belong, and to hold it together with the parish church, even although the provostship also involves cure of souls, but provided that cure is not neglected in either. At the end of two years, however, he must exchange one or the other for a benefice compatible with the remainder, or else resign the parish, or the provostship.[1]

Avignon, 7 Kal. Dec., anno 13 ; expedited, 11 Kal. Jan., anno 13 [22 Dec., 1390].

5 December, 1390   Reg Aven 265, 241-2

To the bishop of Dunblane, the dean of St Pierre, Avignon, and the dean of Dunblane. Mandate to collate Conghan Machabei, priest of Argyll diocese, to the treasurership of Argyll, which is a dignity with cure, but not the greatest after that of the bishop, value not exceeding 12 marks sterling, vacant by the death of the late Maurice Clerici. At that time bishop Martin of Argyll conferred the office on Congan, who then held it for four years, although he was only in his twenty-third year at the time of promotion and not dispensed from defect of age. A certain Christian Johannis also held it for three years, but without ever being ordained to holy orders and he has since taken lay vows.

Avignon, Non. Dec., anno 13 ; expedited, 19 Kal. Feb., anno 13 [14 Jan., 1391] ; consigned, 14 Kal. Feb., anno 13 [19 Jan., 1391].

23 December, 1390   Reg Aven 266, 103-3v

To the archdeacon of the Isles, Sodor diocese. Mandate to collate Celestine Colini, clerk of Sodor diocese, to the perpetual vicarage of the parish church of St Columba de Sorbi, on the island of

---

[1] This letter duplicates that of 2 Aug., 1390, see p 153 above.

Trryech, same diocese, value not exceeding 9 marks sterling, vacant by the death of Murcard Laurence, and notwithstanding that it is unlawfully occupied at present by Donald Fynlay, priest of Sodor diocese.[1]
Avignon, 10 Kal. Jan., anno 13; expedited, 6 Id. Apr., anno 13 [8 Apr., 1391]; consigned, 4 Id. Apr., anno 13 [10 Apr., 1391].

23 December, 1390   Reg Aven 266, 44v–45

To the prior of St Andrews, the chancellor of Aberdeen and the official of St Andrews. Mandate to collate John Steyl, professed monk of the monastery of Londoris, o.s.b., St Andrews diocese, and said to be of noble birth, to the priorship of Coldinghame, same order and same diocese, vacant by the free resignation of William Rede, made into the hands of bishop Walter of St Andrews. The priory is a dependency of Dunfermline and is usually ruled by one of the monks of that monastery, and so John is to be admitted to the monastic choir of Dunfermline in virtue of this collation.[2]
Avignon, 10 Kal. Jan., anno 13; expedited, 2 Non. Feb., anno 13 [4 Feb., 1391]; consigned, 8 Id. Feb., anno 13 [6 Feb., 1391].

17 January, 1391   Reg Aven 268, 426

To the bishop of Glasgow. Mandate to confirm the exchange effected between the abbot and convent of Saydil, Lismore diocese, and the abbot and convent of Crosraguier, Glasgow diocese, of the chapel of the Holy Trinity de Kyldormne and the parish church of Inchemernok, Sodor diocese. This exchange was made thirty years ago, but without obtaining the consent of the local bishop, and so the abbot of Saddell petitions for papal confirmation in spite of this irregularity.[3]
Avignon, 16 Kal. Feb., anno 13; expedited, 9 Kal. Jul., anno 14 [23 June, 1392].
SRO Vat. Trans., i, no. 65; printed: *Highland Papers*, iv, 142–4.

[1] See *CPP*, i, 575.   [2] Cf *CPP*, i, 575.
[3] This letter is repeated on fo. 237, but the text is almost completely illegible. The date of expedition is given as 3 Id Apr., anno 13 [11 Apr., 1391].

1 February, 1391   Reg Aven 265, 165-6

To Robert, bishop of Dunkeld. Provision to the bishopric of Dunkeld, being transferred there from the bishopric of Orkney, the former bishopric being vacant by the death of Bishop John. Avignon, Kal. Feb., anno 13 ; expedited, 12 Kal. Mar., anno 13 [18 Feb., 1391] ; consigned, 10 Kal. Mar., anno predicto [20 Feb., 1391]. Concurrent mandate to the chapter of Dunkeld, the clergy, the faithful, the vassals, and to king Robert.

6 February, 1391   Reg Aven 266, 489-9v

To the official of Glasgow. Mandate to collate John de Hawic, B.DEC., priest, canon of Glasgow, to the perpetual vicarage of the parish church of Dunlop, Glasgow diocese, value not exceeding 15 marks sterling, vacant by the free resignation of Henry de Wardlau, made into the hands of his uncle, the late cardinal Walter, who then provided John, his chaplain and commensal, to the living. John, doubting the validity of this provision, has petitioned the pope for confirmation. Avignon, 8 Id. Feb., anno 13 ; expedited, 17 Kal. Apr., anno 13 [16 Mar., 1391] ; consigned, 11 Kal. Apr., anno 13 [22 Mar., 1391].

21 March, 1391   Reg Aven 266, 95v-96

To John de Douglas, M.A., B.LEG., dean of Moray. Provision to the deanship of Moray, which is the greatest dignity of the cathedral after that of the bishop and is normally elective, vacant on account of the revocation of the dispensation granted to Robert, then bishop-elect of Orkney, to retain it along with the bishopric. John is dispensed to hold the parish church of New[lands], Glasgow diocese, together with the deanery, provided that the cure of souls is not neglected, and on condition that within two years he will have exchanged one or other of the benefices for another benefice compatible with the remaining one, or at the end of that time he must resign the deanery.[1]

[1] See *CPP*, i, 575.

Avignon, 12 Kal. Apr., anno 13 ; expedited, 8 Id. Apr., anno 13 [6 Apr., 1391] ; consigned, 7 Id. Apr., anno 13 [7 Apr., 1391].
Concurrent mandate to the deans of Glasgow and St Pierre, Avignon, and the official of Glasgow.

21 March, 1391   Reg Aven 268, 232v

Ad futuram rei memoriam. Revocation of the dispensation granted to Robert, bishop of Orkney, to retain the deanship of Moray, which he held at the time of his promotion, along with the bishopric of Orkney.
Avignon, 12 Kal. Apr., anno 13.

20 April, 1391   Reg Aven 266, 196v-7

To Duncan Petyt, provost of St Andrews. Mandate to accept the resignation of the deanship of Dunkeld from Thomas Senescalli and the archdeaconship of Brechin from Robert de Cardeny, together with a canonry of Dunkeld and prebend of Cref, the latter both pertaining to lay patronage, and to effect an exchange of benefices, providing Thomas to the archdeaconry of Brechin, which involves cure, but is not elective, nor is it a major dignity of the cathedral, and to the canonry and prebend, and Robert to the deanship of Dunkeld, which is the major dignity of the cathedral, is normally elective and involves cure of souls.
Avignon, 12 Kal. Maii, anno 13 ; consigned, Non. Aug., anno 13 [5 Aug., 1391].

17 May, 1391   Reg Aven 265, 404-5

To Elisaeus Adougan, canon of Glasgow. Provision to a canonry of Glasgow with expectation of a prebend, if vacant at or after 6 Id. Jun. [8 June], notwithstanding that he holds the provostship of the church of Lincludan and the parish church of Kyrkmaho, both in Glasgow diocese.
Avignon, 16 Kal. Jun., anno 13 ; expedited, Kal. Jul., anno 13 [1 July, 1391] ; consigned, 3 Non. Jul., anno 13 [5 July, 1391].
Concurrent mandate to the abbots of Paisley and Holywood, and the official of Glasgow.

21 May, 1391   Reg Aven 265, 62v

To Sir James de Douglas, knight, and Egidia his wife, St Andrews diocese. Indult for a plenary remission of their sins to be granted at the hour of death by a confessor of their own choice.
Avignon, 12 Kal. Jun., anno 13.

21 May, 1391   Reg Aven 268, 323

To Annabella, queen of Scotland. Indult to choose her own confessor.
Avignon, 12 Kal. Jun., [anno 13].

21 May, 1391   Reg Aven 268, 451v

To Peter de Stratherne, rector of the parish church of Cochquen, Glasgow diocese. More ample dispensation, having already been dispensed from illegitimacy of birth, being born of a priest and an unmarried woman, in order to receive holy orders and hold a benefice even with cure, in virtue of which he obtained the parish church, that he may now hold one, two, or three benefices without cure, even if a canonry and prebend, or office, without having to mention his defect or the dispensation when petitioning for future graces.
Avignon, 12 Kal. Jun., anno 13 ; expedited, 2 Id. Oct., anno 15 [14 Oct., 1393].

21 May, 1391   Reg Aven 269, 391v-2

Ad futuram rei memoriam. Declaration with regard to the interpretation of the faculty granted to the bishop of St Andrews [16 Nov., 1378] to confer on worthy persons presented to him by the late king Robert of Scotland, canonries of the following dioceses, distributed in the following manner, with reservation of an equal number of prebends : two canonries of Glasgow, and likewise two of Dunkeld, Aberdeen, Moray, Ross, Caithness, Brechin and Dunblane, with precedence over all others in obtaining effect to these graces, exception being made only for papal familiars. Hesitation has been expressed over precisely which papal familiars

are intended in this case. Therefore, to remove all doubt in this matter, familiars are declared to be those who are continual commensals and also those upon whom expectative graces were conferred in a roll dated 3 Non. Nov., anno 1 [3 Nov., 1378].
Avignon, 12 Kal. Jun., anno 13 ; expedited, 3 Non. Jul., anno 14 [5 July, 1392] ; consigned, 7 Id. Jul., anno 14 [9 July, 1392].
SRO Vat. Trans., i, no. 66.

23 May, 1391   Reg Aven 266, 238v-9

To the bishop, the chanter and the chancellor of Glasgow. Mandate to collate Thomas de Butil, B.DEC., provost of the chapel of St Mary de Mayboyl, Glasgow diocese, to the archdeaconry of Whithorn, which is not the greatest dignity of the cathedral and is not elective, vacant by the death of Patrick Macdowil, clerk of Galloway diocese, or vacant because the said Patrick, having had peaceful possession of the archdeaconry for more than a year, neglected to be ordained priest within the prescribed limit of time, and notwithstanding that Richard Smerles, priest of Glasgow diocese, occupies it unlawfully at present. Thomas is dispensed to retain the provostship, which is a simple office without cure, and the perpetual vicarage of the parish church of Loychruton, Glasgow diocese, and the two expectative graces he received from the pope of a benefice with or without cure in the gift of the prior and chapter of Whithorn [18 Apr., 1390] and of the prioress and convent of Nortberwyk [1 Feb., 1388] remain valid.
Avignon, 10 Kal. Jun., anno 13 ; expedited, 9 Kal. Jul., anno 13 [23 June, 1391] ; consigned, 6 Kal. Jul., anno 13 [26 June, 1391].

30 May, 1391   Reg Aven 268, 323v

To William Ramsay, B.DEC., priest, canon of Dunkeld. Dispensation to retain the parish church of Tanadas, St Andrews diocese, even after the papal letters granting him a dignity, parsonage, or office have obtained their effect [21 Dec., 1387].[1]
Avignon, 3 Kal. Jun., anno 13.

[1] The original text is almost completely destroyed and mutilated, so that this is largely a reconstruction of the letter, based on what is contained in the rubric (f. 9), which is also difficult to read.

31 May, 1391   Reg Aven 266, 551v-2v

To the bishop of Sodor, the abbot of Crossraguel, and the chancellor of Glasgow. Mandate to collate Alexander de Bute, priest of Glasgow diocese, to the perpetual vicarage of the parish church of Kylmacolme, same diocese, vacant by the free resignation of William de Incheenane, made into the hands of bishop Walter of Glasgow, in exchange for the perpetual vicarage of Inchinnan, which Alexander resigned freely into the hands of the same bishop. Alexander has now had possession of the vicarage of Kilmacolm for several years, but he doubts the validity of his provision and has petitioned for papal confirmation. This is granted, even if the vicarage was vacant by the fact that a certain Robert Clerk, who held it for more than a year, neglected to be ordained priest within the prescribed limit of time.

Avignon, 2 Kal. Jun., anno 13 ; expedited, 3 Id. Jul., anno 13 [13 July, 1391] ; consigned, 16 Kal. Aug., anno 13 [17 July, 1391].

1 June, 1391   Reg Aven 266, 212-12v

To Duncan Petyt, B.U.J., archdeacon of Glasgow. Provision to the archdeaconry of Glasgow with its attached prebend, vacant by the free resignation of Jean, bishop of Tusculum, made into the pope's own hands. Duncan, who is a councillor of king Robert, is dispensed to retain his canonry of Glasgow and prebend of Are and the provostship of St Andrews for a period of three years, after which time he must exchange them for compatible benefices.[1]

Avignon, Kal. Jun., anno 13 ; expedited, 4 Id. Jun., anno 13 [10 June, 1391] ; consigned, 2 Id. Jun., anno 13 [12 June, 1391].

Concurrent mandate to the abbots of Paisley and Kilwinning and the dean of St Agricola, Avignon.

3 June, 1391   Reg Aven 266, 540-40v

To the official of Brechin. Mandate to collate John Oliverii, priest of Ross diocese, who was previously dispensed from illegitimacy of birth, being born of a priest and an unmarried woman, in order

---

[1] See Reg Supp 78, 90.

to be ordained priest and accept a benefice even with cure, to the perpetual vicarage of the parish church of Neutil, St Andrews diocese, vacant by the free resignation of William Gerland, subdean of Moray, who must resign it as a condition of obtaining effect to his provision to a canonry of Moray with expectation of a prebend, parsonage, or office [17 Nov., 1378], no dispensation having been granted him for plurality.[1]
Avignon, 3 Non. Jun., anno 13 ; expedited, Kal. Jul., anno 13 [1 July, 1391] ; consigned, 3 Non. Jul., anno 13 [5 July, 1391].

11 June, 1391   Reg Aven 268, 453

To Hugh de Dalmehoy, B.LEG., archdeacon of Moray. Dispensation to hold the archdeaconry, which involves cure of souls, together with a parish church, and to exchange them for similar or dissimilar benefices with or without cure, provided they are not two parishes, as a measure to supplement the meagre revenues derived from the archdeaconry, on condition that cure is not neglected in any of these offices or benefices.
Avignon, 3 Id. Jun., anno 13 ; expedited, 11 Kal. Aug., anno 16 [22 July, 1394] ; consigned, 3 Kal. Sept., anno 16 [30 Aug., 1394].

16 June, 1391   Reg Aven 266, 547-7v

To the bishop of Sodor, the dean of St Pierre, Avignon, and the official of Glasgow. Mandate to collate Maurice Johannis, priest of Argyll diocese, to the parish church of Dunoyng, same diocese, which belongs to lay patronage, vacant by the death of Donald Makcayl, or vacant because John Alexander Macinohham, having held the church for more than a year, neglected to be ordained priest within the prescribed limit of time. After the death of Donald, the parish remained vacant for a long time, until bishop Martin of Argyll provided Maurice on his own authority, although he was only in his twenty-second year at the time, since when he too has held the church for more than a year, but has neglected to receive ordination. Maurice must resign the church and then be reprovided, and he is herewith absolved from all guilt and irregularity.

[1] See *CPP*, i, 575.

Avignon, 16 Kal. Jul., anno 13 ; expedited, 5 Id. Jul., anno 13 [11 July, 1391] ; consigned, 4 Id. Jul., anno 13 [12 July, 1391].

---

17 June, 1391   Reg Aven 266, 452v-3

To the archdeacon of Glasgow. Mandate to appoint Thomas de Glenluysse, professed monk of the monastery of Glenluce, O.CIST., Galloway diocese, to take charge in the meantime of the parish church of Kyrkgumiyne, Glasgow diocese, which is normally served by monks of Holme Abbey, Carlisle diocese ; but on account of the wars in those parts, as well as on account of the Schism, no Englishman may dwell in Scotland, and the parish has been completely neglected. Thomas, who is a priest and engaged in the study of letters, may draw the revenues of the parish.

Avignon, 15 Kal. Jul., anno 13 ; expedited, 8 Kal. Maii, anno 15 [24 Apr., 1393] ; consigned, 4 Kal. Maii, anno 15 [28 Apr., 1393].

---

17 June, 1391   Reg Aven 265, 477v-8

To Thomas de Butyl, B.DEC., priest, canon of Glasgow. Provision to a canonry of Glasgow with expectation of a prebend, notwithstanding that he holds the provostship of the chapel of St Mary de Mayboyll, which is a simple office without cure, and the perpetual vicarage of the parish church of Lochruton, Glasgow diocese, and has been provided by the pope as archdeacon of Whithorn [23 May, 1391], but without as yet having obtained possession, and has expectative graces of benefices with or without cure in the gift of the prior and chapter of Galloway [18 Apr., 1390] and the prioress and convent of Nortberwyk [1 Feb., 1388].

Avignon, 15 Kal. Jul., anno 13 ; expedited, 16 Kal. Oct., anno 13 [16 Sept., 1391] ; consigned, 12 Kal. Oct., anno 13 [20 Sept., 1391]. Concurrent mandate to the abbots of Paisley and Holywood, and the dean of St Agricola, Avignon.

---

4 July, 1391   Reg Aven 267, 31v-32

To the bishop of Argyll, the dean of St Pierre, Avignon, and the official of Glasgow. Mandate to collate Nigel Cambel, clerk of

Dunblane diocese, who was previously dispensed from illegitimacy of birth, being born of noble blood, but in adultery to a married man and an unmarried woman, in order that he might be ordained to holy orders and accept a benefice even with cure, to the parish church of Aran, Sodor diocese, which belongs to lay patronage, vacant by the collation of Bean Johannis to the archdeaconry of the Isles, on condition that before 16 Kal. Sept. [17 Aug.] no third party has a prior claim. Provision to this parish, value not exceeding £20 sterling, has lapsed to the pope on account of the length of time it has remained vacant.[1]

Avignon, 4 Non. Jul., anno 13 ; expedited, 16 Kal. Oct., anno 13 [16 Sept., 1391] ; consigned, 14 Kal. Oct., anno 13 [18 Sept., 1391].

3 August, 1391   Reg Aven 268, 395v–6v

To Guy, bishop of Palestrina, papal nuncio. Statement of the nuncio's financial position with regard to his mission to the kingdoms of England, Scotland and Ireland, the province of Flanders, and the cities and dioceses of Tournai, Cambrai, Liège and Utrecht.

Avignon, 3 Non. Aug., anno 13.

8 August, 1391   Reg Aven 268, 453

To Hugh de Dalmehoy, B.LEG., canon of Moray. In order that the provisions granted him to a canonry of Glasgow with expectation of a prebend [15 Nov., 1378] and to a benefice with or without cure in the gift of the bishop, prior and chapter of St Andrews [19 Aug., 1385] might have speedier effect, the pope grants him precedence over all others, with the exception of cardinals, apostolic notaries, correctors of apostolic letters, masters of requests, papal judges and other papal servants or officials.

Avignon, 6 Id. Aug., anno 13 ; expedited, 2 Kal. Jul., anno 16 [30 June, 1394] ; consigned, 4 Kal. Aug., anno 16 [29 July, 1394].

21 August, 1391   Reg Aven 268, 431–1v

To Abbot Gilbert and the convent of Melrose, O.CIST., Glasgow

---

[1] See *CPP*, i, 576.

diocese. Indult granted to the abbot and his successors to wear a mitre and ring and other pontifical vestments, and to impart the blessing solemnly at the end of Mass, both in the abbey church and in the other churches, which are dependencies of the monastery, even when not fully dependent.

Avignon, 12 Kal. Sept., anno 13 ; expedited, 10 Kal. Mar., anno 15 [20 Feb., 1393].

SRO Vat. Trans., i, no. 67.

16 September, 1391   Reg Aven 268, 366v

To the bishop of Glasgow. Mandate to confirm the foundation, donation and institution of the convent of Southberwyk, O.CIST., St Andrews diocese, made by king David. The prioress and convent have petitioned the pope for confirmation.

Avignon, 16 Kal. Oct., anno 13.

31 October, 1390 × 30 October, 1391   Reg Aven 268, 311-11v

Ad perpetuam rei memoriam. Confirmation of the gift made to the abbot and convent of Holyrood de Edynburgh, O.S.A., St Andrews diocese, of the hospital of St Leonard near Edinburgh, with all its appurtenances, as is more fully contained in certain books drawn up at that time, the entire contents of which are confirmed in every detail.[1]

31 October, 1390 × 30 October, 1391   Reg Aven 268, 314v

It is granted to William Ramsay, canon of Dunkeld, that graces granted to others in that same diocese will not be prejudicial to him.[2]

---

[1] The register has been extensively damaged by water and some folios are mutilated. Apart from the opening phrase, no other part of this confirmation is legible, but its contents are summarised in the rubric on f. 8.

[2] As in the case of the previous letter, no part of this bull can be read and its contents are surmised only from what is provided in the rubric on f. 8.

18 November, 1391   Reg Vat 304, 11-11v

To the bishops of Argyll and Sodor, and the dean of St Pierre, Avignon. Mandate to provide Machabee Patricii to the parish church of St Fynan on Islay, Argyll diocese, vacant by the death of Roderick Maccathayl, last rector. John, lord of the Isles, patron of the church, presented Machabee to the chapter of Argyll, the bishopric being vacant at the time, and he was provided by them. This was confirmed by bishop John of Argyll, but Machabee has petitioned for papal confirmation.

Avignon, 14 Kal. Dec., anno 14; expedited, 5 Id. Jan., anno 14 [9 Jan., 1392]; consigned, 2 Id. Jan., anno 14 [12 Jan., 1392].

6 December, 1391   Reg Vat 302, 148v-9

To Conghan Macabei, priest, archdeacon of Argyll. Provision to the archdeaconry of Argyll, which is not a major dignity, but involves cure and is normally elective, value not exceeding 30 marks sterling, provision on this occasion being reserved to the pope. When the archdeaconry fell vacant by the promotion of John to the bishopric of Argyll, the pope provided Alexander de Wardlau [22 Nov., 1387], but he died before taking possession, whereupon the pope provided John Leche [14 Nov., 1388], who subsequently resigned it freely into the hands of Jean, bishop of Amiens, through his proxy, John Tretim, rector of the parish church of Greyo, Langres diocese. At present the archdeaconry is unlawfully occupied by David Marchard, priest of Argyll diocese. Upon obtaining possession, Conghan must resign the treasurership of Argyll, which is considered to be a dignity.

Avignon, 8 Id. Dec., anno 14; expedited, Id. Jan., anno 14 [13 Jan., 1392]; consigned, 18 Kal. Feb., anno 14 [15 Jan., 1392].

22 December, 1391   Reg Vat 302, 335-6

To the official of St Andrews. Mandate to provide Thomas Trailh, M.A., rector of the parish church of Fetchrressach, St Andrews diocese, to a canonry of Aberdeen with expectation of a prebend, and parsonage, perpetual administration, or office without cure, notwithstanding that he has received provision to a canonry of Moray with expectation of a prebend [17 Nov., 1378], but on condition that he resigns the parish church upon obtaining possession of a parsonage. Thomas is said to be studying theology.[1]
Avignon, 11 Kal. Jan., anno 14; consigned, 3 Non. Mar., anno 14 [5 Mar., 1392].

28 December, 1391   Reg Vat 303, 91v

To the bishop of Argyll, the archdeacon of Argyll, and Colin Cristini, canon of Argyll. Mandate to collate Donald Moricii, clerk of Sodor diocese, to the perpetual vicarage of the parish church of St Columba in Mule, same diocese, value not exceeding £5 sterling, vacant because the late Maruice Macsiri,[2] last vicar, having obtained peaceful possession for a year, neglected to be ordained priest within the prescribed limit of time. At present the vicarage is occupied unlawfully by Brice Clerici.[3]
Avignon, 5 Kal. Jan., anno 14; expedited, 3 Non. Feb., anno 14 [3 Feb., 1392]; consigned, 8 Id. Feb., anno 14 [6 Feb., 1392].

13 January, 1392   Reg Aven 269, 292-2v

To Nigel Cristini, priest of Sodor diocese. Dispensation to accept a dignity with or without cure, provided it is not the greatest dignity of a cathedral after that of the bishop, or the principal dignity of a collegiate church. From his petition it appears that Nigel was already dispensed from defect of birth, being born of a Benedictine monk in priest's orders and an unmarried woman, in order that he might be promoted to holy orders and accept a benefice, even if

---

[1] See Reg Supp 79, 16v.
[2] The name has been cancelled out in the original text and 'Macsiri' has been entered in the margin, but what was originally written looks much nearer to 'McFyn'.
[3] This provision is listed in the rubrics contained in Reg Aven 270, 603v.

with cure; and in virtue of this dispensation he was collated to the parish church of St Symoge, Argyll diocese. He received a more ample dispensation from cardinal Walter, papal legate, enabling him to hold, one, two, or three benefices, even if one was with cure. He resigned the first parish and obtained the parish church of St Molrwe, same diocese, and later he transferred to the parish church of St Bertan, vacant by the death of Mark, the last rector. Nigel was presented to the living by the king of Scots, the true patron, and the bishop and chapter admitted him to the parish, which was raised at the same time to the status of a prebend of the cathedral and Nigel was admitted as a canon. Pietro, cardinal priest of S. Pietro *in Vinculis*, was instructed verbally to authorize the bishop of Sodor to confirm this and to dispense Nigel to retain the parish church, canonry and prebend. Nigel has petitioned the pope for permission to accept a dignity with or without cure, if canonically provided, in order to augment his income, which is very meagre. He is said to have studied canon and civil law for three years. He need not mention his defect of birth or dispensation when petitioning for future graces.

Avignon, Id. Jan., anno 14; expedited, 3 Non. Mar., anno 14 [5 Mar., 1392]; consigned, 5 Id. Mar., anno 14 [11 Mar., 1392].

1 February, 1392   Reg Vat 302, 217v-18v

To Walter de Danyelston, LIC.ART., canon of Glasgow. Provision to a canonry of Glasgow with expectation of a prebend, and dignity with or without cure, or parsonage, or office without cure, even if the dignity is normally elective, but not the major one, notwithstanding that he holds a canonry and prebend of Aberdeen, or was provided by the pope to the parish church of Fin, Glasgow diocese, without ever obtaining possession. The letters of provision cease to be valid whenever he obtains possession of a dignity, or parsonage, in virtue of this present provision. Walter is said to be nobly born and to be studying civil law at Avignon.[1]

Avignon, Kal. Feb., anno 14; expedited, 14 Kal. Aug., anno 15 [19 July, 1393]; consigned, 11 Kal. Aug., anno 15 [22 July, 1393].

P   [1] See *CPP*, i, 577.

Concurrent mandate to the abbots of Paisley and Kilwinning, and the dean of St Agricola, Avignon.

4 February, 1392   Reg Vat 303, 51-51v

To David de Seton, priest, canon and archdeacon of Ross. Provision to a canonry, prebend, and the archdeaconry of Ross, which is a dignity, or parsonage with cure, and normally elective, vacant by the resignation of Jean, bishop of Tusculum, made freely into the pope's own hands. The cardinal was previously dispensed to hold the archdeaconry [3 Dec., 1381].[1]
Avignon, 2 Non. Feb., anno 14; expedited, 15 Kal. Mar., anno 14 [15 Feb., 1392]; consigned, 14 Kal. Mar., anno 14 [16 Feb., 1392].
Concurrent mandate to the bishop of Amiens, the treasurer of Moray, and the official of Paris.

25 May, 1392   Reg Vat 304, 268-8v

To Alexander Trail, LIC.LEG., rector of the parish church of Kilmany, St Andrews diocese. Whereas Alexander in person has freely resigned the parish church of Munimosk, Aberdeen diocese, and Laurence Trail, through his proxy, John Triht, clerk, has freely resigned the parish church of Kylmanx, St Andrews diocese, both into the hands of Giovanni, cardinal priest of S. Anastasia, in order to effect an exchange of benefices. Wherefore the pope confers the parish church of Kilmany, vacant by this resignation, on Alexander, notwithstanding that he already holds canonries and prebends of Aberdeen and Moray.
Avignon, 8 Kal. Jun., anno 14; expedited, Id. Sept., anno 14 [13 Sept., 1392]; consigned, 15 Kal. Oct., anno 14 [17 Sept., 1392].
Concurrent mandate to the dean of St Pierre, Avignon, and the officials of Aberdeen and Moray.

25 May, 1392   Reg Vat 304, 269-9v

To Laurence Trayl, rector of the parish church of Monymusk, Aberdeen diocese. Whereas Laurence, through his proxy, John

---

[1] This provision is listed in the rubrics contained in Reg Aven 270, 602v.

Triht, clerk, has freely resigned the parish church of Kilmany, St Andrews diocese, and Alexander Trayl in person has freely resigned the parish church of Munimosk, Aberdeen diocese, both into the hands of Giovanni, cardinal priest of S. Anastasia, in order to effect an exchange of benefices. Wherefore the pope confers on Laurence the parish church of Monymusk, vacant by this resignation.
Avignon, 8 Kal. Jun., anno 14; expedited, 16 Kal. Oct., anno 14 [16 Sept., 1392]; consigned, 13 Kal. Oct., anno 14 [19 Sept., 1392]. Concurrent mandate to the prior of St Andrews, the dean of St Agricola, Avignon, and the archdeacon of St Andrews.

27 May, 1392   Reg Vat 302, 277-7v

To the abbots of Scone and Arbroath, and the official of Dunkeld. Mandate to collate John de Lychcon, rector of the parish church of Dysert, St Andrews diocese, to the prebend of Brechin, which he obtained in virtue of a papal provision to the canonry and prebend of Brechin, vacant by the death of the late William Dalgarnok, canon of Brechin [1 Nov., 1378]. John has petitioned the pope for confirmation and this is granted, even if the prebend is considered vacant by the deaths of William Darganok, or John de Alwas, or Gilbert de Lyle, and John is to have precedence over all others in obtaining effect to this collation.
Avignon, 6 Kal. Jun., anno 14; expedited, 2 Non. Jul., anno 14 [6 July, 1392]; consigned, 7 Id. Jul., anno 14 [9 July, 1392].

27 May, 1392   Reg Vat 303, 464v-5v

To the archdeacon of Lothian, St Andrews diocese. Mandate to collate Henry de Lychton, nobly born, deacon of Brechin diocese, to the perpetual vicarage of the parish church of Markinche, St Andrews diocese, to which he was provided by John de Lichon, rector of the parish church of Ysert, same diocese, the vicar general of bishop Walter of St Andrews, who authorized him specially to do this, after the death of John de Kynros.[1]
Avignon, 6 Kal. Jun., anno 14; expedited, 7 Id. Aug., anno 15 [7 Aug., 1393]; consigned, 3 Id. Aug., anno 15 [11 Aug., 1393].

[1] This provision is listed in the rubrics contained in Reg Aven 270, 612v.

9 June, 1392   Reg Aven 269, 391v

To the bishops of St Andrews, Glasgow and Aberdeen. Mandate
to enquire into the marriage of Alexander, earl of Buchan, and
Euphemia, countess of Ross, which was contracted *per verba legitima
de presenti*. They remained together only for a short time and the
marriage has been the cause of wars, plundering, arson, murders,
and many other damages and scandals, and it is likely that more will
happen if they remain united in this union. Having called together
the parties, the bishops are to pass canonical sentence on the case.[1]
Avignon, 5 Id. Jun., anno 14; expedited, 3 Non. Jul., anno 14 [5
July, 1392]; consigned, 7 Id. Jul., anno 14 [9 July, 1392].
SRO Vat. Trans., iv, no. 57.

9 June, 1392   Reg Aven 269, 397

To Murdach, son of Robert, earl of Fife, and Isabella, daughter of
Duncan, earl of Lennox, St Andrews and Glasgow dioceses.
Dispensation from the impediment to marriage arising from the
fourth degree of consanguinity and spiritual affinity. Isabella was
related in the fourth degree of consanguinity to Joan, deceased wife
of Murdach, while Isabella's father, before her birth, was godfather
at baptism to Murdach.
Avignon, 5 Id. Jun., anno 14.
SRO Vat. Trans., iv, no. 58.

9 June, 1392   Reg Vat 304, 133v-4v

To the official of Glasgow. Mandate to collate Malcolm Cristini,
priest of Lismore diocese, to the parish church of St Modan in
Cogallo, same diocese, vacant by the resignation of Duncan de
Bute, last rector, made freely into the hands of bishop John of
Lismore. The bishop provided Malcolm to the living by his ordinary
authority, but since this provision has been contested, Malcolm has
petitioned the pope for confirmation.
Avignon, 5 Id. Jun., anno 14; expedited, 5 Id. Jul., anno 14 [11
July, 1392]; consigned, 3 Id. Jul., anno 14 [13 July, 1392].

[1] Followed by further commissions on 5 Dec., 1392, see p 181 below.

9 June, 1392   Reg Vat 304, 164-4v

To the official of Glasgow. Mandate to collate John de Congallo, priest of Lismore diocese, to the parish church of the Three Holy Brethern de Kenlochgoyl, same diocese, vacant by the transfer of John Malcolm by ordinary authority to the parish church of St Peter the Deacon, Lismore diocese. John de Congallo was presented to the living by the true patron, Colin Cambel, donzel of that diocese, and instituted by bishop Martin of Lismore, but his presentation and institution have been contested and he has petitioned the pope for confirmation.
Avignon, 5 Id. Jun., anno 14; expedited, 6 Kal. Aug., anno 14 [27 July, 1392]; consigned, 4 Kal. Aug., anno 14 [29 July, 1392].

12 September, 1392   Reg Aven 269, 466-7

To Walter, bishop of St Andrews. Mandate to provide Adam de Duffton, priest, monk of the monastery of Cupro, O.CIST., St Andrews diocese, as abbot of the monastery of Balmurynach, same order, said diocese, the office being vacant by the resignation of abbot John Plater, made into the hands of abbot Gilbert of Melros. Provision of an abbot to the monastery was reserved to the pope, and the abbatial blessing is to be imparted on Adam and his oath of fidelity to the Apostolic See, made in the prescribed form and duly sealed, is to be sent to the pope as soon as possible.
Avignon, 2 Id. Sept., anno 14; expedited, 13 Kal. Oct., anno 14 [19 Sept., 1392]; consigned, 12 Kal. Oct., anno 14 [20 Sept., 1392].
SRO Vat. Trans., i, no. 68.

12 September, 1392   Reg Aven 269, 467-7v

To William de Conyngham, rector of the parish church of Bothans, St Andrews diocese. More ample dispensation, having already been dispensed from defect of birth, being born out of wedlock to a nobleman and an unmarried woman, in order that he might be ordained priest and be provided to the parish church of Bothans, that he may now hold three benefices with or without cure, even if canonries and prebends, elective dignities, parsonages, administra-

tions, or offices, even if the dignity is the greatest of a cathedral, or the principal one of a collegiate church, without having to mention his defect or the dispensation when petitioning for future graces.
Avignon, 2 Id. Sept., anno 14; expedited, 13 Kal. Oct., anno 14 [19 Sept., 1392]; consigned, 11 Kal. Oct., anno 14 [21 Sept., 1392].

13 September, 1392   Reg Aven 269, 460v

To Adam de Duffton, monk of the monastery of Cupar, o.cist., St Andrews diocese. Appointment as an honorary chaplain of the pope.[1]
Avignon, Id. Sept., anno 14; expedited, 13 Kal. Oct., anno 14 [19 Sept., 1392]; consigned, 11 Kal. Oct., anno 14 [21 Sept., 1392].

23 September, 1392   Reg Aven 269, 473v

To Adam de Duffton, priest, papal chaplain, monk of the monastery of Cupar, o.cist., St Andrews diocese. Dispensation from defect of birth, being born out of wedlock, that he may be provided to any administration, office, or dignity of the Cistercian Order, even the office of abbot.[2]
Avignon, 9 Kal. Oct., anno 14; expedited, 6 Kal. Oct., anno 14 [26 Sept., 1392]; consigned, 5 Kal. Oct., anno 14 [27 Sept., 1392].

23 September, 1392   Reg Vat 303, 27v-28v

To John de Hallis, abbot of the monastery of Newbattle, o.cist., St Andrews diocese. Provision as abbot of the monastery of Newbattle, vacant by the death of abbot Hugh, during whose lifetime provision was reserved to the pope. John is a priest and a professed monk of the monastery of Melros, same order, Glasgow diocese.
Avignon, 9 Kal. Oct., anno 14; expedited, 10 Kal. Jan., anno 15 [23 Dec., 1392]; consigned, 3 Non. Jan., anno 15 [3 Jan., 1393].

---

[1] In Reg Aven 268, 573v it is recorded that Adam de Duffton was received as an honorary papal chaplain and took the customy oath on 23 Dec., 1392.
[2] This provision is listed in the rubrics contained in Reg Aven 270, 601v.

Concurrent mandate to the convent of Newbattle, the vassals, the abbot of Melrose, and king Robert.

SRO Vat. Trans., i, no. 69.

27 September, 1392   Reg Vat 304, 418v-19

To the official of St Andrews. Mandate to reserve to William Thomas, priest of Glasgow diocese, the perpetual vicarage of the parish church of Oueston, same diocese, to be vacated by Brice de Oueston on account of incompatibility of benefices.

Avignon, 5 Kal. Oct., anno 14; expedited, 4 Kal. Oct., anno 14 [28 Sept., 1392]; consigned, 3 Kal. Oct., anno 14 [29 Sept., 1392].

12 October, 1392   Reg Aven 269, 139v-40

To William de Forfare, B.DEC., priest, canon of St Mary's de Jedburgh, O.S.A., Glasgow diocese. Reservation of a benefice with or without cure usually held by the canons of Jedburgh or St Andrews, even if a priory, administration, or office, in the gift of the abbot and convent of Jedburgh, or the prior and convent of St Andrews, together or separately, value not exceeding 30 marks sterling.

Avignon, 4 Id. Oct., anno 14; expedited, 16 Kal. Dec., anno 15 [16 Nov., 1392]; consigned, 15 Kal. Dec., anno 15 [17 Nov., 1392].

Concurrent mandate to the abbots of Melrose and Newbattle, and the dean of St Agricola, Avignon.

20 October, 1392   Reg Aven 269, 523-3v

To the bishop, chanter and chancellor of Glasgow. Mandate to enforce the Constitution of Benedict XII and ensure that William de Forfar, B.DEC., professed canon of St Mary's de Jeddeworth, O.S.A., Glasgow diocese, be allowed to attend a university, while receiving an annual pension from the abbot and convent of his monastery.

Avignon, 13 Kal. Nov., anno 14.

SRO Vat. Trans., i, no. 70.

31 October, 1391 × 30 October, 1392   Reg Aven 270, 622v

A mandate is issued to collate Michael de Balcongy to a benefice in the gift of the bishop and chapter of St Andrews.[1]

31 October, 1391 × 30 October, 1392   Reg Aven 270, 627

An indult is granted to abbot Gilbert of Melrose to visit certain monasteries by proxy.

31 October, 1391 × 30 October, 1392   Reg Aven 270, 627

Colin Cristini is dispensed to hold two incompatible benefices.

31 October, 1391 × 30 October, 1392   Reg Aven 270, 628

Appeal of the pope to the prelates throughout the realm of Scotland to make known publicly the miserable state of the city of Smyrna, to move the people in those parts to extend a helping hand for the assistance and defence of that city, a charitable work which will obtain for them the remission of their sins.[2]

31 October, 1391 × 30 October, 1392   Reg Aven 270, 631

A dispensation is granted that John de Douglas may be admitted to the clerical state and promoted to holy orders, notwithstanding his illegitimate birth, and that he may accept any ecclesiastical benefice.

---

[1] The following eight Scottish entries appear only in the rubrics contained in Reg Aven 270, 600-1 which in part correspond with the contents of Reg Vat 303, 1-541, but unfortunately for these eight the corresponding letters have not been found in any other register of Clement VII and it must be presumed that a complete register of his fourteenth pontifical year has been lost.

[2] For the considerable influence that Clement VII exercised over the Latin Church in the East, cf. N. Valois, *La France et le Grand Schism d'Occident*, ii (Paris, 1896), 218-24. This bull to the Scottish Church should be taken in conjunction with the appeal that the pope made to Christendom on behalf of Smyrna which was under continual threat from the Turks and had been devastated by an earthquake, in Reg Aven 269, 326-7, dated 4 Non. Jan., anno 14 [2 Jan., 1392].

31 October, 1391 × 30 October, 1392   Reg Aven 270, 636v

Confirmation is granted of the collation and provision made to John Barber of the parish church of Tarnas, Aberdeen diocese.

31 October, 1391 × 30 October, 1392   Reg Aven 270, 637v

A mandate is issued that certain monks of the monastery of Neubotil, St Andrews diocese, be received into other houses of the Cistercian Order in the realm of Scotland.

31 October, 1391 × 30 October, 1392   Reg Aven 270, 638

A dispensation is granted to Michael de Balcongy that he may accept a parish church that belongs to lay patronage.

15 November, 1392   Reg Aven 273, 565v

To Duncan Petit, priest of Glasgow diocese. Whereas Duncan was collated by ordinary authority to the archdeaconry of Galloway, which is a dignity with cure, and also to the parish church of Kellis, Galloway diocese, which he believed to be united to the archdeaconry, and he has held these now for many years without obtaining a dispensation. Moreover, he had himself ordained priest within two months of receiving this collation and he has frequently exercised his holy orders. He has also accepted many other benefices with and without cure, which have been obtained by papal and ordinary authority. Others have said, however, that the archdeaconry and the parish church are not united and Duncan has resigned them. Wherefore the pope *motu proprio* absolves Duncan from all irregularity and infamy, because he was the secretary of the late king David, and also *motu proprio* he confers the benefices on him anew.

Avignon, 17 Kal. Dec., anno 15 ; expedited, 16 Kal. Feb., anno 16 [17 Jan., 1394] ; consigned, 12 Kal. Feb., anno 16 [21 Jan., 1394].

24 November, 1392   Reg Vat 306, 134-4v

To James Beset, LIC.DEC., canon of St Andrews, O.S.A., perpetual vicar of the parish church of Kilgour, St Andrews diocese. Whereas James in person freely resigned the perpetual vicarage of the parish church of Forgrund, St Andrews diocese, and William de Balmyle, through his proxy, William de Nary, freely resigned the perpetual vicarage of the parish church of Kylgour, same diocese, both into the hands of Giles, bishop of Nimes, in order to effect an exchange of benefices. James was provided by the pope to the vicarage of Kilgour, vacant by this resignation, but doubt has arisen about the validity of his provision on the grounds that at the time of the exchange neither had a right to the respective vicarages, since the vicarage of Kilgour in the past was served by canons of St Andrews, o.s.a., whereas the vicarage of Forgan was served by the secular clergy, and his vicarage is said to be still vacant. James has petitioned the pope for confirmation and this is hereby granted, together with a dispensation to retain the priory of Loch Levyn, o.s.a., St Andrews diocese, to which he has also been provided by the pope, even although it involves cure, provided that in the priory and the vicarage the cure of souls is not neglected.

Avignon, 8 Kal. Dec., anno 15; expedited, 8 Kal. Maii, anno 15 [24 Apr., 1393]; consigned, 6 Kal. Maii, anno 15 [26 Apr., 1393].

Concurrent mandate to the bishop of Dunkeld, the dean of St Agricola, Avignon, and the official of Dunkeld.

24 November, 1392   Reg Vat 306, 181-2

To William de Balmyle, perpetual vicar of the parish church of Forgan, St Andrews diocese. Whereas William, through his proxy, William de Nary, freely resigned the perpetual vicarage of the parish church of Kylgour, St Andrews diocese, and James Beset freely resigned the perpetual vicarage of the parish church of Forgan, same diocese, both into the hands of Giles, bishop of Nimes, in order to effect an exchange of benefices. William was provided by the pope to the vicarage of Forgrund, vacant by this resignation, but doubt has arisen about the validity of his provision on the grounds that at the time of the exchange neither had a right to the respective vicarages, since the vicarage of Forgan in the past was served by the secular clergy, whereas the vicarage of Kilgour was served by canons of St Andrews, o.s.a. William has petitioned the

pope for confirmation of his provision and this is hereby granted him.
Avignon, 8 Kal. Dec., anno 15; expedited, 8 Kal. Maii, anno 15 [24 Apr., 1393]; consigned, 6 Kal. Maii, anno 15 [26 Apr., 1393]. Concurrent mandate to the bishop of Dunkeld, the prior of St Andrews, and the dean of St Agricola, Avignon.

5 December, 1392   Reg Aven 272, 569

To the bishops of St Andrews, Glasgow and Aberdeen. Mandate to enquire into the marriage of Alexander, earl of Buchan, and his wife Euphemia, who in her petition to the pope accuses him of having committed adultery with Mariette Nilzarre, a woman of Ross diocese, of having had issue by her and of continuing to live in concubinage with her, to the great peril of his soul, injury to his wife, as well as the grave scandal given to many others. He has detained his wife's goods and property. The bishops are to call together the parties concerned and to grant Euphemia a separation from bed and board, together with the restoration of her belongings. Avignon, Non. Dec., anno 15; expedited, 19 Kal. Jan., anno 15 [14 Dec., 1392]; consigned, 18 Kal. Jan., anno 15 [15 Dec., 1392]. SRO Vat. Trans., iv, no. 59.

5 December, 1392   Reg Aven 272, 569

To the same. Identical commission as the previous one, except that the name of the woman accused of committing adultery with the earl is given as Mariette Enyenachyn.
Avignon, Non. Dec., anno 15; consigned, 12 Kal. Jan., anno 15 [21 Dec., 1392].
SRO Vat. Trans., iv, no. 60.

1 February, 1393   Reg Vat 305, 3v-8v; 306, 1-6

To Pedro, cardinal deacon of S. Maria in Cosmedin, papal nuncio. Appointment as papal nuncio to the kingdom of Scotland, the provinces of Flanders, Brabant, and Hainaut, and the cities and dioceses of Liège and Utrecht.

Avignon, Kal. Feb., anno 15.
Likewise to the kingdoms of England and Ireland. Likewise to the kingdom of France. [There then follows a long list of the extensive faculties granted to the nuncio under this same date, to facilitate his mission.][1]

2 February, 1393   Reg Aven 272, 372-2v

To Master John Geyn, professor o.s.a.e. of Glasgow diocese. Appointment as an honorary chaplain of the pope.[2]
Avignon, 4 Non. Feb., anno 15; expedited, 2 Non. Jun., anno 15 [4 June, 1393]; consigned, 2 Non. Jun., anno 15 [4 June, 1393].

15 April, 1393   Reg Vat 305, 197-8

To William Ramsay, B.DEC., priest, canon and archdeacon of Brechin. Provision to a canonry and the archdeaconry of Brechin, value not exceeding 20 marks sterling, vacant by the free resignation of Thomas Senescalli, made at the Roman Curia by his proxy, John Trich, into the hands of Guillaume, cardinal deacon of S. Angelo. It is said by some that the archdeaconry, which is not elective, may be held only by the canons. William is provided even if the archdeaconry is a dignity, parsonage, or office, but not the greatest dignity of the cathedral after that of the bishop, and he is dispensed to hold it together with the parish church of Tanadas, St Andrews diocese, and notwithstanding that he has received from the pope provision to a canonry of Dunkeld with expectation of a prebend, and dignity, parsonage, or office, with or without cure [21 Dec., 1387], on condition that the cure of souls is not neglected in any of these benefices.
Avignon, 17 Kal. Maii, anno 15; expedited, 2 Kal. Jun., anno 15 [31 May, 1393]; consigned, 8 Id. Jun., anno 15 [6 June, 1393].
Concurrent mandate to the deans of Dunkeld and of St Pierre, Avignon, and the official of St Andrews.

---

[1] For the list of the extensive faculties granted to the nuncio, who later became Pope Benedict XIII, under this same date to facilitate his mission *see* Reg Vat 305, 10-13, 17-21v.
[2] In Reg Aven 268, 579v it is recorded that Hugh de Dalmehoy took the oath on John Geyn's behalf on 21 June, 1393, as is testified in a notarial instrument drawn up by Jean Faber of Toul.

19 April, 1393   Reg Aven 273, 393v

To John de Balnawys, canon of the church of Abernethy, Dunblane diocese. Dispensation to retain his canonry of Abbyrnethy together with the perpetual vicarage of the parish church of Collessy, St Andrews diocese, notwithstanding a contrary statute of the founder, confirmed by papal authority, which prohibits the canons from holding a second benefice involving residence.
Avignon, 13 Kal. Maii, anno 15; expedited, 2 Kal. Jun., anno 15 [31 May, 1393]; consigned, 8 Id. Jun., anno 15 [6 June, 1393].

21 April, 1393   Reg Vat 306, 326-6v

To the abbot of Fearn, Ross diocese. Isaac de Monroy freely resigned a canonry of Ross and the prebend of Cantayne into the hands of bishop Alexander of Ross, and the parish church of Tyry, Aberdeen diocese, into the hands of bishop Gilbert of Aberdeen, and Thomas Hale freely resigned the chancellorship of Ross into the hands of the said bishop of Ross, in order to effect an exchange of benefices. Thomas was provided by ordinary authority to the canonry and prebend of Ross, and instituted to the parish church of Tyrie, after due presentation to the bishop of Aberdeen by James de Lyndesay, layman, true patron of the church. Isaac received collation to the chancellorship of Ross by ordinary authority, but since doubts have been raised about the validity of his collation and the chancellorship is said to be still vacant, he has petitioned the pope for confirmation and the abbot is hereby commissioned to grant him this.
Avignon, 11 Kal. Maii, anno 15; expedited, 7 Id. Aug., anno 15 [7 Aug., 1393]; consigned, 3 Id. Aug., anno 15 [11 Aug., 1393].

26 April, 1393   Reg Aven 273, 183

To Alexander de Hadinton, canon of the cathedral of St Andrews, o.s.a. Indult for a plenary remission of his sins to be granted at the hour of death by a confessor of his own choice.
Avignon, 6 Kal. Maii, anno 15.

28 April, 1393   Reg Aven 273, 361v-2

To Cuthbert de Brechyn, priest, chanter of Brechin. Dispensation to accept a second benefice with cure and hold it together with the chantership of Brechin, which is a dignity with cure, value not exceeding 20 marks sterling.
Avignon, 4 Kal. Maii, anno 15; expedited, 6 Id. Maii, anno 15 [10 May, 1393]; consigned, 6 Id. Maii, anno 15 [10 May, 1393].

3 May, 1393   Reg Vat 305, 191-2

To the prior of Restennet, the dean of St Agricola, Avignon, and the official of Brechin. Mandate to collate Cuthbert de Brechin, priest of Dunkeld diocese, to the chantership of Brechin and the annexed benefices. Upon the death of the late Alexander Dog, bishop Stephen provided Cuthbert to the chantership, which is a non-elective dignity with cure, value not exceeding 20 marks sterling and he has enjoyed peaceful possession for six years. Since his tenure is now disputed on the grounds that the chantership was vacant, not by the death of Alexander Dog, but rather by the promotion by the pope of Salomon Ra as dean of Dunkeld [3 Dec., 1381], Cuthbert has petitioned the pope for confirmation. He studied Arts at Paris.
Avignon, 5 Non. Maii, anno 15; expedited, 6 Id. Maii, anno 15 [10 May, 1393]; consigned, 6 Id. Maii, anno 15 [10 May, 1393].

4 May, 1393   Reg Vat 306, 311-12

To James Biset, LIC.DEC., prior of the priory of Loch Leven, O.S.A., St Andrews diocese. Provision as prior of the priory of Loch Leven, which is a dependency of St Andrews, O.S.A., and is usually served by one of the canons. It is neither a dignity, nor a parsonage, nor is it elective, value not exceeding £40 sterling. It is vacant by the provision by the pope of Robert de Monros as prior of St Andrews [19 Apr., 1387], which is the greatest dignity after that of the bishop, or by the resignation of David Bell, a former prior and papal chaplain, or by the resignation of the said Robert de Monros, made fraudulently outwith the Roman Curia. James is dispensed to retain the perpetual vicarage of the parish church of Kylgour, St Andrews diocese [24 Nov., 1392], together with the priory, which also involves cure of souls.

Avignon, 4 Non. Maii, anno 15; expedited, 19 Kal. Sept., anno 15 [14 Aug., 1393]; consigned, 5 Kal. Sept., anno 15 [28 Aug., 1393].

Concurrent mandate to the bishop of Brechin, the abbot of Arbroath, and the dean of St Pierre, Avignon.

12 May, 1393   Reg Aven 271, 96v-97

To the deans of Argyll and St Agricola, Avignon, and the official of Glasgow. Mandate to confirm the collation of Duncan Patricii, priest of Sodor diocese, to the perpetual vicarage of the parish church of St John the Evangelist on the island of Mula. The vicarage was vacated by the resignation of Kenneth Macadam, made into the hands of bishop Michael of Sodor, whereupon Duncan was presented to the living by abbot Fingon of Hy, o.s.b., to whom the right of presentation belongs by ancient and time honoured custom, and Duncan was instituted by the bishop and has had peaceful possession ever since, but he has petitioned the pope for confirmation of his provision.

Avignon, 4 Id. Maii, anno 15; expedited, 2 Kal. Jun., anno 15 [31 May, 1393]; consigned, 4 Non. Jun., anno 15 [2 June, 1393].

20 May, 1393   Reg Aven 272, 422v

To John de Douglas, B.LEG., dean of Moray. Extension of the dispensation to retain the parish church of Newlandis, Glasgow diocese, together with the deanship of Moray, which is a major dignity with cure, the period of two years since his provision being elapsed [21 Mar., 1391], after which time he was to exchange one or other of these for another compatible benefice, or resign the deanship. This extension is granted at the petition of his kinswoman, queen Annabella of Scotland, because the income from the deanship is so meagre and has been greatly reduced on account of the wars that have been waged in those parts. The parish church of Newlands belongs to lay patronage, and cure of souls must not be neglected in either benefice.

Avignon, 13 Kal. Jun., anno 15; expedited, 15 Kal. Jul., anno 15 [17 June, 1393]; consigned, 13 Kal. Jul., anno 15 [19 June, 1393].

22 May, 1393   Reg Aven 273, 432

To Patrick de Palding, M.A., canon of Moray. Dispensation to hold a canonry and prebend of Moray together with the parish church of Lundi, St Andrews diocese, and accept a dignity, parsonage, or office, with cure, even if the dignity is the greatest of a cathedral, or principal one of a collegiate church, provided cure of souls is not neglected in the parish or in the benefice involving cure. Patrick declares himself a kinsman of king Robert.

Avignon, 11 Kal. Jun., anno 15; expedited, 6 Id. Jul., anno 15 [10 July, 1393]; consigned, 11 Kal. Aug., anno 15 [22 July, 1393].

24 May, 1393   Reg Vat 306, 246-6v

To John de Karale, perpetual vicar of the parish church of Banff, Aberdeen diocese. Whereas the pope empowered the abbot of Paseleto and two other executors to confer, or reserve, twelve benefices with or without cure in each of the cathedrals, cities, and dioceses of Scotland, even if canonries and prebends, dignities, parsonages, or offices, in whosesoever gift, for suitable persons to be named by king Robert. And whereas recently John, through his proxy, William de Nary, clerk of St Andrews diocese, has freely resigned the deanship of Brechin, and Andrew de Kyle in person has resigned the perpetual vicarage of the parish church of Banff, both into the hands of Giovanni, cardinal priest of S. Anastasia, in order to effect an exchange of benefices. Wherefore the pope confers on John the said vicarage of Banff, vacant by this resignation, even although it is said that the abbot of Paisley had reserved a benefice for Andrew, who was thereby obliged to resign the vicarage upon obtaining possession of a dignity, parsonage, or office with cure.

Avignon, 9 Kal. Jun., anno 15; expedited, 12 Kal. Jul., anno 15 [20 June, 1393]; consigned, 11 Kal. Jul., anno 15 [21 June, 1393].

Concurrent mandate to the deans of Dunblane and St Agricola, Avignon, and the archdeacon of Moray.

24 May, 1393   Reg Vat 306, 267-8

To Andrew de Kyle, dean of Brechin. Whereas the pope empowered the abbot of Paseleto and two other executors to confer, or reserve, twelve benefices with or without cure in each of the cathedrals, cities, and dioceses of Scotland, even if canonries and prebends, dignities, parsonages, or offices, in whosesoever gift, for suitable persons to be named by king Robert. And whereas recently Andrew in person has freely resigned the perpetual vicarage of the parish church of Bamffe, Aberdeen diocese, and John de Karale, through his proxy, William de Nary, clerk of St Andrews diocese, has freely resigned the deanship of Brechin, both into the hands of Giovanni, cardinal priest of S. Anastasia, in order to effect an exchange of benefices. Wherefore the pope confers on Andrew the deanship of Brechin, which is the greatest dignity after that of the bishop and is normally elective, even if it involves cure, vacant by this resignation, and even although it is said that the abbot of Paisley had reserved a benefice for Andrew, who was thereby obliged to resign the vicarage upon obtaining possession of a dignity, parsonage, or office with cure.
Avignon, 9 Kal. Jun., anno 15; expedited, 12 Kal. Jul., anno 15 [20 June, 1393]; consigned, 11 Kal. Jul., anno 15 [21 June, 1393]. Concurrent mandate to the deans of Aberdeen, Dunblane, and St Agricola, Avignon.

26 May, 1393   Reg Aven 272, 422

To Robert Adyson, perpetual vicar of the parish church of Colmanell, Glasgow diocese. Dispensation to hold the perpetual chaplaincy of the chapel of the Holy Trinity in the parish church of St John the Baptist at Are, Glasgow diocese, which entails personal residence by the intention of the founder, together with the perpetual vicarage of the parish church of Colmanell, same diocese, which he should have resigned upon obtaining provision to the chaplaincy,

Q

or resigning the vicarage, to accept a similar or dissimilar benefice, provided the cure of souls is not neglected.

Avignon, 7 Kal. Jun., anno 15; expedited, 18 Kal. Jul., anno 15 [14 June, 1393]; consigned, 14 Kal. Jul., anno 15 [18 June, 1393].

26 May, 1393   Reg Aven 273, 9-9v

To Robert Adyson, perpetual vicar of the parish church of Colmanell, Glasgow diocese. Indult to derive the revenues of the perpetual vicarage of the parish church of Colmanell, Glasgow diocese, together with those of the perpetual chaplaincy of the chapel of the Holy Trinity in the parish church of St John the Baptist at Are, same diocese, exception being made for daily distributions, if there are such, just as if he was resident personally in both.

Avignon, 7 Kal. Jun., anno 15.

Concurrent mandate to the abbot of Crossraguel, the dean of Glasgow, and Thomas de Butil, canon of Glasgow.

30 May, 1393   Reg Aven 272, 402v-3

To all Christ's faithful. Indulgence of one year and forty days is granted to all who visit the parish church of St John the Evangelist in Arduis de Mulle, Sodor diocese, on the principal feasts of the year, the feast of St John the Evangelist [27 Dec.] and on the feast of the Dedication of the church, and fifty days indulgence during their octaves and the six days after Pentecost, and contribute towards its upkeep.

Avignon, 3 Kal. Jun., anno 15; expedited, 4 Id. Jun., anno 15 [10 June, 1393].

SRO Vat. Trans., i, no. 71; printed: *Highland Papers*, iv, 144-6.

30 May, 1393   Reg Aven 272, 403

To the bishop of Sodor. Faculty to dispense Hector Macgileeom, donzel, and Mor, daughter of Calen Cambel, damsel, of Sodor and Argyll dioceses, from the impediment to marriage arising from the third and fourth degrees of consanguinity. Notwithstanding their knowledge of this impediment, they have espoused themselves to be married, without subsequent consummation, in order to establish peace and harmony among their families and friends, whereas until now there have only been wars, dissensions, murders and other grave scandals.

Avignon, 3 Kal. Jun., anno 15.

SRO Vat. Trans., iv, no. 61.

31 May, 1393   Reg Aven 272, 409v-10

To Odon Macayd, rector of the parish church of St Coman, Sodor diocese. Provision[1] to the parish church of St Coman, Sodor diocese, notwithstanding that at present it is occupied unlawfully by Andrew Macheacerna, priest of Argyll diocese, who was dispensed from defect of birth, being born of a clerk and an unmarried woman, and received collation to the parish church of St Kewan, Argyll diocese, peaceful possession of which he enjoyed for many years. Upon the death of Dugald Mafinnius, rector of the parish church of St Colman, Andrew moved there uncanonically and obtained collation by authority of the bishop, but lawful provision has lapsed to the pope on account of the period of time that the parish has remained vacant.

Avignon, 2 Kal. Jun., anno 15; expedited, 6 Kal. Jul., anno 15 [26 June, 1393]; consigned, 5 Kal. Jul., anno 15 [27 June, 1393].

31 May, 1393   Reg Vat 306, 255v-6v

To the official of Sodor. Mandate to collate Angus Macayd, clerk of Sodor diocese, to the parish church of St Constantine, Argyll diocese, vacant by the death of Maelmore Mec Clemente. Angus was presented to the parish by John of the Isles, donzel of Sodor diocese and true patron, and this was approved by bishop John of Argyll within the legal limit of time. Angus has had peaceful possession for a year or thereabouts, but since he was only in his twenty-second year at the time of his induction, he has begun to doubt the validity of his tenure and has petitioned the pope for confirmation, which is hereby granted him, together with the necessary dispensation from defect of age.

[1] This provision was made originally on 19 July, 1382, see p 79 above.

Avignon, 2 Kal. Jun., anno 15; expedited, 4 Kal. Jul., anno 15 [28 June, 1393]; consigned, 2 Kal. Jul., anno 15 [30 June, 1393].

7 June, 1393   Reg Vat 306, 235-5v

To Finlay Nigelli, clerk of Sodor diocese. Reservation of a benefice in the gift of the bishop, chapter and single parsons of Sodor, together or separately, to the value of 20 marks sterling with cure, or 15 marks sterling without cure, provided it is not a canonry and prebend.[1]
Avignon, 7 Id. Jun., anno 15; expedited, 6 Kal. Jul., anno 15 [26 June, 1393]; consigned, 5 Kal. Jul., anno 15 [27 June, 1393].
Concurrent mandate to the abbot of Saddell, the dean of St Agricola, Avignon, and Malcolm Cristini, canon of Argyll.

14 June, 1393   Reg Aven 271, 138-9

To Thomas Bel, priest, perpetual vicar of the parish church of Lintrathen, St Andrews diocese. Provision to the perpetual vicarage with cure of the parish church of Lintrecyyn, St Andrews diocese, value not exceeding 20 silver marks, vacant by the transfer of John de Harunk, familiar of cardinal Walter, bishop of Glasgow, to the perpetual vicarage of Dunlop, Glasgow diocese, made by the cardinal's ordinary authority.
Avignon, 18 Kal. Jul., anno 15; expedited, 12 Kal. Aug., anno 15 [21 July, 1393]; consigned, 10 Kal. Aug., anno 15 [23 July, 1393].
Concurrent mandate to the dean of St Agricola, Avignon, the chanter of Brechin, and the treasurer of Glasgow.

15 June, 1393   Reg Aven 273, 406v-7

To John de Douglas, scholar of St Andrews diocese. Whereas John was born out of wedlock to a nobleman and an unmarried woman and is not yet of age to obtain a benefice with cure, being only in his seventeenth year. Previously[2] he was dispensed from his defect of birth in order to enter the clerical state and be promoted to all holy

---

[1] See *CPP*, i, 577.   [2] See p 178 above.

orders, and to accept one, two, three, or even more benefices, even if canonries and prebends, and one of them with cure, or a dignity, parsonage, or office, with permission to exchange them at will for similar or dissimilar benefices, without mentioning his defect when petitioning for future graces. But whereas at that time John was actually only in his fifteenth year, the pope now dispenses him from defect of age, at the petition of his kinswoman, queen Annabella of Scotland, and grants the same effect to the original dispensation, as if express mention had been made therein of the fact that John was only in his fifteenth year, so that the validity may not be contested. Moreover, John may even be promoted to the rank of a bishop, or accept a major dignity of a cathedral, even one that is normally elective.

Avignon, 17 Kal. Jul., anno 15; expedited, Kal. Jul., anno 15 [1 July, 1393]; consigned, 4 Non. Jul., anno 15 [4 July, 1393].

17 June, 1393   Reg Aven 271, 231-iv

To the archdeacon of Galloway. Mandate to confirm, after due enquiry, the collation of John de Crugilton, priest of Galloway diocese, to the parish church of Crugilton, same diocese, value not exceeding 15 marks sterling. John was presented to the living by Archibald de Douglas, lord of Galloway, the true patron of the church, after the death of Roland Matkyo, and was instituted by bishop Thomas of Galloway, but he doubts the validity of this institution on the grounds that the church was really vacant by the death of the late William de Crugilton, and so John has petitioned the pope for confirmation.

Avignon, 15 Kal. Jul., anno 15; expedited, 11 Kal. Feb., anno 16 [22 Jan., 1394]; consigned, 9 Kal. Feb., anno 16 [24 Jan., 1394].

17 June, 1393   Reg Aven 272, 389v

To Thomas, lord of Erskyn, knight, and his wife Joan, of St Andrews diocese. Indult to have Mass celebrated in their presence on a portable altar by some worthy priest.

Avignon, 15 Kal. Jul., anno 15.

SRO Vat. Trans, i, no. 72.

17 June, 1393   Reg Aven 273, 548-8v

Ad perpetuam rei memoriam. Confirmation, granted at the petition of
abbot Finlay and the convent of Soulseat, O.PREMON., Galloway
diocese, of the union of the church of St Medan de Lerynnys, same
diocese, to the said monastery, by cardinal Walter, legate *a latere*
to Scotland and Ireland, to augment the income of the monastery,
which is greatly reduced and which is in a ruinous and collapsed
condition on account of the wars in those parts, with insertion
of the letters of the cardinal, sealed with his green wax seal, and
dated: *Datum sub sigillo quo dudum utebamur ut episcopus Glasguen.
apud Glasgu xj^{ma} die mensis Aprilis anno Domini millesimo CCC^{mo}
octuagesimo sexto et pontificatus domini nostri Clementis divina
providentia pape septimi anno octavo.* The church was vacant by the
resignation of Finlay Ahanna, made freely into the cardinal's
hands.
Avignon, 15 Kal. Jul., anno 15; expedited, 6 Id. Jan., anno 16 [8
Jan., 1394]; consigned, 2 Id. Jan., anno 16 [12 Jan., 1394].
SRO Vat. Trans., i, no. 73.

17 June, 1393   Reg Vat 305, 226v-7v

To John Barry, priest of Glasgow diocese. Reservation of a canonry
and prebend of Astorga and the archdeaconry of Parramo, whenever
vacated by the promotion of Alfonso to the bishopric of Astorga.
John is said to be of noble birth and this reservation is granted at the
petition of king Henry of Castille and Leon.
Avignon, 15 Kal. Jul., anno 15; expedited, 12 Kal. Dec., anno 16
[20 Nov., 1393]; consigned, 11 Kal. Dec., anno 16 [21 Nov., 1393].
Concurrent mandate to the dean of St Agricola, Avignon, and the
officials of Zamora and Leon.

19 June, 1393   Reg Aven 271, 115v

To Bean Johannis Andree, dean of Argyll. Confirmation, granted
at the petition of king Robert on behalf of his chaplain, of the
provision of Bean to the deanship of Argyll [18 Jan., 1389], vacant
by the free resignation of James Johannis into the hands of bishop

John of Argyll, to whom acceptance of the resignation, collation and provision belonged by ancient and approved custom. This provision was approved of by Robert Senescalli, earl of Ffiffe, true patron of the deanery. At that time Bean held the parish church of St Monewog, Argyll diocese, which the bishop, with the consent of all the canons resident in the diocese, united to the deanery of Argyll in order to augment the meagre revenues of the latter, and this met with the approval of Donald de Yle, lord of the Isles, true patron of the church.

Avignon, 13 Kal. Jul., anno 15; expedited, 14 Kal. Aug., anno 15 [19 July, 1393]; consigned, 5 Kal. Aug., anno 15 [28 July, 1393].

23 June, 1393   Reg Aven 271, 131-iv

To the abbot of Saddell, O.CIST., Argyll diocese. Mandate to confirm, after due enquiry, the provision of James Macgilleylam, priest of Glasgow diocese, to the perpetual vicarage of the parish church of St Merin de Inverkype, same diocese, made by the ordinary authority of bishop Walter of Glasgow, after the death of Maurice Mackerayche. James has had peaceful possession, but he has petitioned the pope for confirmation.

Avignon, 9 Kal. Jul., anno 15; expedited, 4 Id. Jul., anno 15 [12 July, 1393]; consigned, 17 Kal. Aug., anno 15 [16 July, 1393].

27 June, 1393   Reg Aven 273, 423-3v

Ad perpetuam rei memoriam. Confirmation, granted at the petition of the abbot and convent of the monastery of Sagadyl, O.CIST., Argyll diocese, of the various endowments made to the said monastery, which was founded by the late Reginald, son of Somorledi, king of the Isles, to the glory of God, under the invocation of the Virgin Mary, and with the permission of the Apostolic See. For the sustenance of the abbot and convent he endowed the monastery with ten pennyworths from Balebeam, five pennyworths from the valley of Saddell, five pennyworths from Stesthayn in Hareyn, Sodor diocese, the sum total value of which lands does not exceed 30 marks annually of the usual money in circulation in Scotland. Then the late Roderick, son of Reginald, gifted one pennyworth of land at Thorsradyl and half a pennyworth of ground at Wgladal, the annual value of which does not exceed 6 marks. John de Yle, lord of the Isles, has donated half a pennyworth of land at Darneychan, the annual value of which does not exceed 2 marks, and Christine Calem has gifted the island of Daavhara, which is worth only 5 shillings a year. The pope herewith confirms these endowments.

Avignon, 5 Kal. Jul., anno 15; expedited, 6 Id. Jul., anno 15 [10 July, 1393]; consigned, 5 Id. Jul., anno 15 [11 July, 1393].

SRO Vat. Trans., i. no. 74; printed: *Highland Papers*, iv, 146-9.

29 June, 1393   Reg Vat 305, 294v, 297-7v

To the deans of Dunkeld and St Pierre, Avignon, and the official of St Andrews. Mandate to collate Thomas Bel, priest, perpetual vicar of the parish church of Luntrechyn, St Andrews diocese, to a canonry of Glasgow and the prebend of Raynfreu, vacant by the death of the late Henry de Arthourli, a familiar and commensal of cardinal Walter, notwithstanding that the pope provided Thomas to the vicarage only recently [14 June, 1393]. He studied canon law for three years at Orleans and is still pursuing his studies.

Avignon, 3 Kal. Jul., anno 15; expedited, 7 Kal. Aug., anno 15 [26 July, 1393]; consigned, 5 Kal. Aug., anno 15 [28 July, 1393].

30 June, 1393   Reg Aven 273, 461v-2

To Duncan Petit, B.U.J., archdeacon of Glasgow. Indult, valid for three years, to visit by deputy, even on the same day, two churches, monasteries, or other ecclesiastical places, and the persons thereof, in the archdeaconry of Glasgow, and to receive the procurations due to him in ready money to the amount of thirty silver Tournois, twelve being equal to one gold florin of Florence. Those, however, who cannot pay in full, are to pay according to their means, and those who cannot pay at all are not to be compelled.

Avignon, 2 Kal. Jul., anno 15; expedited, 2 Kal. Aug., anno 15 [31 July, 1393]; consigned, 4 Non. Aug., anno 15 [2 Aug., 1393].

Concurrent mandate to the abbot of Paisley, the dean of Glasgow, and the archdeacon of Teviotdale.

12 July, 1393   Reg Aven 273, 465

To all Christ's faithful. Indulgence of one year and forty days is granted to all who visit the chapel of the Holy Trinity in the parish church of Inverkipe, Glasgow diocese, on the principal feasts of the year, the feast of the Holy Trinity [first Sunday after Pentecost], and on the feast of the Dedication of the chapel, and fifty days indulgence during their octaves and the six days after Pentecost, and contribute towards the completion of the fabric.
Avignon, 4 Id. Jul., anno 15 ; expedited, 7 Kal. Aug., anno 15 [26 July, 1393] ; consigned, 2 Kal. Aug., anno 15 [31 July, 1393].
SRO Vat. Trans., i, no. 75.

12 July, 1393   Reg Vat 306, 26v-27

To the bishops of Argyll and St Andrews. Mandate to provide Macratius, priest, professed monk of the monastery of St Mary de Sagadel, O.CIST., Argyll diocese, as abbot of the said monastery, vacant by the death of abbot Patrick, during whose lifetime provision was specially reserved to the pope. Unaware of this reservation, the convent elected Macratius as abbot and the election was confirmed by John, abbot of Melifont, Armagh diocese, to whom the right of confirmation belongs by ancient and approved custom. Abbot John, however, has adhered to Pierino de Thomacellis [Boniface IX] and so Macratius has petitioned the pope for confirmation. The bishops are commissioned to absolve him from excommunication, irregularity and infamy, to provide him as abbot, and to receive his oath of fidelity to the Apostolic See, which must be sent to the pope as soon as possible.
Avignon, 4 Id. Jul., anno 15 ; expedited, 7 Id. [   ],[1] anno 15.

12 July, 1393   Reg Vat 306, 310v-11

To the dean of St Pierre, Avignon, Nicholas de Irwyne, canon of Glasgow, and the official of Glasgow. Mandate to collate Malcolm de Bute, priest of Sodor diocese, to the perpetual vicarage of the

[1] The month has been omitted from the date, but it could only have been '7 Id Aug.' [7 Aug.], or '7 Id. Sept.' [7 Sept.], or '7 Id. Oct.' [9 Oct.].

parish church of St Blaan de Kyngarth, same diocese, value not exceeding £7 sterling, vacant by the death of Maurice Doncani. Avignon, 4 Id. Jul., anno 15; expedited, 19 Kal. Sept., anno 15 [14 Aug., 1393]; consigned, 17 Kal. Sept., anno 15 [16 Aug., 1393].

25 July, 1393   Reg Vat 306, 380v-1v

To Patrick de Huyston, canon of Glasgow. Provision to a canonry of Glasgow and the prebend of Renfru, vacant through the transfer by papal authority of the late Adam de Tynnyngham, canon of Glasgow, to another canonry of Glasgow and the prebend of Barlanark, or vacant by the consecration of the late Walter as bishop of Glasgow, notwithstanding that Patrick has an expectative grace of a benefice with or without cure of the cathedral, city, or diocese of Glasgow, even if a canonry and prebend, dignity, parsonage, or office.
Avignon, 8 Kal. Aug., anno 15; expedited, 7 Kal. Sept., anno 15 [26 Aug., 1393]; consigned, 6 Kal. Sept., anno 15 [27 Aug., 1393]. Concurrent mandate to the abbots of Paisley and Kilwinning and the dean of St Pierre, Avignon.

24 August, 1393   Reg Vat 305, 312v-13v

To William de Nary, M.A., canon of Moray. Provision to a canonry of Moray and the prebend of Botarry, vacant by the death at the Roman Curia of the late Christian de Cromdale, papal chaplain, notwithstanding that he holds the parish church of Kerymton, St Andrews diocese. William is studying civil law and is in his third years of lectures.
Avignon, 9 Kal. Sept., anno 15; expedited, 9 Kal. Oct., anno 15 [23 Sept., 1393]; consigned, 9 Kal. Oct., anno 15 [23 Sept., 1393]. Concurrent mandate to the bishop of St Andrews, the dean of St Pierre, Avignon, and the official of Aberdeen.

1 December, 1393   Reg Vat 307, 477v

To all Christ's faithful. Indulgence of one year and forty days is granted to all who visit the parish church of St Mary de Ederham,

St Andrews diocese, which is noted for the miracles performed there, that in the past have attracted countless pilgrims, on the principal feasts of the year, the feast of St Michael the Archangel [29 Sept.], and the Dedication of the church, and fifty days indulgence during their octaves and the six days after Pentecost, and contribute towards its upkeep.

Avignon, Kal. Dec., anno 16.

SRO Vat. Trans., i, no. 76.

5 January, 1394   Reg Vat 307, 12-12v

To the bishops of Glasgow and Dunkeld. Mandate to enforce the nomination of abbot John to the monastery of Neubotil, O.CIST., St Andrews diocese, to which he was provided by the pope after the death of the late abbot Hugh [23 Sept., 1392]. John was admitted to the temporalities of the abbey by king Robert, who holds them in feu, but Donald, the prior, and the convent refused to admit him as their abbot on the pretext of tyranny and they appealed to the Apostolic See. Abbot John also has petitioned the pope in this matter.

Avignon, Non. Jan., anno 16; expedited, 2 Kal. Mar., anno 16 [28 Feb., 1394]; consigned, 4 Non. Mar., anno 16 [4 Mar., 1394].

SRO Vat. Trans., i, no. 77.

7 February, 1394   Reg Vat 307, 371-1v

To Malcolm de Aula, canon of Glasgow. Mandate to reserve to John Twnnok, priest, rector of the parish church of Henryland, Glasgow diocese, a benefice usually assigned to the secular clergy in the gift of the abbot and convent of Kalcho, O.S.B., St Andrews diocese, together or separately, to the value of 40 marks sterling with cure, or 18 marks sterling without cure, if vacant on the 13 Kal. Mar. [17 Feb.] or thereafter, on condition that he resigns the parish church upon obtaining possession of a benefice with cure.

Avignon, 7 Id. Feb., anno 16; expedited, 2 Kal. Mar., anno 16 [28 Feb., 1394]; consigned, 6 Non. Mar., anno 16 [2 Mar., 1394].

17 February, 1394   Reg Vat 307, 120v-1

To Richard Smerles, rector of the parish church of Hutton, Glasgow diocese. Provision to the parish church of Hutton, Glasgow diocese, value not exceeding 25 marks sterling, vacant by the provision by the pope of Thomas Ewar to the parish church of Glencarn, same diocese [18 Jan., 1379], or vacant because the said Thomas, having obtained peaceful possession of the parish church, neglected to be ordained priest within the prescribed limit of time, or vacant for whatsoever reason, and notwithstanding that at present John de Molnj occupies it unlawfully.

Avignon, 13 Kal. Mar., anno 16; expedited, 3 Kal. Mar., anno 16 [27 Feb., 1394]; consigned, 2 Kal. Mar., anno 16 [28 Feb., 1394].

Concurrent mandate to the abbots of Sweetheart and Holywood, and the dean of St Pierre, Avignon.

9 May, 1394   Reg Aven 274, 389-90

To the dean of Glasgow. Mandate to collate John de Fayrle, priest of Glasgow diocese, as rector of the parish church of Sankar, same diocese, value not exceeding £20 sterling, vacant because William Macmoryn, having held the parish church for more than a year, neglected to be ordained priest within the prescribed limit of time. John was presented to the living by John de Crechton, patron of the church, and instituted by bishop Matthew of Glasgow. He has enjoyed peaceful possession for more than two years, but doubts have arisen regarding the validity of his institution, and he has petitioned the pope for confirmation.

Avignon, 7 Id. Maii, anno 16; expedited, 10 Kal. Jun., anno 16 [23 May, 1394]; consigned, 3 Kal. Jun., anno 16 [30 May, 1394].

9 May, 1394   Reg Vat 307, 508v-9

To Walter, bishop of St Andrews, and John de Caron, canon of Aberdeen. Whereas, as is contained in the petition of Robert, king of Scots, and his eldest son, David, earl of Carreyk, the monastery of Neubotil, o.cist., St Andrews diocese, which lies near the borders of Scotland and England, as a result of the wars which have waged

in those parts, has been burned down and destroyed by the English and is in great need of repair. The revenues of the monastery are insufficient for this work and for the maintenence of the monks. The king and the earl are willing to undertake the restoration of the monastery, but have been dissuaded from doing so, because abbot John, who was provided by the pope [23 Sept., 1392], is exceedingly ungrateful to the earl and hateful to him, and only at great detriment and scandal can he be allowed to remain in possession. On the other hand, if a suitable person were to be provided as abbot, one who is pleasing to the king and the earl, then they are prepared to repair the monastery, and protect and defend it. Therefore, they have petitioned the pope to find a suitable remedy ; they have no particular person to present, but will accept whomsoever the convent elect. The pope commissions the bishop and the canon to enquire fully about this matter and report back to him as soon as possible. If the facts are as stated, they are to remove abbot John from office. Avignon, 7 Id. Maii, anno 16 ; expedited, 4 Non. Jun., anno 16 [2 June, 1394] ; consigned, 3 Non. Jun., anno 16 [3 June, 1394].
SRO Vat. Trans., i, no. 78.

16 May, 1394   Reg Aven 274, 443v

To the dean and archdeacon of Glasgow, and John Wyschard, canon of Glasgow. Mandate to collate John de Fayerle, priest of Glasgow diocese, to the perpetual vicarage of the parish church of Craufor, same diocese, value not exceeding 20 marks sterling, vacant by the death of the late John de Cranford, otherwise called Sytosycsariast, and notwithstanding that David de Camera, canon of Holyrood de Edymburgh, occupies the vicarage unlawfully.
Avignon, 17 Kal. Jun., anno 16 ; expedited, 4 Non. Jul., anno 16 [4 July, 1394] ; consigned, 2 Non. Sept., anno 16 [4 Sept., 1394].

19 May, 1394   Reg Vat 307, 220v-1

To the official of St Andrews. Mandate to collate Gilbert Knycht, priest of St Andrews diocese, to the perpetual vicarage of the parish church of Fordon, same diocese, vacant by the death of Robert Wy. Gilbert was provided to the living by bishop Walter of St Andrews, but doubting the validity of his provision, he has petitioned the pope for confirmation.

Avignon, 14 Kal. Jun., anno 16; expedited, 16 Kal. Jul., anno 16 [16 June, 1394]; consigned, 7 Kal. Jul., anno 16 [24 June, 1394].

23 May, 1394   Reg Vat 307, 544

To Richard de Ayton, layman, and Christine Sibalde, woman, of St Andrews diocese. Dispensation from the impediment to marriage arising from the fourth degrees of consanguinity and affinity.

Avignon, 10 Kal. Jun., anno 16.

SRO Vat. Trans., iv, no. 62.

10 July, 1394   Reg Vat 307, 297-7v

To James Biset, LIC.DEC., prior of St Andrews, O.S.A. Provision to the office of prior of St Andrews, which is the greatest dignity of the cathedral after that of the bishop and involves cure of souls, vacant by the death of prior Robert de Monros. Unaware that provision was specially reserved to the pope, the chapter, on the fixed day and having summoned all who had a right to be present, elected James as prior and he consented to his election. In fact, however, the election was invalid and so the pope confers the priorship on him. It is usually held by one of the canons. James is dispensed to retain the perpetual vicarage of the parish church of Kilgour, St Andrews diocese, provided cure of souls is not neglected, but he must relinquish all claim to the priory of Loch Leven, O.S.A., same diocese, over which there has been litigation at the papal court.

Avignon, 6 Id. Jul., anno 16; expedited, 19 Kal. Sept., anno 16 [14 Aug., 1394]; consigned, 15 Kal. Sept., anno 16 [18 Aug., 1394]. Concurrent mandate to the abbot of Cambuskenneth, the dean of St Pierre, Avignon, and the official of St Andrews.

10 July, 1394   Reg Vat 307, 583v

To Malcolm de Karryncors, LIC.ART., clerk of St Andrews diocese. More ample dispensation, having already been dispensed from defect of birth, being born of a married man and an unmarried woman, in order that he might receive all grades of holy orders and accept a benefice, even one with cure, that he may now accept any number of benefices, with or without cure, even if they are canonries and prebends, dignities, parsonages, administrations, or offices, and even if the dignities are the greatest of cathedrals, or principal ones of collegiate churches, with permission to exchange them freely for similar or dissimilar benefices, without mentioning his defect or the dispensation in future petitions for graces. This is granted him because of his noble parentage.

Avignon, 6 Id. Jul., anno 16; expedited, 14 Kal. Jan., anno 1 [19 Dec., 1394]; consigned, 10 Kal. Jan., anno 1 Benedicti pape XIII [23 Dec., 1394].

24 July, 1394   Reg Vat 307, 565v

To Hugh de Dalmehoy, LIC.LEG., archdeacon of Moray. Hugh has freely resigned a canonry and prebend of Moray, made by proxy into the hands of bishop Alexander of Moray, while Duncan Petit has also freely resigned the archdeaconry of Moray, made personally into the hands of the said bishop, who by ordinary authority provided Duncan to the canonry and prebend, and Hugh to the archdeaconry, thereby effecting an exchange of benefices. The revenues of the archdeaconry, which is with cure, are very meagre, so the pope dispenses Hugh to accept a parish church, if conferred upon him canonically, and hold it together with the archdeaconry, provided cure of souls is not neglected. This is not to prejudice the other expectative grace he received from the pope of a benefice with or without cure in the gift of the bishop, prior and chapter of St Andrews [19 Aug., 1385].

Avignon, 9 Kal. Aug., anno 16; expedited, 11 Kal. Sept., anno 16 [22 Aug., 1394]; consigned, 3 Kal. Sept., anno 16 [30 Aug., 1394].

10 August, 1394   Reg Vat 307, 344-4v

To the dean of Glasgow, and John Vaus and John Haubic, canons of Glasgow. Whereas, as is contained in the petition of William de Govan, priest of Glasgow diocese, the bishop of Dunblane, the abbot of Pasleto, and the official of Glasgow received a mandate from the pope to reserve in all the cathedrals, cities and dioceses of Scotland, twelve benefices with or without cure, of whatsoever value and in the gift of whomsoever, for suitable persons to be named by king Robert for provision to one, two, three, or even more of these benefices, with precedence over others in obtaining effect to the reservation. The king named William to one of these benefices and abbot John of Paisley reserved one to him. Subsequently, when the perpetual vicarage of the parish church of Monkton, Glasgow diocese, fell vacant by the death of the late Robert de Bour, last vicar, William, who held the perpetual vicarage of the parish church of Sybaldly, same diocese, on pretext of his nomination and reservation, obtained collation to the vicarage and has held it for more than a year. Doubts have arisen about the validity of the provision and the vicarage is said to be still vacant, so at the petition also of king Robert he seeks confirmation from the pope, and this is hereby granted him without prejudice to the reservation of another benefice with or without cure in the cathedral, city, or diocese of Glasgow, as contained in the original reservation, but on obtaining a benefice with cure, he must resign the vicarage.

Avignon, 4 Id. Aug., anno 16; expedited, 6 Kal. Sept., anno 16 [27 Aug., 1394]; consigned, 3 Kal. Sept., anno 16 [30 Aug., 1394].

14 August, 1394   Reg Vat 307, 567

To the bishop of Glasgow. Faculty to dispense John Henrici, donzel, and the noblewoman Margaret, daughter of Thomas de Kirkpatrik, knight, of Glasgow diocese, from the impediment to marry arising from the third and fourth degrees of affinity, because previously John had committed fornication with Evota, daughter of Dei Mechehan, who is related to Margaret in the third and fourth degrees of consanguinity from the same descent.

Avignon, 19 Kal. Sept., anno 16.

SRO Vat. Trans., iv, no. 63.

INDEX

Place-names are indexed under the modern form of the name, where this has been identified, followed in parenthesis by the forms given in the text. Cross-references have been supplied to the remoter of these forms. Personal names are indexed as they appear in the text with remoter forms following in parenthesis and cross-references again being supplied where necessary. Only persons in actual possession of a particular office or benefice have been accredited with the title to it, and other claimants will be found by reference to the entry relating to the office or benefice itself.

R

CADDER (Cader), vicar of, see
Bricii, Walter: vicarage of, 11-12
Caithness, archdeacon of, see
Forestarii, William: archdeaconry
of, 74: bishop of, lvi; see also
Drumbreck, Malcolm de; Man,
Alexander: bishopric of, 68:
canon of, see Eddenham, Thomas
de; Gerland, William; Spyny,
William de: canonry and prebend
of, lvi, 6, 8, 16, 38, 74, 99, 162:
chapter of, 68: dean of, 16: elect
of, see Man, Alexander
Calabre, William de, canon of
Aberdeen, 2, 154
Calder (Caldore), parish church of,
157: vicar of, see Bothwyle,
Gilbert de
Calem, Christine, 194
Cambel, Colin (Calen), 175, 188:
his daughter Mor, see Mor
Cambel, John, lord of Glaston, 142
Cambel, Nigel, clerk, 166-7
Cambrai, bishop of, see Geneva,
Robert of: canon of, see
Jausserand, Armand: cities and
diocese of, 19, 167: nuncio to
cities and diocese of, see Guy,
bishop of Palestrina
Cambuskenneth (Cambuskynech,
Cambuskyneth), abbey of, 29,
32, 36, 40, 66-67: abbot of, 22,
36, 48-49, 65, 98, 141, 200; see
also William: canon of, see
Dersy, John de: convent of, 22, 32,
36
Cambuslang, parish church of, 123,
126, 129, 131, 146-7: rector of,
see Merton, John de
Cambusnethan (Chambusnathan),
vicar of, see Petyern, John:
vicarage of, 4
Camera, David de, canon of Holyrood, vicar of Crawford, 127n,
199
Camera, Gilbert de, priest, 51

Camera, Robert de, rector of
Arbuthnott, 50-51, 99
Camera, Stephen de, priest, 10
Camera, William de, clerk, 2
Camera, William de, senior, canon
of Dunkeld, rector of Hailes, 2, 10,
47, 155
Canatayne, prebend of, see Contin
Cantoris, John, chaplain, 74
Capello, Pampeo, xxv, xl, xlin,
xlii-xlvi and n, xlviii-xlix
Carale, parish church of, see Crail
Caralle (Carall), John de, canon of
Moray, canon of Ross and
prebendary of Cullicudden, rector
of Muckhart, 32, 37
Cardeny, Robert de, archdeacon of
Brechin, canon of Dunkeld and
prebendary of Crieff, dean of
Dunkeld, 161
Carguill, Thomas de, canon of
Aberdeen, vicar of Logie-Durno,
52
Carmelite order, 147
Carnne, John de, rector of Idvies, 58
Carnoten, Thomas de, priest, 14
Caron (Karon), Alexander de,
canon of Aberdeen, 18, 35
Caron, Alexander de, professor of
canon and civil law, 55
Caron, John de, canon of Aberdeen,
canon of Glasgow and prebendary
of Stobo, canon of Moray, rector
of Ratho, 9, 38, 40, 57, 142, 149,
153, 198-9
Caron, John de, priest, 32
Carpentras, xxxviiin: canon of, see
Curtibus, Giles de
Carrick (Carreyk), David, earl of,
see Senescalli, David
Carrick, John, earl of, and Athol,
seneschal of Scotland, see
Senescalli, John
Carrington (Kerymton), parish
church of, 196: rector of, see
Nary, William de

bishop of, 21, 32, 74, 102, 160; *see
also* Bur, Alexander: bishopric of,
liv: canon of, *see* Aerd, John de;
Boerii, Peter; Caralle, John de;
Caron, John de; Cornel, Richard
de; Cromdale, Cristin de;
Dalmehoy, Hugh de; Forg, John
de; Gerland, William; Greenlaw,
Gilbert de; Kilconkar, Thomas
de; Man, Alexander; Marr,
David de; Nary, William de;
Spalding, Patrick de; Strevelyn,
David de; Trayl, Alexander;
Trayl, Thomas; Trebrim, David
de; Tynyngham, Adam de;
Wardlau, Henry de; Wardlau,
Walter de; Wysse, Robert:
canonry and prebend of, lvii, 2,
6-7, 9-10, 13, 15, 23, 37-38, 47, 54,
69, 72, 75, 98, 100, 103, 113, 115,
128, 135, 151, 162, 165, 170, 172,
186; *see also* Advie and Cromdale,
Botarie, Duffus, Kinnoir, Spynie:
cathedral of, 160: chanter of, *see*
precentor: chaplain in diocese of,
see Abirkerdir, John de; Cantoris,
John: chaplaincy in diocese of,
74-75: dean of, lvii; *see also*
Douglas, John de; Sinclair,
Robert de; Trayl, Walter:
deanery of, 100, 102, 160-1, 185:
official of, 8, 43, 73, 172: precentor
of, 2, 8, 15-16, 118; *see also* Spyny,
William de: precentorship of, 88,
128: sacristanship of, 133: sub-
chanter of, 88; *see also* Aerd, John
de: sub-dean of, *see* Gerland,
William de: treasurer of, 172
More, John, canon of Glasgow and
prebendary of Ayr, papal chaplain,
116, 120
Moricii, Donald, clerk, 170
Morins, vicarage of, *see* Mearns
Muckhart (Mathard, Mocard),
parish church of, 32, 37: rector of,
see Carralle, John de

Muffald, Gilbert de, canon of
Glasgow and prebendary of
Eddlestone, vicar of Dumfries,
115-16, 149-50
Mull (Moll), parish church of St
Columba in, *see* Kilcolmkill
Mull (Mula, Mulle), parish church
of St John the Evangelist in Ard
of, *see* Torosay
Mull (Mula), parish church of St
John the Evangelist on the island
of, *see* Killean
Mundavilla, John de, canon of
Holyrood, 127n
Munterdove (Monterduffy), parish
church of, 76: rector of, *see*
Gilbert, prior of Whithorn;
Lorimer, William
Murdach, son of Robert, earl of
Fife, *see* Senescalli
Murrawe, John, earl of, *see* Dunbar
Musselburgh (Mouschilburg,
Muschilburgh, Muschulburgh),
chaplain of the hospital of, *see*
Cornel, Richard de: chaplaincy
of the hospital of, 118: hospital of
St Mary Magdalene at, 118: vicar
of, *see* Cornel, Richard de;
Torrech, Thomas de: vicarage of,
108-9, 118

NAPLES, xixn, xxxviii: minister at
court of, *see* Hamilton, William
Richard
Napoleon, the emperor, xxviii
Nary, William de, canon of Moray
and prebendary of Botarie, rector
of Carrington, 9, 180, 186-7, 196
Neut, John, priest, 13
Navarre, king of, xxxviii
Nevay (Nevet), parish church of,
134: rector of, *see* Grahame, John
de; Oggistoune, John; Sanctoclaro,
Godfrey de
Newbattle (Neubotil, Newbotil,
Newbotill), abbacy of, 176, 197:

T

MEMBERSHIP

*Membership of the Scottish History Society
is open to all who are interested in the history of Scotland.
For an annual subscription of £5·00
members normally receive one volume each year.
Enquiries should be addressed to
the Honorary Secretary or the Honorary Treasurer
whose addresses are given overleaf.*

REPORT

of the 87th Annual Meeting

The 87th Annual Meeting of the Scottish History Society was held in the Rooms of the Royal Society, George Street, Edinburgh, on Saturday, 15 December 1973, at 11.15 a.m. Monsignor David McRoberts, Chairman of Council, was in the Chair.

The Report of Council was as follows:

The eighth and ninth volumes of the Fourth Series, the two volumes of *Papers on Sutherland Estate Management: 1802-1816*, edited by Mr R. J. Adam, were issued to members during the year. This work has aroused great interest both among members and the general public, and it has already received favourable reviews. The tenth volume in the series, *William Melrose in China: letters of a Scottish tea merchant, 1845-1855*, edited by Professor Hoh-Cheung Mui and his wife, Lorna H. Mui, is in the final stages of preparation and will be issued to members with this report. Mr Iain Brash's volume of *Papers on Scottish Electoral Politics, 1832-1850*, is also well advanced.

The Council records with great sorrow the death on 23 March 1973 of Dr Annie I. Dunlop. Dr Dunlop, who had been a member of the Society for over fifty years, produced the first of the eight volumes she edited for the Society in 1927. Her loyal service as a member of Council and her unstinting generosity to the Society, finally marked by a substantial legacy, will long be remembered. Council feels that an appropriate work being prepared by the Society should be dedicated to her memory. This will be a *Calendar of letters relating to Scotland of Pope Clement VII, 1378-1394*, to be edited by the Right Rev. Monsignor Charles Burns of the Vatican Archives; it will include a memoir of Dr Dunlop by Dr Ian B. Cowan, Honorary Treasurer of the Society.

The Council also notes with regret two further deaths, of Sir James Fergusson of Kilkerran on 25 October 1973, and of Mr William Stevenson, a present member of the Council of the Society, on 27 July 1973. Their practical and unwavering support of the Society for many years will be sorely missed.

With the termination of the agreement with the Kraus-Thomson Reprint Corporation for reprinting the first series of our publications because such an extensive programme was not economically viable, Council has throughout the year been considering ways of making at least some of the Society's out-of-print volumes available again to members. In negotiations with the Scottish Academic Press agreement has been reached in principle for the Press to reprint certain volumes for general sale, the volumes to be available to individual members at a generous discount. Some details have yet to be worked out, but it is expected that the first batch of reprints, to include the three volumes of *The Lyon in Mourning* and *Scottish Population Statistics*, will be available in the coming year. Further information about these reprints will be circulated to members as soon as possible.

Monsignor David McRoberts has completed his four-year term of office as Chairman of Council. His quiet and competent manner of managing Council affairs has been of great benefit to the Society. Council has appointed as his successor to that position Professor R. H. Campbell, who will take up his duties after the Annual Meeting.

Members of Council who retire in rotation at this time are Mr Alexander D. Cameron, Mr Bruce Lenman and Miss Margaret D. Young. There are two further vacancies, caused by the appointment of Professor Campbell to be Chairman of Council, and by the death of Mr Stevenson. The following will be proposed to the Annual Meeting for election to Council: Mr E. J. Cowan, Mr J. J. Robertson, Miss M. B. H. Sanderson, Rev. Dr D. Shaw, Mr N. F. Shead.

During the past year seven members have died, seven have resigned, and six have been removed from the list of members for non-payment of subscription. New members numbered thirty-six. The membership, including 231 libraries, now totals 736, compared with 720 in 1972.

In presenting the Annual Report, Monsignor McRoberts discussed in more detail the points raised in the Report, emphasising that the new agreement for the reprinting of certain selected volumes would bring back into circulation useful volumes too long out of print, and provide publicity for the Society.

The Hon. Treasurer reported a satisfactory balance, indicating that the recent raising of the subscription had brought in a substantial and necessary increase in funds. Nevertheless this satisfactory situation was more apparent than real when costs of production were continuously increasing.

Mr J. Simpson moved the adoption of the Annual Report; this was seconded and duly approved.

Mr W. D. H. Sellar, seconded by Mrs Jean Monro, nominated for election as ordinary members of Council Mr E. J. Cowan, Mr J. J. Robertson, Dr Margaret H. B. Sanderson, Rev. Dr D. Shaw, and Mr N. F. Shead; and they were duly elected.

An address entitled 'Roads and routes in medieval Scotland' prepared by the President, Professor G. W. S. Barrow, was read in his absence by the Honorary Secretary.

Professor G. Donaldson proposed a vote of thanks to the President, and to Dr Rae for reading his paper; and Mr R. G. Cant thanked Monsignor McRoberts both for chairing the meeting in the absence of the President and for his services to the Society during his term of office as Chairman of Council.

ABSTRACT ACCOUNT OF CHARGE AND DISCHARGE OF THE
INTROMISSION OF THE HONORARY TREASURER for
1 November 1972 to 31 October 1973

I. GENERAL ACCOUNT

CHARGE

I. Cash in Bank at 1 November 1972		
1. Sum at credit of Savings Account with Bank of Scotland		£2,863·21
2. Sum at credit of Current Account with Bank of Scotland		291·45
3. Sum at credit of Savings Account with Edinburgh Savings Bank		59·99
4. Sum at credit of Special Investment Account with Edinburgh Savings Bank		948·61
		£4,163·26
II. Subscriptions received		2,190·32
III. Past Publications sold		294·72
IV. Interest on Savings Accounts with Bank of Scotland and Edinburgh Savings Bank		210·44
V. Grant from Leverhulme Trust		750·00
VI. Grant from Carnegie Trust		250·00
VII. Income Tax Refund (1971-2)		159·60
VIII. Donations		1,055·00
IX. Sums drawn from Bank Current Account	£4,771·42	
X. Sums drawn from Bank Savings Account	—	
		£9,073·34

DISCHARGE

I. Cost of publications during year (*Sutherland Estate Papers*)		£2,135·01
Cost of printing Annual Report, Notices and Printers' Postages, etc.		149·62
		£2,384·63
II. Brochure		48·84
III. Insurance premiums		28·13
IV. Miscellaneous Payments		109·82
V. Sums lodged in Bank Current Account	£4,991·09	
VI. Sums lodged in Bank Savings Account	£6,282·25	

VII. Funds at close of this account;
1. Balance at credit of Savings Account with Bank of Scotland £5,204·05
2. Balance at credit of Current Account with Bank of Scotland 219·67
3. Balance at credit of Savings Account with Edinburgh Savings Bank 62·05
4. Balance at credit of Special Investment Account with Edinburgh Savings Bank 1,016·15

6,501·92

£9,073·34

GLASGOW, *22 November 1973.* I have examined the General Account of the Honorary Treasurer of the Scottish History Society for the year from 1 November 1972 to 31 October 1973 and I find the same to be correctly stated and sufficiently vouched.

I. M. M. MACPHAIL
Auditor

SCOTTISH HISTORY SOCIETY

LIST OF MEMBERS

1975-1976

ABBOT, D. M., Esq., 9 Ravelston House Loan, Edinburgh EH4 3LY
ADAM, Professor R. J., Cromalt, Lade Braes, St Andrews KY16 9ET
ADAMS, I. H., PH.D., 58 Blackett Place, Edinburgh EH9
ADAMSON, Duncan, 39 Roberts Crescent, Dumfries, CD4 27RS
ADAMSON, Miss Margot R., 100 Handside Lane, Welwyn Garden City, Herts.
AGNEW, Sir Crispin, of Lochnaw, Bt., c/o Regimental Headquarters, Royal Highland Fusiliers, 518 Sauchiehall Street, Glasgow G3
ALDERSON, John J., Havelock, Victoria, 3465, Australia
ALEXANDER, Joseph, Trust, per J. A. Carnegie & Smith, solicitors, Bank of Scotland Buildings, Kirriemuir, Angus.
ALLENTUCK, Professor Marcia, B.A., PH.D., 5 West 86 Street, Apt. 12B, New York, N.Y. 10024, USA
ANDERSON, J. Douglas, F.S.A. SCOT., 16 Grantley Gardens, Glasgow
ANDERSON, Mrs Marjorie O., West View Cottage, Lade Braes Lane, St Andrews KY16
ANGUS, G., 73 Findlay Gardens, Edinburgh EH7
ANGUS, Rev. J. A. K., T.D., M.A., The Manse, 90 Albert Road, Gourock, Renfrewshire
ANNAND, A. McK., T.D., F.S.A., SCOT., Magdalen, High Street, Findon, Worthing, Sussex
ANNAND, James K., 174 Craigleith Road, Edinburgh EH4
ANTON, Professor A. E., 41 Braid Farm Road, Edinburgh EH10 6LE
ARKLE, Douglas G., F.S.A. SCOT., Airthrey, 91 Keptie Road, Arbroath, Angus
ARMET, Miss Catherine M., Mount Stuart, Rothesay, Isle of Bute
ARMSTRONG, Campbell, 66 North Kilmeny Crescent, Wishaw, Lanarkshire ML2 8RS
ARMSTRONG, Murdo, Royal Bank House, Muir of Ord, Ross-shire
ASH, Miss Marinell, M.A., PH.D., B.B.C., Queen Street, Edinburgh
ASPLIN, P. W., Strathcraig, Loganswell, Newton Mearns, Glasgow

BACSICH, Mrs Anna B., 11 Ashton Road, Glasgow G12
BAIN, Miss Sheila M., M.A., M.ED, Dept of Geography, University of Aberdeen AB9 2UB
BAIRD, Miss Mary Myrtle, Scottish Record Office, H.M. General Register House, Edinburgh EH1 3YY
BANKS, Noel, Wolverton, Stratford-on-Avon, Warwickshire
BANNERMAN, John W. M., PH.D., Arrochy Beg, Balmaha, Stirlingshire
BARNES, Professor Thomas G., D.PHIL., Department of History, University of California, Berkeley, California, 94720, USA
BARR, Mrs A. R., Bonahaven, Colintraive, Argyll

BARROW, Professor G. W. S., Department of Modern History, The University of St Andrews, Fife KY16 9AJ (*President*)

BAXTER, John, 65 Canterbury Road, Redcar, Yorks.

BECKET, Miss Lindsay D., 2 St Michaels Court, Keere Street, Lewes, Sussex

BENNETT, Miss Josephine M., B.L., 91 Victoria Road, Dunoon, Argyll

BERNARD, K. N., B.A., F.S.A. SCOT., 21 Machrie Drive, Clyde Arran, Helensburgh, Dunbartonshire

BIGWOOD, Mrs A. R., 38 Primrose Bank Road, Edinburgh EH5 3JF

BIRD, A. G., 49 Woldcarr Road, Anlaby Road, Hull, Yorks HU3 6TP

BOGIE, Rev. A. P., M.A., The Manse, Forgan, Newport-on-Tay, Fife DD6 8RB

BONNAR, Maurice K., 1 Dubbs Road, Port Glasgow

BRASH, J. I., M.A. (OXON.), Department of History, University of Western Australia, Nedlands, W.A., 6009

BRENNAN, James S., No 1 Cottage, Dalcross Station, Dalcross, by Inverness

BRISTOL, Major Nicholas M. V., Breacachadh Castle, Isle of Coll, Coll

BROUN LINDSAY, Lady, Colstoun, Haddington, East Lothian

BROWN, Jennifer M., M.A., PH.D., Scottish History Department, The University, Glasgow G12 8QG

BRUCE, Fraser F., M.A., LL.B., 18 Delnie Road, Inverness

BRUCE, Iain, 39 Comely Bank Road, Edinburgh EH4

BRYSON, William, 16 Jubilee Street, Mornington, Dunedin, New Zealand

BUCHANAN, John, 67 Great King Street, Edinburgh EH3 6RP

BUCKROYD, Mrs Julia, 60 Highlands Court, Highland Road, Gipsy Hill, London, SE19

BUIST, Frank F., Faireyknowe, by Arbroath, Angus

BULLIVANT, Mrs Margaret S., Brockhampton, Bringsty, Worcester

BULLOCH, Rev. James, D.D., Manse of Stobo, Peebles

BURNS, Right Rev. Monsignor Charles, Archivio Segreto, Citta de Vaticano, Roma, Italy

BURNS, David M., M.A., W.S., 7 Heriot Row, Edinburgh EH3 6HU

BURNS, R. R. J., M.A., LL.B., 7 India Street, Edinburgh EH3 6HA

BURRELL, Professor Sydney A., A.B., PH.D., Department of History, Boston University, Bay State Road, Boston, Mass., 02215, USA

BURTON, Mrs Frances J., M.A., PH.D., 75 Silverknowes Gardens, Edinburgh EH4 5NB

CADELL, Patrick, B.A., 11A Tipperlinn Road, Edinburgh EH10 5ET

CAIRD, Professor J. B., D.DE L'UNIV., Department of Geography, The University, Dundee DD1

CAIRNS, Mrs Trevor, B.A., 4 Ashmore Terrace, Sunderland, Co. Durham SR2 7DE

CALDER, Dr Angus, 6 Buckingham Terrace, Edinburgh EH4 3AB

CAMERON, Alexander D., 14 Esplanade Terrace, Edinburgh EH15 2ES
CAMERON, Donald W., 15 Baberton Mains Gardens, Edinburgh EH17 3BY
CAMERON, The Hon. Lord, 28 Moray Place, Edinburgh EH3
CAMPBELL, Colin, P.O. Box 8, Belmont 78, Massachusetts, USA
CAMPBELL, J. L., of Canna, D.LITT., LL.D., Isle of Canna, Inverness-shire
CAMPBELL, Peter H., Levensholme, Tyneview Road, Haltwhistle, Northumberland
CAMPBELL, Professor R. H., Department of History, University of Stirling, Stirling (*Chairman of Council*)
CAMPBELL-PRESTON, Lt.-Col., Ardchattan Priory, Connel, Argyll
CANAVAN, Vincent J., LL.B., 2 Borlum Road, Inverness
CANT, R. G., 2 Kinburn Place, St Andrews KY16
CARMICHAEL, Major G. B., Three Ways, Cold Ash, Newbury, Berks.
CARMICHAEL, P. O., Arthurstone, Meigle, Perthshire
CARNEGIE, B. Grant, Wellburn, Northmuir, Kirriemuir, Angus
CAROON, Robert G., B.A., B.D., 910 N. Third Street, Milwaukee, Wisc., 53203, USA
CHAMBERS, J. W., B.SC., M.B., CH.B., F.R.C.P.(GLASG.), 14 Woodburn Road, Glasgow G43 2TN
CHECKLAND, Professor S. G., PH.D., Department of Economic History, The University, Glasgow G12 8QG
CHEYNE, Rev. Professor A. C., B.LITT., B.D., 11 Tantallon Place, Edinburgh EH9
CHITNIS, A. C., B.A., M.A., PH.D., Department of History, University of Stirling, Stirling
CHRISTIE, William, M.A., 306 Blackness Road, Dundee DD2 1SB
CLARK, Ian D. L., PH.D., Bishop's College, 224 Lower Circular Road, Calcutta 17, India
CLAVERING, R. J., Lucarne House, 56 Farnley Road, Menston, Ilkley, Yorks.
CLOW, Robert, G. M., John Smith & Son (Glasgow) Ltd., 57-61 St Vincent Street, Glasgow G2
COCKBURN, Miss Sara, M.A., Retreat Cottage, Laigh, Fenwick, Ayrshire
COHEN, Mrs M. C., 8 Norfolk Road, London NW8
COLLINS, Denis, F., M.A., LL.B., Stirling House, Craigiebarn Road, Dundee DD4 7PL
COLQUHOUN, Rev. John, Free Presbyterian Manse, Glendale, Skye
COSH, Miss Mary, M.A., 63 Theberton Street, London N1
COWAN, Edward J., M.A., Department of Scottish History, William Robertson Building, 50 George Square, Edinburgh EH8 9JY
COWAN, Ian B., PH.D., 119 Balshagray Avenue, Glasgow G11 7EG (*Hon. Treasurer*)

U

COWE, F. M., 10 Ravensdowne, Berwick-upon-Tweed
CRAWFORD, Iain A., M.A., The Dower House, Thriplow, Nr. Royston, Hertfordshire
CRAWFORD, Thomas, M.A., 61 Argyll Place, Aberdeen
CREGEEN, E. R., Eaglesview, Auchterarder, Perthshire
CRORIE, William D., B.SC., 34 Dumyat Drive, Falkirk, Stirlingshire
CROSBIE, George, M.A., East Crookboat, Sandilands, By Lanark, Lanarkshire
CROSS, Mrs Margaret B., 13 Grange Road, Edinburgh EH9 1UQ

DAICHES, Professor D., Downsview, Wellhouse Lane, Burgess Hill, Sussex RH15 0BN
DARRAGH, James, M.A., 103 Deakin Leas, Tonbridge, Kent
DAVIES, Miss Katharine L., PH.D., 198 Dalkeith Road, Edinburgh, EH16
DAVIS, E. D., Craigie College of Education, Beech Grove, Ayr KA8 0SR
DE BEER, E. S., 31 Brompton Square, London SW3
DEVINE, Dr. T. M., Department of History, McCance Building, University of Strathclyde, Glasgow
DIACK, William G., 20 Howes View, Bucksburn, Aberdeen
DICKSON, D., 17 Laurel Avenue, Lenzie, Dunbartonshire G66 4RX
DILWORTH, Rev. A. Mark, Fort Augustus Abbey, Fort Augustus, Inverness
DIXON, George A., 13 Thirlestane Road, Edinburgh, EH9
DOCHERTY, Rev. Henry, PH.L., 8 Crookston Grove, Glasgow G52
DONALDSON, Professor Gordon, D.LITT., Preston Tower Nursery Cottage, Prestonpans, East Lothian, EH32 9EN
DONALDSON, Rear Admiral Vernon D'Arcy, 36 Tregunter Road, London SW10
DOUGLAS, Gordon G., 3390 Norman Drive, Reno, Nevada, 89509, USA
DRAFFEN, George S., of Newington, M.B.E., Meadowside, Balmullo, Leuchars, Fife KY16 0AW
DRALLE, Professor Lewis A., M.A., PH.D., Department of History, Wichita State University, Kansas 67508, USA
DRUMMOND-MURRAY, P., Old Hadlow House, Hadlow Down, Nr Uckfield, Sussex
DRYSDALE, Charles D., M.B.E., 17 Orchil Crescent, Auchterarder, Perthshire
DUNBAR, John G., F.S.A., Royal Commission, Ancient & Historical Monuments (Scotland), 52-54 Melville Street, Edinburgh EH3 7HF
DUNCAN, Archibald, Ovenstone House, by Pittenweem, Fife
DUNCAN, Professor Archibald A. M., Department of Scottish History, The University, Glasgow G12 8QH
DUNLOP, Rev. A. Ian, 11 Bellevue Place, Edinburgh EH7 4BS
DUNLOP, Professor D. M., D.LITT., 423 West 120th Street, New York, N.Y. 10027, USA

DURACK, Mrs Isabel J., 87 Comiston Drive, Edinburgh EH10
DURKAN, J., PH.D., 14 Newfield Square, Glasgow G42 8BP

ELLIOT, Mrs Margaret R., B.A., 8 Easter Belmont Road, Edinburgh
EH12 6EX
EWING, Mrs Winifred, M.P., LL.B., 52 Queen's Drive, Glasgow G42 8BP

FARQUHARSON, R. 20 Monaro Crescent, Red Hill, ACT 2603,
Australia
FENTON, Alexander, M.A., 132 Blackford Avenue, Edinburgh EH9 3HH
FERGUSON, William, PH.D., Scottish History Department, William
Robertson Building, 50 George Square, Edinburgh EH8 9JY
FERGUSON, W. K., M.A., 82 St Quivox Road, Prestwick, Ayrshire
FINDLAY, Donald R., 52 Morningside Road, Edinburgh EH10
FINLAYSON, G., Department of History, The University, Glasgow
G12 8QG
FISHER, Ian, B.A., Royal Commission, Ancient & Historical Monuments
(Scotland), 52-54 Melville Street, Edinburgh EH3 7HF
FLATT, Roy Francis, 6 Comrie Street, Crieff, Perthshire PH7 4AX
FLECK, John M. M., M.A., Ard-Coile, Conon Bridge, Ross-shire N7 8AE
FLEMING, A. M. H., Glenfintaig House, Spean Bridge, Inverness-shire,
PH34 4DX
FLEMING, Mrs M. J. P., M.B., CH.B., 17 Graham Park Road, Gosforth,
Newcastle-upon-Tyne
FOSTER, Mrs Linda, B.A., Hilton View, Pattiesmuir, Nr. Dunfermline,
Fife
FOTHRINGHAM, H. Steuart, of Grantully, F.S.A.SCOT., Grantully
Castle, Aberfeldy, Perthshire PH15 2EG
FRASER, Mrs Agnes P. D.A., F.S.A., SCOT. 76 Moira Terrace, Edinburgh
EH7
FRASER, Lady Antonia, 52 Campden Hill Square, London W8
FRASER, Barclay S., Viewforth, Glebe Road, Cramond, Edinburgh
FRASER, The Hon. Lord, 30 Cleaver Square, London, SE11 4EA
FYFE, Ronald, 74 Mile End Avenue, Aberdeen

GALBRAITH, The Hon. T. G. D., M.P., 2 Cowley Street, London SW1
GAULD, Miss Mary B., 29 Beechgrove Terrace, Aberdeen AB2 4DR
GAULDIE, Mrs Enid, B.PHIL, Waterside, Invergowrie, by Dundee
GIBSON, Dr J. A., M.D., D.R.C.O.G., M.R.C.G.P., Foremount House,
Kilbarchan, Renfrewshire
GIBSON, Miss Kathleen C. S., D.A., 21 Buckstone Road, Edinburgh
EH10
GILFILLAN, J. B. S., Edenkerry, Helensburgh, Dunbartonshire G84 7HQ
GILL, W. M., M.A., Woodburn, Cairnryan, Stranraer, Wigtownshire
GILLANDERS, Farquhar, M.A., The University, Glasgow G12 8QQ

GLADSTONE, John, Capenoch, Penpont, Dumfriesshire
GLEN, F. J., St Margaret's Hospital, Crossgate, Durham
GORRIE, D. C. E., M.A., 54 Garscube Terrace, Edinburgh EH12
GOULDESBROUGH, Peter, LL.B., Scottish Record Office, H.M. General Register House, Edinburgh EH1 3YY
GOURLAY, Miss Teresa, M.A., 4 Thorburn Road, Edinburgh EH13
GRAHAM, Norman W., Suilven, Kings Road, Longniddry, East Lothian
GRAHAM, Thomas, M.A., 21A Rosebery Street, Aberdeen AB2 4LN
GRANGE, R. W. D., Aberdour School, Burgh Heath, nr. Tadworth, Surrey
GRANT, I. D., 94 Polwarth Gardens, Edinburgh EH11 1LJ
GRANT, Miss I. F., LL.D., 35 Heriot Row, Edinburgh EH3
GRANT, Ian R., 72 Dundas Street, Edinburgh
GRANT, Miss Margaret W., 3 Ben Bhraggie Drive, Golspie, Sutherland
GRANT-PETERKIN, K., B.A., Invererne, Forres, Moray
GRAY, Charles, The Cathedral Manse, Dunblane, Perthshire
GRIEVE, Miss Hilda E. P., B.E.M., B.A., 153 New London Road, Chelmsford, Essex CM2 0AA
GROVES, William N., 5 Staikhill, Lanark ML11 7PW

HAIG, Miss Lilian S., 30 Hazel Avenue, Kirkcaldy, Fife
HALDANE, A. R. B., C.B.E., W.S., Foswell, Auchterarder, Perthshire
HALL, John N. S., 27 Carseloch Road, Alloway, Ayr
HALLIDAY, J., 10 Argyle Street, Maryfield, Dundee
HALLIDAY, Rev. Canon R. T., B.D., Holy Cross Rectory, 18 Barnton Gardens, Edinburgh EH4 6AF
HAMPTON, Gordon B. I., 809 Tak Shing House, 20 Des Voeux Road Central, Hong Kong
HANHAM, Professor H. J., PH.D., School of Humanities and Social Science, Massachusetts Institute of Technology, Cambridge, Mass., 02139, USA
HANNAH, Alexander, Roebucks, Hollybank Road, Hookheath, Woking, Surrey
HARGREAVES, Professor John D., 146 Hamilton Place, Aberdeen
HARRISON, E. S., The Bield, Elgin, Moray
HAWORTH, John C., PH.D., 519 Witherspoon Drive, Springfield, Illinois, 62704, USA
HAWS, Charles H., B.A., Department of History, Old Dominion University, Norfolk, Virginia 23508, USA
HAY, Professor Denys, 31 Fountainhall Road, Edinburgh EH9
HAY, Frederick G., M.A., Department of Political Economy, The University, Glasgow G12 8QG
HAY, George, F.S.A., 29 Moray Place, Edinburgh EH3 6BX
HAY, Col. R. A., New Club, 86 Princes Street, Edinburgh EH2 2BB
HAYES, David, Landmark, Carrbridge, Inverness-shire
HEDDLE, Miss Joan, 4 Cliff Court, Military Road, Rye, Sussex, TN36

HENDERSON, Mrs M. I. O. Gore-Browne, 41 Cluny Gardens, Edinburgh EH10 6BL

HENDERSON, W. R., Cedar Grove, Dirleton, North Berwick, East Lothian

HENDERSON-HOWAT, Mrs A. M. D., 7 Lansdowne Crescent, Edinburgh EH12

HESKETH, Lady, Towcester, Northamptonshire

HILTON, Miss Margaret, B.A., Malvern Girls' College, Great Malvern

HOPE, Col. Archibald J. G., Luffness, Aberlady, East Lothian

HORN, Miss B. L. H., 5 Rothesay Terrace, Edinburgh EH3 7RY

HORRICKS, Miss Christine L., B.A., 5 Avon Close, Saltburn-by-Sea, Yorks.

HOUSTON, Professor George, Department of Political Economy, The University, Glasgow G12 8QG

HOWATSON, William, M.A., Cairn Park, Templand, Lockerbie, Dumfriesshire

HOWELL, Roger, Jr., M.A., PH.D., Department of History, Bowdoin College, Brunswick, Maine 04011, USA

HUIE, A. W., 15 Louisville Avenue, Aberdeen

HUME, John R., B.SC., 28 Partickhill Road, Glasgow G11 5BP

HUNTER, Mrs Jean, M.S., Stromcrag, 2 Mary Street, Dunoon, Argyll

HUNTER, R. L., F.S.A., 74 Trinity Road, Edinburgh EH5

HUNTER, R. L. C., LL.B., Department of Jurisprudence, University of Dundee, Dundee DD1

HUNTER SMITH, Norval S., M.A., Instituut voor Algemene Taalwetenschap, Spui 21, Amsterdam, Holland

HUTTON, B. G., 9 Wilton Road, Edinburgh EH16 5NX

IIJIMA, Keiji, B.LITT., 4-34-8 Yayoi-cho, Nakano-Ku, Tokio, Japan

INNES, Malcolm, of Edingight, M.A., LL.B., Court of the Lord Lyon, H.M. New Register House, Edinburgh EH1 3YT

IREDELL, Godfrey W., LL.M., PH.D., D.P.A., F.S.A. SCOT., Woodlands, Braithwaite, Keswick, Cumbria CA12 5TW

JAMIESON, Morley, 57 West Holmes Gardens, Musselburgh, Midlothian

JOHN, Stanley, DIPL. RTC., 34 Killermont Place, Kilwinning, Ayrshire, KA13 6PZ

JOHNSON, Mrs Christine, 5 Johnsburn Road, Balerno, Midlothian

KANE, Patrick, A.L.A., 83 Carvale Avenue, Salsburgh, Shotts ML7 4NF

KAUFFMAN, Christopher J., A.B., M.A., 519 Donne Avenue, St Louis, Missouri 63130, USA

KEAN, A. A., M.A., LL.B., Tannachy, Forres, Moray

KEILLAR, Ian J., 80 Duncan Drive, Elgin, Moray

KELLY, F. N. Davidson, St Gerardine's, 30 Old Kirk Road, Edinburgh EH12

KENNEDY, A., Craigmullen, Dundrennan, Kirkcudbright DG6 4QF

KENNEDY, James, B.SC., 9 Segton Avenue, Kilwinning, Ayrshire

KIDD, Matthew P., Corrie Doon, Queen Victoria Street, Airdrie ML6 0DL

KILPATRICK, P. J. W., Pythouse, Tisbury, Salisbury, Wilts

KINLOCH, Sir John, Aldie Cottage, Fossoway, nr. Kinross

KINNIBURGH, T. C., No 2 Flat 1, Albion Villas, Folkestone, Kent

KIRK, David C., Croft End, 117 Foxley Lane, Purley, Surrey CR2 3HQ

KIRK, James, PH.D., Woodlea, Dunmore, by Falkirk

KIRKPATRICK, H. S., F.S.A. SCOT., c/o Dr D. Cohen, 17 Springpool, Keele University, Staffs.

LAMBIE, Brian, Gairland, Biggar, Lanarkshire ML12 6DN

LAWRIE, John J., 51 Colcokes Road, Banstead, Surrey

LAWSON, William A., 3 Mansionhouse Road, Paisley

LEE, Professor Maurice, Jr., Douglass College, Rutgers University, New Brunswick, New Jersey, 08903 USA

LEGGE, Professor M. D., B.LITT., 191A Woodstock Road, Oxford OX2 7AB

LENMAN, Bruce P., M.A., M.LITT., 6 Irvine Crescent, St Andrews KY16 8LG

LESLIE, The Hon. J. W., East Kintrockat, Brechin, Angus

LILBURN, Alistair J., B.SC., Newlyn, Aboyne, Aberdeenshire AB3 5HE

LILBURN, Gavin C., c/o National Liberal Club, Whitehall Place, London SW1

LOCKETT, G. D., M.B.E., Clonterbrook House, Swettenham, Congleton, Cheshire

LOCKHART, Douglas G., The Mound, 23 King's Crescent, Elderslie, Renfrewshire

LOCKHART, S. F. MacDonald, Newholm, Dunsyre, Carnwath, Lanarkshire ML11 8NQ

LOGUE, Kenneth J., 4 Oxford Street, Edinburgh EH8 9PJ

LOLE, F. P., Seaton Cote, Branthwaite Lane, Seaton, Workington, Cumberland

LORIMER, Hew, R.S.A., Kellie Castle, Pittenweem, Fife

LYTHE, Professor S. G. E., Department of Economic History, University of Strathclyde, McCance Building, Richmond Street, Glasgow G1

MACALLISTER, R. B., 34 Thomas Telford Road, Langholm, Dumfriesshire

McALLISTER, R. I., 6 Ogilvie Place, Bridge of Allan, Stirlingshire

MACARTHUR, D., 8 Dempster Terrace, St Andrews KY16

McARTHUR, James N., M.A., Stirling High School, Torbrex, Stirling

McAULAY, Alexander C., 30B Glenacre Road, Cumbernauld, Glasgow G67 2MZ

MACAULAY, James M., M.A., PH.D., 6 Hamilton Drive, Glasgow G12 8DR

McCAFFREY, J. F., PH.D., 12 Balmoral Drive, Cambuslang, Glasgow

McCOSH, Bryce K., of Huntfield, Quothquan, Biggar, Lanarkshire

MACDONALD, Mrs C., 1 Windsor Street, Edinburgh 7

MACDONALD, D., 10 Pearce Avenue, Corstorphine, Edinburgh 12

MACDONALD, Hector, M.A., PH.D., c/o National Library of Scotland, George IV Bridge, Edinburgh EH1 1EW

MACDONALD, J. M., Bruach, Sidinish, Locheport, North Uist

MACDONALD, Rev. R., S.T.L., Reul nu Mara, Brandon Street, Dunoon PA23 8BU

MACFARLANE, L. J., F.S.A., 113 High Street, Old Aberdeen

MACFARQUHAR, Roderick, 8 Glencairn Crescent, Edinburgh EH12

McFAULDS, John, 2F Milton Street, Airdrie ML6 6JN

McINNES, Alan I., 13 North Gardiner Street, Glasgow G11

MACINNES, Rev. John, PH.D., D.D., Eastcott, Fortrose, Ross-shire

MACINTOSH, Farquhar, M.A., 212 Colinton Road, Edinburgh EH14 1BP

MACINTYRE, J. Archibald, B.A., M.A., Department of Sociology, University of Guelph, Guelph, Ontario, Canada

MACINTYRE, Robert D., M.B., CH.B., J.P., 8 Gladstone Place, Stirling

MacINTYRE, Stuart, M.A., 57 Wills Street, Kew, Victoria, Australia, 3101

MACIVER, I. F., M.A., c/o National Library of Scotland, George IV Bridge, Edinburgh EH1 1EW

MACKAY, Rev. Hugh, M.A., F.S.A. SCOT., The Manse, Duns, Berwickshire

MACKAY, Miss Margaret L., 3 Braid Mount, Edinburgh EH10

MACKAY, Rev. P. H. R., M.A., Clola, 1 Dirleton Road, North Berwick

MACKAY, R. L., O.B.E., M.C., M.D., 5 The Parklands, Finchfield, Wolverhampton

MACKAY, William, O.B.E., Upper Glassburne, by Beauly

MACKAY, William, 4 St Barnabas Road, Cambridge

MACKECHNIE, Miss Catherine B., 59 Polwarth Street, Glasgow G12

MACKECHNIE, Donald, Schoolhouse, Bridge of Douglas, Inveraray, Argyll

MacKECHNIE, John, M.A., B.D., 41 Orchard Place, Chatham, Ontario, Canada

MACKENZIE, Mrs P. C., The Cottage, Upper Clatford, Andover, Hants.

MACKIE, Professor J. D., C.B.E., M.C., LL.D., 67 Dowanside Road, Glasgow G12

MACLACHLAN, H. S., 18 Clarence Street, Clydebank, Dunbartonshire G81 2HU

MACLEAN, Rev. Ewan A., 12 Tantallon Place, Edinburgh EH9

MACLEAN, James N. M., ygr., of Glensanda, B.LITT., PH.D., Department of History, University of Edinburgh, William Robertson Building, 50 George Square, Edinburgh EH8 9JY

MACLEAN, Dr J., Van Neckstraat 102, 's-Gravenhage 1, Netherlands
MACLEAN, Mrs L. M., of Dochgarroch, Hazelbrae House, Glen Urquhart, Inverness IV3 6TJ
McLELLAN, Miss Maureen A., M.A., 32 Royal Circus, Edinburgh EH3
MACLEOD, Innes F., M.A., Department of Extra-mural Studies, 57/59 Oakfield Avenue, Glasgow G12 8LW
MACLEOD, Col. James H. Calder, 80 Whittinghame Court, Glasgow G12
McMAHON, Geo. I. R., M.A., B.LITT., Homerton College, Cambridge
MACMILLAN, Andrew T., C.A., 20 Garscube Terrace, Edinburgh EH12 6BQ
McMILLAN, N. W., LL.B., 160 West George Street, Glasgow G2 2LA
McNAUGHT, James, Kilneiss, Moniaive, Thornhill, Dumfriesshire
MACNAUGHTON, Miss Catherine, Oakbank Cottage, St Fillans, Perthshire
McNEILL, Sheriff Peter G. B., 185 Nithsdale Road, Glasgow G41
McNUTT, Miss Margaret R., M.A., DIP.ED., 384 North Deeside Road, Cults, Aberdeen
MACPHAIL, Angus N., 3 Denton Avenue, Gledhow, Leeds 8
MACPHAIL, I. M. M., PH.DR., Rockbank, Barloan Crescent, Dumbarton
MACPHAIL, W. D., M.A., B.A., Bretonville, Conon Bridge, Ross-shire
MACPHERSON, Captain J. Harvey, F.S.A. SCOT., Dunmore, Newtonmore, Inverness-shire
MACQUEEN, Professor John, School of Scottish Studies, University of Edinburgh, 27 George Square, Edinburgh EH8 9LD
McROBERTS, Right Rev. Monsignor David, S.T.L., F.S.A., 16 Drummond Place, Edinburgh
MACHIN, G. I. T., D.PHIL., Department of Modern History, The University, Dundee DD1 4HN
MACK, Donald W., 88 Brownside Road, Cambuslang, Glasgow
MAGRUDER, Thomas G., Jr., 331 North Henry Street, Williamsburg, Virginia 23185, USA
MANNING, Mrs Doreen Caraher, B.A., Gowanlea, Willoughby Street, Muthil by Crieff, Perthshire PH5 2AE
MARSHALL, Rev. James S., M.A., 4 Claremont Park, Edinburgh EH6 7PH
MARSHALL, Miss Rosalind K., PH.D., 11 St Clair Terrace, Edinburgh EH10 5NW
MARWICK, W. H., 5 Northfield Crescent, Edinburgh EH8 7PU
MATTHEW, Mrs Irene W., Whinniehill Cottage, Allander Toll, Milngavie, Glasgow G62 6EW
MAXWELL, Stuart, F.S.A. SCOT., 23 Dick Place, Edinburgh EH9
MEEK, Donald E., Department of Celtic, University of Glasgow G12
MENZIES, George M., 34 Brighton Place, Edinburgh EH15 1LT
MICHAEL, James, O.B.E., Achtemrack, Drumnadrochit, Inverness-shire
MILLER, Jonathan, Wellcraig, Tayport, Fife

MILNE, Miss Doreen J., PH.D., Department of History, King's College, Old Aberdeen AB9 2UB

MINTO, B. L. J., C.A., 164 South Street, St Andrews, Fife KY16

MITCHELL, Brian, 5 Park View, Brechin, Angus

MITCHELL, Miss Rosemary, M.A., 24 Alexandra Place, Oban, Argyll

MITCHISON, Mrs R., Great Yew, Ormiston, East Lothian EH35 5NJ

MONCRIEFFE, Sir Iain, PH.D., F.S.A., House of Moncreiffe, Bridge of Earn, Perthshire

MOORE, Edwin, Merry Leazes West, Hexham, Northumberland

MOORE, Hugh P. Esq., 1906 Montezuma Way, West Coving, California, 91791, USA

MOORE, R. L., 11 Ribble Avenue, Rainhill, Prescott, Lancs. L35 0NJ

MORPETH, R. S., 11 Albert Terrace, Edinburgh EH10

MORRIS, F. G., 45 Potton Road, Everton, Sandy, Beds SG19 2LE

MUI, Hoh-cheung, PH.D., Department of History, Memorial University, St John's, Newfoundland, Canada

MULHOLLAND, R., 2 Farr Cottages, Farr, Strathnairn, Inverness-shire

MUNRO, D. J., M.A., 7 Midfield Drive, Barnehurst, Bexley Heath, Kent

MUNRO, Mrs R. W., 15A Mansionhouse Road, Edinburgh EH9 1TZ

MUNRO, R. W., 15A Mansionhouse Road, Edinburgh EH9 1TZ

MURCHISON, Very Rev. Dr T. M., 10 Mount Stuart Street, Glasgow G14 3YL

MURDOCH, Mrs S. M., Aird House, Badachro, Gairloch, Ross-shire

MURRAY, A. L., PH.D., LL.B., 33 Inverleith Gardens, Edinburgh EH3

MURRAY, David, Maclay, Murray & Spens, 169 West George Street, Glasgow G2 2LA

MURRAY, Murdoch D., M.R.C.V.S., 3 Gardiner Grove, Edinburgh EH4 3RT

NAUGHTON, Miss J. M., M.A., 9 Summerside Street, Edinburgh EH6

NEIL, J. K., The Viewlands, Blakeshall, nr. Kidderminster, Worcs.

NEILLY, Miss Margaret, R.G.N., 9 Woodmuir Road, Whitburn, West Lothian

NICHOLSON, C. B. Harman, Galleria Passarella 1, 20122-Milan, Italy

NICHOLSON, R. G., Department of History, Wellington College, University of Guelph, Guelph, Ontario, Canada

NICOL, Miss Mary P. M.A., 15 Falcon Road West, Edinburgh EH10

NICOLL, Mrs I. M., Westcroft, Wardlaw Gardens, St Andrews KY16

NIMMO, Mrs A. E., 9 Succoth Gardens, Edinburgh EH12

NOBLE, John, Ardkinglas, Cairndow, Argyll

NORBY, Mrs Eunice, 207 Mary Avenue, Missoula, Montana, USA

NOTMAN, R. C., B.L., W.S., c/o Morton, Fraser and Milligan, W.S., 15-19 York Place, Edinburgh EH1 3EL

NUTTER, Bryan, 21 Taywood Close, Poulton-Le-Fylde, nr. Blackpool FY6 7EY

OLIVER, Col. W. H., M.B.E., Blain, Nether Blainslie, Galashiels TD1 2PR, Selkirkshire

PAGE, R. A., 47 Pittenweem Road, Anstruther, Fife KY10 3DT
PALMER, Kenneth W., 4 Cumin Place, Edinburgh EH9 2JX
PARKER, Major H. F., Torlochan, Gruline, Isle of Mull, Argyll
PATTULLO, David, Fairhaven, Elie, Fife
PATTULLO, Miss Nan, 29 Ormidale Terrace, Edinburgh EH12
PHILLIPSON, N. T., History Department, University of Edinburgh, William Robertson Building, 50 George Square, Edinburgh EH8 9JY
PRAIN, Sheriff A. M., Castellar, Crieff, Perthshire
PREBBLE, John, F.R.S.L., Shaw Coign, Alcocks Lane, Burgh Heath, Tadworth, Surrey

RAE, Miss Isobel, Dunlugas Cottage, Nairn
RAE, Thomas I., PH.D., National Library of Scotland, George IV Bridge, Edinburgh EH1 1EW (*Honorary Publications Secretary*)
RAMSAY, Alan D. M., Bolland of Galashiels, Selkirkshire
REID, Professor W. Stanford, Department of History, University of Guelph, Guelph, Ontario, Canada
RITCHIE, Alexander, 19 Langside Drive, Kilbarchan, Renfrewshire
RITCHIE, James S., M.A., 42 Dudley Gardens, Edinburgh EH6 4PS
ROACH, William M., PH.D., 156 Brownside Road, Burnside, Rutherglen, Glasgow G73 5AZ
ROBERTSON, F. W., PH.D., 17 Sinclair Terrace, Wick, Caithness
ROBERTSON, James J., LL.B, Faculty of Law, University of Dundee, Dundee DD1
ROBERTSON, Miss Kathleen, M.A., 120 Albert Road, Gourock, Renfrewshire
ROBERTSON, Lewis, C.B.E., The Blair, Blairlogie, Stirling FK9 5PX
ROBERTSON, The Hon. Lord, 49 Moray Place, Edinburgh EH3 6DT
RODGER, George N., 9 The Cross, Forfar, Angus DD8 1BX
ROSS, Rev. Anthony, O.P., S.T.L., 24 George Square, Edinburgh EH8 9LD
ROSS, Douglas H., Killorn, Milngavie, Glasgow
ROSS, Ian S., Department of English, University of British Columbia, Vancouver V6T 1W5, B.C., Canada
RUSSELL, D. F. O., Rothes, Markinch, Fife KY7 6PW
RUSSELL, Miss Florence M., 95 Victoria Road, Dunoon, Argyll, PA23 7AD

SANDERSON, Miss Elizabeth C., 28 Highfield Crescent, Linlithgow, West Lothian
SANDERSON, Miss Margaret H. B., PH.D., 28 Highfield Crescent, Linlithgow, West Lothian
SCARLETT, James D., 9 Bellevue Terrace, Edinburgh EH7 4DT
SCOTLAND, James, M.A., LL.B., M.ED., 67 Forest Road, Aberdeen
SCOTT, David, 22 Blomfield Road, London, W9 1AD

SCOTT, J. G., M.A., 10 Abbotsford Court, Colinton Road, Edinburgh EH10 5EH

SCOTT, P. H., 40 House o'Hill Road, Blackhall, Edinburgh EH4 2AN

SCOTT, R. Lyon, Braeside, Loanhead, Midlothian

SCOTT, Thomas H., M.A., B.L., 1 Thimblehall Place, Dunfermline

SCOTT, W. W., 26 Braid Hills Road, Edinburgh EH10 6HY

SEFTON, Rev. H. R., PH.D., Department of Church History, King's College, Aberdeen AB9 2UB

SELLAR, W. D. H., 2 Bellevue Terrace, Edinburgh EH7

SEMPLE, Walter G., 47 Newark Drive, Glasgow G41

SERVICE, Commander Douglas, of Torsonce, 16 Redington Road, Hampstead, London NW3 7RG

SHARP, Brian, 12 Shelley Drive, Bothwell, Glasgow G71 8TA

SHARP, Buchanan, B.A., M.A., College V, University of California, Santa Cruz, California, USA

SHAW, Major C. J., of Tordarroch, M.B.E., T.D., D.L., Newhall, Balblair, Conon Bridge, Ross-shire

SHAW, Rev. Duncan, PH.D., 4 Sydney Terrace, Edinburgh EH7

SHEAD, N. F., 16 Burnside Gardens, Clarkston, Glasgow

SHEARER, J. G. S., M.A., 36 Snowdon Place, Stirling

SHEPHERD, James P., M.A., 14 East Fettes Avenue, Edinburgh EH4 1AN

SIMPSON, Eric J., 1 Pinewood Drive, Dalgety Bay, Dunfermline, Fife

SIMPSON, Grant G., PH.D., F.S.A., Department of History, University of Aberdeen, Taylor Building, King's College, Old Aberdeen AB9 2UB

SIMPSON, John M., Scottish History Department, William Robertson Building, 50 George Square, Edinburgh EH8 9JY

SINCLAIR, Alexander, M.A., DIP.M.S., A.M.B.I.M., 16 Kensington Drive, Bearsden, Glasgow G61 2HG

SINCLAIR, John N., Hamarsland, 12 Lovers Loan, Lerwick, Shetland ZE1 OBA

SKINNER, Basil C., 10 Randolph Cliff, Edinburgh EK3 7UA

SLADE, H. Gordon, T.D., A.R.I.B.A., 15 Southbourne Gardens, London SE12

SLIMMINGS, Sir William K. M., C.B.E., D.LITT., C.A., 62 The Avenue, Worcester Park, Surrey

SMAIL, James E., 2 Bright's Crescent, Edinburgh EH9 2DA

SMITH, Mrs Annette, Kingarth, Lade Braes, St Andrews KY16 9ET

SMITH, David B., LL.B., 30 Great King Street, Edinburgh EH3

SMITH, Harold, M.A., 13 Newhailes Crescent, Musselburgh, Midlothian

SMITH, J. A., B.ED., 108 Queen Victoria Drive, Glasgow G14 9BL

SMOUT, Professor T. C., PH.D., 19 South Gillsland Road, Edinburgh EH10

SMYTHE, Thomas, 4 Whorterbank, Lochee, Dundee

SOUTHESK, The Rt. Hon. The Earl of, K.C.V.O., Kinnaird Castle, Brechin, Angus

STARKEY, A. M., PH.D., History Department, Adelphi University, Garden City, NY, 11530, USA

STENHOUSE, B. A., 6/14 Orchard Brae Avenue, Edinburgh EH4 2HP
STEVENSON, David, B.A., 15 Binghill Park, Milltimber, Aberdeenshire AB1 OEE (*Honorary Secretary*)
STEWART, H. C., Netherton, Wellside Road, Falkirk, Stirlingshire
STEWART, Robert G., 12 Nutt Road, Auburn, New Hampshire, 03032 USA
STIRLING, Matthew, 20 Westbourne Terrace, London W2
STONES, Professor E. L. G., PH.D., F.S.A., History Department, The University, Glasgow G12 8QG
STRACHAN, M. F., M.B.E., 7 Napier Road, Edinburgh EH10
STRAWHORN, John, PH.D., 2 East Park Avenue, Mauchline, Ayrshire
STUART, Peter Maxwell, Traquair House, Innerleithen, Peeblesshire EH44 6PW
SUNTER, J. R. M., M.A., 30 March Road, Blackhall, Edinburgh EH4 3TB
SUTHERLAND, The Countess of, Uppat House, Brora, Sutherland
SWAINSTON, Mrs A. Y. Imrie, 8 Sheldon Avenue, London N6

TAYLOR, David B., M.A., F.S.A. SCOT., Delvine, Longforgan, byDundee
TAYLOR, W., PH.D., 25 Bingham Terrace, Dundee
TENNANT, Charles, Greymount, Alyth
THOMPSON, F. G., Arnish, 31 Braeside Park, Balloch, Inverness, Inverness-shire
THOMS, David, Strathview, Trinity Road, Brechin, Angus
THOMSON, A. G., PH.D., 30 Forth Street (1st Flat), Edinburgh EH1 3LH
THOMSON, A. McLay, F.R.H.S., 94 Baldwin Avenue, Glasgow G13 2QU
THOMSON, J. A., Summerhill House, Annan, Dumfriesshire
THOMSON, J. A. F., D.PHIL., History Department, The University, Glasgow G12 8QG
THOMSON, James M., 27 Kilrymont Road, St Andrews, Fife KY16
THORNBER, Iain, Ardtornish, Morvern, Oban, Argyll PA34 5UZ
TODD, J. M., Redbourn House, Main Street, St Bees, Cumberland
TREVOR-ROPER, Professor H. R., Chiefswood, Melrose
TROUP, J. A., St Abbs, 34 Hillside Road, Stromness, Orkney
TURNER, Professor A. C., College of Letters and Science, University of California, Riverside, California 92502, USA

URQUHART, Kenneth T., ygr., of Urquhart, 4713 Orleans Blud Jefferson, La., 70121, USA

VEITCH, Rev. Thomas, M.A., F.S.A. SCOT., St Paul's and St George's Rectory, 53 Albany Street, Edinburgh EH1
VON GOETZ, Richard B., Chesterhill, Newport-on-Tay, Fife

WALKER, Professor David M., Q.C., PH.D., LL.D., 1 Beaumont Gate, Glasgow G12

WALLACE, J. C., M.A., 9 Spottiswoode Street, Edinburgh EH9 1EP
WALLS, Andrew F., M.A., B.LITT., Department of Religious Studies, King's College, Old Aberdeen AB9 2UB
WALSH, Rev. James, L.S.H., St Peter's College, Cardross, Dunbartonshire G82.5EU
WALTON, Mrs P. M. Eaves, 55 Manor Place, Edinburgh EH3
WARD, Rev. David F., Chaplaincy for University Catholics, 172 Perth Road, Dundee
WATSON, Miss Elspeth G. Boog, Pitsligo House, Edinburgh EH10 4RY
WATSON, Miss Janet, 138 Chamberlain Road, Glasgow G13
WATSON, T. A., M.A., 8 Melville Terrace, Anstruther, Fife
WATT, Donald E. R., Department of Medieval History, St Salvator's College, St Andrews KY16
WEBSTER, A. Bruce, F.S.A., 5 The Terrace, St Stephens, Canterbury, Kent
WEDGWOOD, Dame C. V., 22 St Ann's Terrace, London NW8 6PJ
WEIR, Thomas E., U.S.N.R., B.D., PH.D., Correctional Facility, Camp Lejeune, NC 28542, USA
WHITEFORD, Rev. D. H., Q.H.C., B.D., PH.D., Gullane Manse, Gullane, East Lothian
WHITTY, Naill R., 44 Garscube Terrace, Edinburgh EH12
WHYTE, Donald, 4 Carmel Road, Kirkliston, West Lothian
WILLIAMSON, John, New Grunnasound, Bridge End, Shetland
WILLOCK, Professor I. D., Department of Jurisprudence, University of Dundee, Dundee DD1
WILLS, Mrs Peter, Allan Gowan, 109 Henderson Street, Bridge of Allan, Stirlingshire
WILSON, Miss Florence Eva, 164 Forest Avenue, Aberdeen AB1 6UN
WILSON, Sir Garnet, LL.D., St Colmes, 496 Perth Road, Dundee DD5 1LS
WILSON, Gordon, Department of History, College of Education, Bothwell Road, Hamilton
WILSON, Miss Isabel J. T., 2 Segton Avenue, Kilwinning, Ayrshire KA16 6LQ
WISKER, R. F., 17 Merridale Lane, Wolverhampton, WV3 9RD
WITHRINGTON, D. J., M.ED., History Department, King's College, Old Aberdeen AB9 2UB
WYLIE, Lawrence A., 127 Benito Avenue, Santa Cruz, California, 95060, USA

YOUNG, Mrs E. M., M.A., F.R.G.S., Beechwoods, Killishaws Road, Dalry, Ayrshire KA24 4LL
YOUNG, Kenneth G., LL.B., W.S., Dunearn, Auchterarder, Perthshire
YOUNG, Miss Margaret D., 1 Craiglockhart Gardens, Edinburgh EH14 1ND

YOUNG, Mrs Margaret D., 73 Kingslynn Drive, Glasgow G44 4JB

YOUNG, R. M., Rustlings, 389 Cross Lane, Congleton, Cheshire CW12 3JX

YOUNGSON, Professor A. J., D.LITT., Research School of Social Science, Australian National University, PO Box 4, Canberra ACT 2600, Australia

Aberdeen College of Education
Aberdeen Public Library
Aberdeen University Library
Adelaide University Barr Smith Library, Australia
Adelphi University Swirbul Library, Garden City, Long Island, NY., USA
Alabama University Library, Ala., USA
Alberta University Library, Edmonton, Canada
Angus and Kincardine County Library
Arbroath Public Library, Montrose
Argyll County Library, Dunoon
Auckland University Library, New Zealand
Ayr Carnegie Public Library
Ayr, Craigie College of Education

Baillie's Institution Free Library, Glasgow
Banff County Library, Portsoy
Belfast Library and Society for Promoting Knowledge (Linenhall Library)
Bibliothèque Nationale, Paris, France
Birmingham Public Libraries
Birmingham University Library
Blackwell Ltd., Oxford
Boston Athenaeum, Mass., USA
Boston Public Library, Mass., USA
Boston University Libraries, Mass., USA
Bowdoin College Library, Brunswick, Maine, USA
Bristol University Library
British Columbia University Library, Vancouver, Canada
British Library, Boston Spa
Brown University Library, Providence, Rhode Island, USA
Bute County Library, Rothesay

Calgary University Library
California University at Berkeley Library, USA
California University at Davis Library, USA
California University at Los Angeles Library, USA
California University at Riverside Library, USA
California University at San Diego, USA
Cambridge University Library
Cape Breton College, Sydney, Nova Scotia
Capetown University J. W. Jagger Library, South Africa
Cardiff Free Library
Chicago University Library, Ill., USA
Cincinnati University General Library, Ohio, USA

Cleveland Public Library, Ohio, USA
Coatbridge Carnegie Public Library
Columbia University Library, New York, NY, USA
Copenhagen Royal Library, Denmark
Cornell University Library, Ithaca, NY, USA

Dalhousie University Library, Halifax, Canada
Dartmouth College Library, Hanover, NH, USA
Delaware University Memorial Library, Newark, USA
Denny High School
Duke University Library, Durham, NC, USA
Dumbarton Public Library
Dumfries County Library
Dundee College of Education
Dundee Public Library
Dundee University Library
Dunfermline Public Library
Dunoon Tulloch Free Library
Durham University Library

Ealing Central Library
East Anglia University Library, Norwich
East Lothian County Library, Haddington
Edinburgh City Corporation
Edinburgh, Hope Trust
Edinburgh, Moray House College of Education
Edinburgh New Club
Edinburgh Public Library
Edinburgh University. Fraser Chair of Scottish History
Edinburgh University Library
Edinburgh University, Scottish History Department
Enoch Pratt Free Library, George Peabody Department, Baltimore, Md.,
    USA
Episcopal Church of Scotland Theological Library, Edinburgh
Exeter University Library

Falkirk, Callendar Park College of Education
Falkirk Public Library
Flinders University of South Australia, Bedford Park
Folger Shakespeare Library, Washington, DC, USA
Forfar Public Library
Fort Wayne and Allen County Public Library, Ind., USA
Free Church of Scotland Library, Edinburgh

Georgia University Library, Athens, USA
Glasgow Art Gallery and Museum

Glasgow, Jordanhill College of Education
Glasgow University Library
Glasgow University, Scottish History Class Library
Glasgow University, Scottish History Department
Glencoe, 1745 Association and National Military History Society
Golspie High School
Gothenburg University Library, Sweden
Grangemouth Victoria Public Library
Guelph University Library, Canada

Hamilton College of Education
Harvard College Library, Cambridge, Mass., USA
Houston University Library, Tex., USA
Hull University Library
Huntington Library and Art Gallery, San Marino, Calif., USA

Illinois University Library, Urbana, USA
Indiana University Library, Bloomington, USA
Inverness Divisional Library
Inverness Public Library
Inverness Royal Academy
Iowa State University Libraries, Iowa, USA

Kilmarnock Public Library
Kirkcudbrightshire County Library, Castle Douglas
Kirkintilloch William Patrick Memorial Library

Lambeth Palace Library, London
Lancaster University Library
Leeds Reference Library
Leeds University Brotherton Library
Leicester University Library
Library of Congress, Washington, DC, USA
Liverpool University Library
London Corporation Guildhall Library
London Library
London University, Institute of Historical Research Library
London University Library
London University, Queen Mary College Library
London University, School of Economics and Political Science Library
London University, University College Library
Los Angeles Public Library, Calif., USA
Louvain Université Catholique, Bibliothèque Centrale, Belgium
Loyola University E. M. Cudahy Memorial Library, Chicago, Ill., USA

x

McGill University Library, Montreal, Canada
McMaster University Mills Memorial Library, Hamilton, Canada
Manchester Public Library
Manchester University, John Rylands Library
Maryland University McKeldin Library, College Park, USA
Melbourne University Library, Australia
Miami University Library, Oxford, Ohio, USA
Michigan State University Library, East Lansing, USA
Michigan University General Library, Ann Arbor, USA
Minnesota University Library, Minneapolis, USA
Missouri University General Library, Columbia, USA
Mitchell Library, Glasgow
Montreat Historical Foundation of Presbyterian Reformed Churches, NC,
    USA
Motherwell Public Libraries

Nashville University Joint Library, Tenn., USA
National Library of Australia, Canberra
National Library of Canada, Ottawa
National Library of Ireland, Dublin
National Library of Scotland, Edinburgh
National Library of Wales, Aberystwyth
National Museum of Antiquities of Scotland, Edinburgh
National Trust for Scotland, Edinburgh
Nebraska University Library, Lincoln, USA
Netherlands Royal Library, The Hague
Newberry Library, Chicago, Ill., USA
Newcastle-upon-Tyne Public Library
Newcastle-upon-Tyne University Library
New College Library, Edinburgh
New England University Library, Armidale, Australia
Newfoundland Memorial University Library, St John's, Canada
New South Wales Library, Sydney, Australia
New York General Theological Seminary Library, NY, USA
New York Public Library, NY, USA
New York State Library, Albany, USA
New York State University at Buffalo Lockwood Memorial Library, USA
New York University Libraries, NY, USA
Northumberland County Library, Morpeth
Northwestern University Library, Evanston, Ill., USA
Notre Dame University Library, Ind., USA
Nottingham Free Public Library

Ohio State University Library, Columbus, USA
Oregon University Library, Eugene, USA
Orkney County Library, Kirkwall

Oxford University, All Souls College Library
Oxford University, Balliol College Library
Oxford University Bodleian Library
Oxford University, Worcester College Library

Paisley College of Technology
Pennsylvania Historical Society, Philadelphia, USA
Pennsylvania State University Patee Library, University Park, USA
Pennsylvania University Library, Philadelphia, USA
Perth and Kinross County Library
Perth Sandeman Public Library
Princeton Theological Seminary Library, NJ, USA
Princeton University Library, NJ, USA
Public Record Office, London

Queen's University Library, Belfast

Reading University Library
Renfrew District Libraries, Paisley
Rochester University Library, NY, USA
Royal College of Physicians Library, Edinburgh
Royal Scottish Geographical Society, Edinburgh
Rutgers University Library, New Brunswick, NJ, USA

St Andrews Hay Fleming Library
St Andrews University Library
St Andrews University, Scottish History Library
St Benedict's Abbey, Fort Augustus
St Francis Xavier University Library, Antigonish, Canada
St Peter's College, Cardross
Saltire Society, Edinburgh
Sancta Maria Abbey, Nunraw, Haddington
Scottish Central Library, Edinburgh
Scottish Genealogy Society, Edinburgh
Scottish Record Office, Edinburgh
Scottish Reformation Society, Edinburgh
Sheffield City Libraries
Sheffield University Library
Signet Library, Edinburgh
Society of Antiquaries, London
Society of Australian Genealogists, Sydney, NSW, Australia
Society of Genealogists, London
Southern California University Library, Los Angeles, Calif., USA
Speculative Society, Edinburgh
Stanford University Library, Calif., USA
Stechart MacMillan Inc., Stuttgart, W. Germany

PUBLICATIONS

Volumes marked with an asterisk are no longer obtainable

FIRST SERIES

*17. LETTERS AND PAPERS ILLUSTRATING THE RELATIONS BETWEEN CHARLES II AND SCOTLAND IN 1650. Ed. SAMUEL RAWSON GARDINER. 1894.

*18. SCOTLAND AND THE COMMONWEALTH. LETTERS AND PAPERS RELATING TO THE MILITARY GOVERNMENT OF SCOTLAND, Aug. 1651-Dec. 1653. Ed. C. H. FIRTH. 1895.

*19. THE JACOBITE ATTEMPT OF 1719. LETTERS OF JAMES, SECOND DUKE OF ORMONDE. Ed. W. K. DICKSON. 1895.

20. 21, 22. THE LYON IN MOURNING, OR A COLLECTION OF SPEECHES, LETTERS, JOURNALS, ETC., RELATIVE TO THE AFFAIRS OF PRINCE CHARLES EDWARD STUART, by BISHOP FORBES. 1746-1775. Ed. HENRY PATON. 3 vols. 1895-96. [Reprint.]

23. ITINERARY OF PRINCE CHARLES EDWARD (Supplement to the Lyon in Mourning). Compiled by W. B. BLAIKIE. 1897. [Reprint.]

*24. EXTRACTS FROM THE PRESBYTERY RECORDS OF INVERNESS AND DINGWALL, 1638-88. Ed. WILLIAM MACKAY. 1896.

*25. THE RECORDS OF THE COMMISSIONS OF THE GENERAL ASSEMBLIES, 1648-49. Ed. Rev. Professor MITCHELL and Rev. JAMES CHRISTIE. 1896.

*26. JOHNSTON OF WARISTON'S DIARY, 1639. Ed. G. M. PAUL—THE HONOURS OF SCOTLAND, 1651-52. Ed. C. R. A. HOWDEN.—THE EARL OF MAR'S LEGACIES, 1722, 1726. Ed. Hon. S. ERSKINE.— LETTERS BY MRS GRANT OF LAGGAN. Ed. J. R. N. MACPHAIL. 1896.

Presented to the Society by Messrs T. and A. Constable

*27. MEMORIALS OF JOHN MURRAY OF BROUGHTON, 1740-1747. Ed. R. FITZROY BELL. 1898.

*28. THE COMPT BUIK OF DAVID WEDDERBURNE, MERCHANT OF DUNDEE, 1587-1630. Ed. A. H. MILLAR. 1898.

*29, 30. THE CORRESPONDENCE OF DE MONTEREUL AND THE BROTHERS DE BELLIÈVRE, FRENCH AMBASSADORS IN ENGLAND AND SCOTLAND, 1645-48. Ed. and trans. J. G. FOTHERINGHAM. 2 vols. 1898-9.

*31. SCOTLAND AND THE PROTECTORATE. LETTERS AND PAPERS RELATING TO THE MILITARY GOVERNMENT OF SCOTLAND, FROM JANUARY 1654 TO JUNE 1659. Ed. C. H. FIRTH. 1899.

*32. PAPERS ILLUSTRATING THE HISTORY OF THE SCOTS BRIGADE IN THE SERVICE OF THE UNITED NETHERLANDS. 1572-1782. Ed. JAMES FERGUSON. Vol. I, 1572-1697. 1899.

*33, 34. MACFARLANE'S GENEALOGICAL COLLECTIONS CONCERNING FAMILIES IN SCOTLAND. Ed. J. T. CLARK. 2 vols. 1900.

Presented to the Society by the Trustees of the late Sir William Fraser, K.C.B.

*35. PAPERS ON THE SCOTS BRIGADE IN HOLLAND, 1572-1782. Ed. JAMES FERGUSON. Vol. II, 1698-1782. 1899.

*36. JOURNAL OF A FOREIGN TOUR IN 1665 AND 1666, ETC., BY SIR JOHN LAUDER, LORD FOUNTAINHALL. Ed. DONALD CRAWFORD. 1900.

*37. PAPAL NEGOTIATIONS WITH MARY QUEEN OF SCOTS DURING HER REIGN IN SCOTLAND. Ed. Rev. J. HUNGERFORD POLLEN. 1901.

*38. PAPERS ON THE SCOTS BRIGADE IN HOLLAND, 1572-1782. Ed. JAMES FERGUSON. Vol. III. 1901.

*39. THE DIARY OF ANDREW HAY OF CRAIGNETHAN, 1659-60. Ed. A. G. REID. 1901.

*40. NEGOTIATIONS FOR THE UNION OF ENGLAND AND SCOTLAND IN 1651-53. Ed. C. STANFORD TERRY. 1902.

*41. THE LOYALL DISSUASIVE. Written in 1703 by Sir ÆNEAS MACPHERSON. Ed. Rev. A. D. MURDOCH. 1902.

*42. THE CHARTULARY OF LINDORES, 1195-1479. Ed. Right Rev. JOHN DOWDEN, Bishop of Edinburgh. 1903.

*43. A LETTER FROM MARY QUEEN OF SCOTS TO THE DUKE OF GUISE. Jan. 1562. Reproduced in Facsimile. Ed. Rev. J. HUNGERFORD POLLEN, 1904.
    Presented to the Society by the Family of the late Mr Scott of Halkshill

*44. MISCELLANY OF THE SCOTTISH HISTORY SOCIETY. Vol. II. 1904.

*45. LETTERS OF JOHN COCKBURN OF ORMISTOUN TO HIS GARDENER, 1727-1743. Ed. JAMES COLVILLE. 1904.

*46. MINUTE BOOK OF THE MANAGERS OF THE NEW MILLS CLOTH MANUFACTORY, 1681-1690. Ed. W. R. SCOTT. 1905.

*47. CHRONICLES OF THE FRASERS; being the Wardlaw Manuscript. By Master JAMES FRASER. Ed. WILLIAM MACKAY. 1905.

*48. PROCEEDINGS OF THE JUSTICIARY COURT FROM 1661 TO 1678. Vol. I, 1661-1669. Ed. Sheriff SCOTT-MONCRIEFF. 1905.

*49. PROCEEDINGS OF THE JUSTICIARY COURT FROM 1661 TO 1678. Vol. II, 1669-1678. Ed. Sheriff SCOTT-MONCRIEFF. 1905.

*50. RECORDS OF THE BARON COURT OF STITCHILL, 1655-1807. Ed. CLEMENT B. GUNN. 1905.

*51, 52, 53. MACFARLANE'S GEOGRAPHICAL COLLECTIONS. Ed. Sir ARTHUR MITCHELL. 3 vols. 1906-8.

*54. STATUTA ECCLESIÆ SCOTICANÆ, 1225-1559. Trans. and ed. DAVID PATRICK. 1907.

*55. THE HOUSE BOOKE OF ACCOMPTS, OCHERTYRE, 1737-39. Ed. JAMES COLVILLE. 1907.

*56. THE CHARTERS OF THE ABBEY OF INCHAFFRAY. Ed. W. A. LINDSAY, Right Rev. Bishop DOWDEN and J. MAITLAND THOMSON. 1908.

*57. A SELECTION OF THE FORFEITED ESTATES PAPERS PRESERVED IN H.M. GENERAL REGISTER HOUSE AND ELSEWHERE. Ed. A. H. MILLAR. 1909.

*58. RECORDS OF THE COMMISSIONS OF THE GENERAL ASSEMBLIES, 1650-52. Fd. Rev. JAMES CHRISTIE. 1909.
*59. PAPERS RELATING TO THE SCOTS IN POLAND. 1576-93. Ed. A. FRANCIS STEUART. 1915.
*60. SIR THOMAS CRAIG'S DE UNIONE REGNORUM BRITANNIÆ TRACTATUS. Ed. and trans. C. SANFORD TERRY. 1909.
*61. JOHNSTON OF WARISTON'S MEMENTO QUAMDIU VIVAS, AND DIARY FROM 1632 TO 1639. Ed. G. M. PAUL. 1911.

SECOND SERIES

*1. THE HOUSEHOLD BOOK OF LADY GRISELL BAILLIE, 1692-1733. Ed. R. SCOTT-MONCRIEFF. 1911.
2. ORIGINS OF THE '45 AND OTHER NARRATIVES. Ed. W. B. BLAIKIE. 1916. [Reprint.]
*3. CORRESPONDENCE OF JAMES, FOURTH EARL OF FINDLATER AND FIRST EARL OF SEAFIELD, LORD CHANCELLOR OF SCOTLAND. Ed. JAMES GRANT. 1912.
*4. RENTALE SANCTI ANDREE; BEING CHAMBERLAIN AND GRANITAR ACCOUNTS OF THE ARCHBISHOPRIC IN THE TIME OF CARDINAL BETOUN, 1538-1546. Trans. and ed. ROBERT KERR HANNAY. 1913.
*5. HIGHLAND PAPERS. Vol. I. Ed. J. R. N. MACPHAIL. 1914.
*6. SELECTIONS FROM THE RECORDS OF THE REGALITY OF MELROSE. Vol. I, 1605-1661. Ed. C. S. ROMANES. 1914.
*7. RECORDS OF THE EARLDOM OF ORKNEY, 1299-1614. Ed. J. S. CLOUSTON. 1914.
*8. SELECTIONS FROM THE RECORDS OF THE REGALITY OF MELROSE. Vol. II, 1662-76. Ed. C. S. ROMANES. 1915.
*9. SELECTIONS FROM THE LETTER BOOKS OF JOHN STEUART, BAILIE OF INVERNESS, 1715-52. Ed. WILLIAM MACKAY. 1915.
*10. RENTALE DUNKELDENSE; BEING THE ACCOUNTS OF THE CHAMBERLAIN OF THE BISHOPRIC OF DUNKELD, 1506-1517. Ed. R. K. HANNAY. 1915.
*11. LETTERS OF THE EARL OF SEAFIELD AND OTHERS, ILLUSTRATIVE OF THE HISTORY OF SCOTLAND DURING THE REIGN OF QUEEN ANNE. Ed. Professor HUME BROWN. 1915.
*12. HIGHLAND PAPERS. Vol. II. Ed. J. R. N. MACPHAIL. 1916.
*13. SELECTIONS FROM THE RECORDS OF THE REGALITY OF MELROSE. Vol. III, 1547-1706. Ed. C. S. ROMANES. 1917.
*14, 15. A CONTRIBUTION TO THE BIBLIOGRAPHY OF SCOTTISH TOPOGRAPHY. Ed. Sir ARTHUR MITCHELL and C. G. CASH. 2 vols. 1917.
*16, 17. PAPERS RELATING TO THE ARMY OF THE SOLEMN LEAGUE AND COVENANT, 1643-1647. Ed. Professor C. SANFORD TERRY. 2 vols. 1917.

*18. WARISTON'S DIARY. Vol. II, 1650-54. Ed. D. HAY FLEMING. 1919.
*19. MISCELLANY OF THE SCOTTISH HISTORY SOCIETY. Vol. III. 1919.
*20. HIGHLAND PAPERS. Vol. III. Ed. J. R. N. MACPHAIL. 1920.

THIRD SERIES

1. REGISTER OF THE CONSULTATIONS OF THE MINISTERS OF EDINBURGH. Vol. I. 1652-1657. Ed. Rev. W. STEPHEN. 1921.
2. DIARY OF GEORGE RIDPATH, MINISTER OF STITCHEL, 1755-1761 Ed. Sir JAMES BALFOUR PAUL. 1922.
3. THE CONFESSIONS OF BABINGTON AND OTHER PAPERS RELATING TO THE LAST DAYS OF MARY QUEEN OF SCOTS. Ed. Rev. J. H. POLLEN. 1922.
4. FOREIGN CORRESPONDENCE WITH MARIE DE LORRAINE, QUEEN OF SCOTLAND (BALCARRES PAPERS). Vol. I, 1537-1548. Ed. MARGUERITE WOOD. 1923.
*5. SELECTIONS FROM THE PAPERS OF THE SIR WILLIAM FRASER. Ed. J. R. N. MACPHAIL. 1924.
 Presented to the Society by the Trustees of the late Sir William Fraser, K.C.B.
*6. PAPERS RELATING TO THE SHIPS AND VOYAGES OF THE COMPANY OF SCOTLAND TRADING TO AFRICA AND THE INDIES, 1696-1707. Ed. GEORGE P. INSH. 1924.
7. FOREIGN CORRESPONDENCE WITH MARIE DE LORRAINE, QUEEN OF SCOTLAND (BALCARRES PAPERS). Vol. II, 1548-1557. Ed. MARGUERITE WOOD. 1925.
*8. THE EARLY RECORDS OF THE UNIVERSITY OF ST ANDREWS, 1413-1579. Ed. J. MAITLAND ANDERSON. 1926.
*9. MISCELLANY OF THE SCOTTISH HISTORY SOCIETY. Vol. IV, 1926.
*10. THE SCOTTISH CORRESPONDENCE OF MARY OF LORRAINE, 1543-1560. Ed. ANNIE I. CAMERON. 1927.
11. JOURNAL OF THOMAS CUNINGHAM, 1640-1654. CONSERVATOR AT CAMPVERE. Ed. ELINOR JOAN COURTHOPE. 1928.
*12. THE SHERIFF COURT BOOK OF FIFE, 1515-1522. Ed. WILLIAM CROFT DICKINSON. 1928.
13, 14, 15. THE PRISONERS OF THE '45. Ed. Sir BRUCE SETON, Bart., of Abercorn, and Mrs JEAN GORDON ARNOT. 3 vols. 1928-9.
16. REGISTER OF THE CONSULTATIONS OF THE MINISTERS OF EDINBURGH. Vol. II, 1657-1660. Ed. Rev. W. STEPHEN. 1930.
17. THE MINUTES OF THE JUSTICES OF THE PEACE FOR LANARKSHIRE, 1707-1723. Ed. C. A. MALCOLM. 1931.
18. THE WARRENDER PAPERS. Vol. I, 1301-1587. Ed. ANNIE I. CAMERON, with Introduction by Principal ROBERT S. RAIT. 1931.

19. THE WARRENDER PAPERS. Vol. II, 1587-1603. Ed. ANNIE I. CAMERON, with introduction by Principal ROBERT S. RAIT. 1932.
20. FLODDEN PAPERS. Ed. MARGUERITE WOOD. 1933.
21. MISCELLANY OF THE SCOTTISH HISTORY SOCIETY. Vol. V. 1933.
22. HIGHLAND PAPERS. Vol. IV. Ed. J. R. N. MACPHAIL, with Biographical introduction by WILLIAM K. DICKSON. 1934.
23. CALENDAR OF SCOTTISH SUPPLICATIONS TO ROME, 1418-1422. Ed. Rev. and Hon. E. R. LINDSAY and ANNIE I. CAMERON. 1934.
24. EARLY CORRESPONDENCE OF ROBERT WODROW. Ed. L. W. SHARP. 1937.
25. WARRENDER LETTERS. CORRESPONDENCE OF SIR GEORGE WARRENDER, LORD PROVOST OF EDINBURGH, 1715. Ed. WILLIAM K. DICKSON. 1935.
26. COMMENTARY ON THE RULE OF ST AUGUSTINE BY ROBERTUS RICHARDINUS. Ed. G. G. COULTON. 1935.
27. SURVEY OF LOCHTAYSIDE, 1769. Ed. MARGARET M. MCARTHUR. 1936.
28. AYR BURGH ACCOUNTS, 1534-1624. Ed. G. S. PRYDE. 1937.
*29. BARONY COURT BOOK OF CARNWATH, 1523-1542. Ed. WILLIAM CROFT DICKINSON. 1937.
30. CHRONICLE OF HOLYROOD. Ed. MARJORIE OGILVIE ANDERSON, with some additional notes by ALAN ORR ANDERSON. 1938.
31. THE JACOBITE COURT AT ROME, 1719. Ed. HENRIETTA TAYLER. 1938.
32. INCHCOLM CHARTERS. Ed. Rev. D. E. EASSON and ANGUS MACDONALD. 1938.
33. MISCELLANY OF THE SCOTTISH HISTORY SOCIETY. Vol. VI. 1939.
34. WARISTON'S DIARY. Vol. III. Ed. J. D. OGILVIE. 1940.
35. MISCELLANY OF THE SCOTTISH HISTORY SOCIETY. Vol. VII. 1941.
36. TWO MISSIONS OF JACQUES DE LA BROSSE, 1543 AND 1560. Ed. G. DICKINSON. 1942.
37. MINUTES OF THE SYNOD OF ARGYLL, 1639-1651. Ed. DUNCAN C. MACTAVISH. 1943.
38. MINUTES OF THE SYNOD OF ARGYLL, 1652-1661. Ed. DUNCAN C. MACTAVISH, with Introduction by J. D. OGILVIE. 1944.
*39. MONYMUSK PAPERS. Ed. HENRY HAMILTON. 1945.
40, 41. CHARTERS OF THE ABBEY OF COUPAR ANGUS. Ed. D. E. EASSON. 2 vols. 1947.
42. ACCOUNTS OF THE COLLECTORS OF THE THIRDS OF BENEFICES, 1561-1572. Ed. GORDON DONALDSON. 1949.
43. MISCELLANY OF THE SCOTTISH HISTORY SOCIETY. Vol. VIII. 1951.
44. SCOTTISH POPULATION STATISTICS. Ed. J. G. KYD. 1952. [Reprint.]
45. THE LETTERS OF JAMES IV, 1505-1513. Calendared by R. K. HANNAY. Edited with Biographical Memoir and Introduction by R. L. MACKIE assisted by ANNE SPILMAN. 1953.

46, 47. ACCOUNT OF THE PROCEEDINGS OF THE ESTATES IN SCOTLAND, 1698-1690. Ed. E. W. M. BALFOUR-MELVILLE. 2 vols. 1954-5.

48. CALENDAR OF SCOTTISH SUPPLICATIONS TO ROME, 1423-1428. Ed. ANNIE I. DUNLOP. 1956.

49. EARLY RECORDS OF ABERDEEN, 1317 and 1398-1407. Ed. WILLIAM CROFT DICKINSON. 1957.

50. MISCELLANY OF THE SCOTTISH HISTORY SOCIETY. Vol. IX. 1958.

51. WIGTOWNSHIRE CHARTERS. Ed. R. C. REID. 1960.

52. JOHN HOME'S SURVEY OF ASSYNT. Ed. R. J. ADAM. 1960.

53. COURT BOOK OF THE BURGH OF KIRKINTILLOCH, 1658-1694. Ed. G. S. PRYDE. 1963.

*54, 55. ACTA FACULTATIS ARTIUM UNIVERSITATIS SANCTI ANDREE, 1413-1588. Ed. ANNIE I. DUNLOP. 2 vols. 1964.

FOURTH SERIES

1. ARGYLL ESTATE INSTRUCTIONS (Mull, Morvern, Tiree), 1771-1805. Ed. ERIC R. CREGEEN. 1964.

2. MISCELLANY OF THE SCOTTISH HISTORY SOCIETY. Vol. X. 1965. (Memoir of Dr E. W. M. Balfour-Melville, by D. B. HORN; Bagimond's Roll for the diocese of Moray, ed. Rev. CHARLES BURNS; Accounts of the King's Pursemaster, 1539-40, ed. A. L. MURRAY; Papers of a Dundee shipping dispute, 1600-4, ed. W. A. McNEILL; A Scottish liturgy of the reign of James VI, ed. GORDON DONALDSON; List of Schoolmasters teaching Latin, 1690, ed. D. J. WITHRINGTON; Letters of Andrew Fletcher of Saltoun and his family, 1715-16, ed. I. J. MURRAY; Sir John Clerk's Observations on the present circumstances of Scotland, 1730, ed. T. C. SMOUT; A Renfrewshire election account, 1832, ed. WILLIAM FERGUSON.)

3. LETTERS OF JOHN RAMSAY OF OCHERTYRE, 1799-1812. Ed. BARBARA L. H. HORN. 1966.

4. THE COURT BOOKS OF ORKNEY AND SHETLAND, 1614-15. Ed. ROBERT S. BARCLAY. 1967.

5. THE MINUTES OF EDINBURGH TRADES COUNCIL, 1859-73. Ed. IAN MACDOUGALL. 1968.

6. THE DUNDEE TEXTILE INDUSTRY, 1790-1885, FROM THE PAPERS OF PETER CARMICHAEL OF ARTHURSTONE. Ed. ENID GAULDIE. 1969.

7. CALENDAR OF SCOTTISH SUPPLICATIONS TO ROME. 1428-32. Ed. ANNIE I. DUNLOP and IAN B. COWAN. 1970.

8, 9. PAPERS ON SUTHERLAND ESTATE MANAGEMENT, 1780-1820. Ed. R. J. ADAM. 2 vols. 1972.

10. WILLIAM MELROSE IN CHINA: THE LETTERS OF A SCOTTISH TEA MERCHANT, 1845-55. Ed. H.-C. MUI and L. H. MUI. 1973.

11. PAPERS ON SCOTTISH ELECTORAL POLITICS, 1832-50. Ed. IAN BRASH. 1974.
12. CALENDAR OF PAPAL LETTERS TO SCOTLAND OF CLEMENT VII OF AVIGNON, 1378-1394. Ed. CHARLES BURNS. 1976.
13. CALENDAR OF PAPAL LETTERS TO SCOTLAND OF BENEDICT XIII OF AVIGNON, 1394-1419. Ed. FRANCIS McGURK. 1976.

In preparation

1. SCOTTISH INDUSTRIAL HISTORY: A MISCELLANY OF DOCUMENTS.
2. TYNINGHAME KIRK SESSION MINUTES, 1615-1650. Ed. D. J. WITHRINGTON.
3. THE LETTERS AND PAPERS OF PETER MAY, LAND SURVEYOR, 1753-1785. Ed. IAN ADAMS.
4. THE CHARTERS OF THE LORDS OF THE ISLES, 1354-1493. Ed. R. W. MUNRO and JEAN MUNRO.
5. NINIAN WINZET AT RATISBON, 1577-1589: LETTERS AND PAPERS FROM THE ARCHIVES OF THE DUKES OF BAVARIA. Ed. Rev. MARK DILWORTH.

RULES

1. The object of the Society is the discovery and printing, under selected editorship, of unpublished documents illustrative of the civil, religious and social history of Scotland. The Society will also undertake to issue reprints of printed works of a similar nature which are out of print and may in exceptional circumstances publish works of reference, if the Council so decides.

2. The affairs of the Society shall be managed by a Council, consisting of a Chairman, Treasurer, Secretary, and twelve elected Members, five to make a quorum. Three of the twelve elected Members shall retire annually in rotation and shall not be eligible for re-election until after the lapse of one year. Nominations for election to membership of Council, duly proposed and seconded by two members of the Society, must be lodged with the Honorary Secretary not later than seven days before the date of the Annual General Meeting.

3. The Annual Subscription to the Society shall be five pounds. The publications of the Society shall not be delivered to any Member whose Subscription is in arrear, and no Member shall be permitted to receive more than one copy of the Society's publications in respect of one Annual Subscription. Volumes issued by the Society may be sold to non-members, if the Council so decides, provided that the cost of any such volume to a non-member shall be greater by at least one-third than its cost to a member.

4. The Society shall normally undertake the issue of its own publications, i.e. without the intervention of a publisher or any other paid agent, but may exceptionally employ a publisher or agent, by decision of Council.

5. The Society shall normally issue one volume each year.

6. An Annual General Meeting of the Society shall be held, normally in the month of December, or otherwise at a date to be determined by the Council.

7. Two stated Meetings of the Council shall be held each year, one in May or June, the other not later than seven days before the date of the Annual General Meeting. The Secretary, on the request of three Members of the Council, shall call a special meeting of the Council.

8. Editors shall receive 20 copies of each volume they edit for the Society.

9. The owners of Manuscripts published by the Society will also be presented with a certain number of copies.

10. The Annual Balance Sheet, Rules and List of Members shall be printed.

11. No alteration shall be made in these Rules except at a General Meeting of the Society. A fortnight's notice of any alterations to be proposed shall be given to the Members of the Council.